STRONG
TO
THE HOOP

STRONG
TO *HOOP*
THE

1,501 BASKETBALL TRIVIA QUESTIONS, QUOTES, AND FACTOIDS FROM EVERY ANGLE

KENNETH A. SHOULER

LYONS
PRESS

Essex, Connecticut

An imprint of Globe Pequot, the trade division of
The Rowman & Littlefield Publishing Group, Inc.
4501 Forbes Blvd., Ste. 200
Lanham, MD 20706
www.rowman.com

Distributed by NATIONAL BOOK NETWORK

British Library Cataloguing in Publication Information available

Library of Congress Cataloging-in-Publication Data

Names: Shouler, Kenneth A., author.
Title: Strong to the hoop : 1,501 basketball trivia questions, quotes, and factoids
    from every angle / Kenneth A. Shouler.
Description: Essex, Connecticut : Lyons Press, [2023]
Identifiers: LCCN 2023023792 (print) | LCCN 2023023793 (ebook) | ISBN
    9781493069842 (trade paperback) | ISBN 9781493069859 (epub)
Subjects: LCSH: Basketball—Records—United States. | Basketball—United
    States—Miscellanea. | Basketball—United States—History. | National Basketball
    Association—History.
Classification: LCC GV885.55 .S54 2023 (print) | LCC GV885.55 (ebook) | DDC
    796.323/6406—dc23/eng/20230531
LC record available at https://lccn.loc.gov/2023023792
LC ebook record available at https://lccn.loc.gov/2023023793

♾️™ The paper used in this publication meets the minimum requirements of
American National Standard for Information Sciences—Permanence of Paper for
Printed Library Materials, ANSI/NISO Z39.48-1992.

INTRODUCTION

When I think of basketball, I think of the ABA and the All-Star Game, of the present decade and those past, of the immortal numbers and the pecking order of the greatest players. So those are the categories that leapt to mind when I thought of this book. My love of the game began more than 50 years ago.

It was May 8, 1970, an earlier date for Game 7 of the National Basketball Association Finals than we have seen since. In Game 6 at the Los Angeles Forum, with Willis Reed sitting on the bench nursing a leg injury, Wilt Chamberlain had his way in the paint and throttled New York to the tune of 45 points and 27 rebounds in a 135–113 massacre. The result of that game made the prospects for success look bleak for the Knicks, to say the least, even with the next game scheduled back at Madison Square Garden.

It was questionable until game time whether Reed would play. A cortisone shot numbed his injury. He dragged his injured leg like a satchel that was a great burden. But he muscled Chamberlain for 25 minutes. Walt Frazier, my favorite player as a boy, took care of the rest. He scored 36 points, assisted on 19 other baskets, and snared seven rebounds, a line I recited to him during an interview for *Hoop* magazine for a 20th anniversary article in 1990. "And four steals," he reminded me. The Knicks led by as many as 30 points during the evening and won 113–99. "Red [Holzman, the head coach] always said, 'Hit the open man.' That night I was the open man," Frazier laughed.

It was the Knicks' first title. New York was all in. It was my first title of any kind, since neither the Yankees nor the football Giants had won any championships since I had started rooting. The Knicks were unique. They had five players who could hit the last shot—Frazier, Reed, Bill Bradley, Dave DeBusschere, and Dick Barnett. The Knicks won a second title—and their last—in 1973. This spring makes 50 years without a fresh banner.

But the allure of 1970s basketball didn't end there.

The categories of this book mirror the game's alluring qualities. Take the ABA, the first category in this volume. While the mid-1970s witnessed the Knicks' decline, the New York Nets of the American Basketball Association were ascendant. They played their first season in Teaneck, New Jersey, in 1967–68. For the 1968–69 season, they moved to the Long Island Arena (the Long Island Ducks of the Eastern Hockey League played hockey on other nights), sometimes called the Commack Arena, in a place once inhabited by Native Americans. At the same venue I also saw early heavy metal with Black Sabbath, preceded by the opening act the James Gang with Joe Walsh (who owned the show). The arena also hosted a great road version of the Broadway sensation *Jesus Christ Superstar*, which I saw with my father.

Now situated in the Nassau Coliseum, the Nets in 1974 were plenty good, good enough for a 55-29 record in their 84-game ABA slate (so it wasn't just a red, white, and blue ball or a 3-point line that the ABA contributed). They had Larry Kenon, Billy Paultz, and a guard with a barrel chest: "Super" John Williamson. Their brightest star was Julius Erving, a 24-year-old from the University of Massachusetts. The Nets' quintet played the Utah Stars in the ABA Finals, boasting Hall of Famer Zelmo Beaty and perennial All-Star Willie Wise. The Nets won in five, behind Erving's 28 points a game and Kenon's 14 rebounds.

After the Indiana Pacers, who had already won three titles, lost to the Kentucky Colonels in 1975, the Nets were at it again in 1976. They took the Denver Nuggets in six, as Erving (37.7 points per game to go with 14 rebounds and five assists) destroyed David Thompson (28 points, six rebounds, and three assists) in the mano-a-mano duel. The Nets closed out the series with a flourish on May 13, 1976, with Erving posting 31 points and 19 rebounds in a 112–106 victory. We said goodbye to the ABA.

Besides the Knicks, Nets, and Pacers winning multiple titles in the 1970s, the Celtics, the post-Russell Celtics that is, won twice. One can get a full picture of the history of the game from a season or team or player. The entire decade had a dynastic feel to it. Two historic teams—the Lakers and the Celtics—succeeded early in the decade, as did a less than historic quintet, the Knicks. But the Knicks, who won the league's first game up in Toronto in 1946, went to three Finals in four years, thus playing the best basketball at any time in their 77-year history.

The Celtics that won in 1974 and 1976 had two young would-be Hall of Famers, Jo Jo White and Dave Cowens, and a veteran. The veteran was John Havlicek, who played guard and small forward and so was labeled a "swing man," in what now seems like arcane language. If I tried, I could not disguise my affection for the Celtics' wiry 6'5" forward. He began his career in 1962, yet another Celtic sixth man, a role that coach Red Auerbach invented and that 25-minute-a-game forward Frank Ramsey had played to perfection starting in 1956. After Bill Russell played his last victorious game against the Lakers in 1969, he said to Havlicek, "It's your team now." Truth be told, it was his team in large measure before that historic season. The statistics won't show it in the early 1960s since, like Ramsey, Hondo was playing fewer minutes as the sixth man.

A legend about Havlicek came to light when an x-ray revealed a lung capacity nearly twice that of a normal person. The revelation explained how he was able to run those ovals from sideline to sideline in the front court, running defenders ragged. He was in on everything the Celtics did, like stealing the inbound pass at the Boston Garden to end the 1965 Finals as Johnny Most screamed over and over in that gravelly voice, "Havlicek stole the ball." He also hit the running, leaning one-handed bank shot with a second left, before Garfield Heard hit the shot to send his Suns into the third overtime in Game 5 of the 1976 Finals. The Celtics won in six games against the desert upstarts. Havlicek averaged just 15 for the series, but shooting guard Jo Jo White was awarded the MVP, posting 21.7 points and 46 minutes per game.

Havlicek had shone brighter in the 1974 Finals, which appeared to belong to the previous year's Most Valuable Player, Dave Cowens. Cowens was one of the evolutionary club of running centers. I can see him yet, trailing on the fast break, taking a pass and rising to the zenith of his jump and letting go that left-handed jumper. The slashing, running centers, who deemphasized playing with their backs to the basket, might have begun with Walt Bellamy, who at 6'11" at the outset of his career could cut to the basket faster than those other three of comparable height, Chamberlain, Russell, and Nate Thurmond. In the 1970s the quick centers were Bob Rule, Willis Reed, and Bob McAdoo, the greatest scorer of the greyhounds, since he won three scoring titles in a row for the Buffalo Braves. Cowens earned his way into the club.

In the 1974 Finals he gave away six inches to another center, Kareem Abdul-Jabbar. Jabbar had the better line. But after Jabbar hit an astounding 15-foot skyhook from the baseline in Game 6 to give the Bucks a double-overtime win, the Celtics traveled to the Milwaukee Arena and won going away, 102–87. Cowens played a great game with 28 points and 14 boards. In the frequent illogic that attends these occasions, the game story was written up as another center outplaying Jabbar. A digression here is appropriate since the same write-ups followed the early career of Chamberlain, who had been outplayed, or so the narrative went, when, in actuality, the rest of his team had been outplayed, while he registered something like 49 points and snatched 31 rebounds. So it was in Milwaukee that Jabbar's Game 7 showed 26 points and 13 rebounds for the game. For the series it was better: 32.6 points, 12 rebounds, and five assists, by far the best line of anyone. Oscar Robertson, playing his last season, was ineffective in the series and missed 11 of 13 shots in Game 7. Havlicek contributed most of the offense for the Celtics. He played an ungodly 47 minutes per contest, averaged 26 points and seven rebounds, and secured the series MVP trophy.

The Lakers only won the championship once in the 1970s, but they played three Finals against the Knicks, one a classic seven-gamer, and two five-game tilts. When they won in 1972, people recall best their 33 straight games from November through January, but they forget how they won the title. It was Chamberlain doing what he did for the last seven years of his career, following that seven-year run of winning scoring titles from 1960 through 1966. He connected on 60 percent of his shots, posting 19 points a game and averaging 22 rebounds. Jerry Lucas, playing the pivot in place of an injured Willis Reed, couldn't keep Chamberlain from setting up camp near the hoop.

No one ever stopped Chamberlain for long. He is the unofficial champion of this book. He owns the NBA record book lock, stock, and barrel. Has anyone but Chamberlain averaged 40 points in a season? No. And the "Big Dipper" did it twice. He averaged a nutty 50.4 points in 1962 and followed that with 44.8 in 1963. Of course, he scored 100 in a contest on March 2, 1962. In 14 seasons he led the circuit in rebounds 11 times. Only Wilt ever averaged 27 rebounds a game, and he did it twice. After seven consecutive scoring titles from 1960 through 1966—when his average never went under 33.5—he had his "transition" season in 1967, with averages of 24.1 points, 24.2 rebounds, and 7.8 assists. That year the Philadelphia Warriors won 68 (the most wins in a season to that point) and Wilt got his first championship.

The history keeps getting made. Damian Lillard and Donovan Mitchell each posted 71 points in games this past season. Historical note: Chamberlain scored 70 or more six times. But Wilt was human after all. He doesn't own the mark for career points. That belongs to LeBron James, who passed Kareem's 38,387 points in February. So, history is present.

The NBA's book of life keeps expanding.

ABA

1. True or False? No player has led the NBA and ABA in scoring.
Answer: True. The two best candidates were Rick Barry and Julius Erving. Both led the ABA in scoring but fell short of leading in the NBA.

2. Rank the following ABA players in career playoff points per game.
A. Dan Issel   B. George Gervin   C. Rick Barry   D. Julius Erving
Answer: 1-C, 33.45 points per game; 2-D, 31.08; 3-B, 25.24; 4-A, 23.81.

3. Who owns Denver's record for points in a game over a season, including ABA and NBA competition?
A. Alex English   B. Spencer Haywood   C. Dan Issel   D. David Thompson
Answer: B. Haywood dropped 30 per game for the Rockets in 1970, the power forward's rookie season out of the University of Detroit.

4. True or False? The ABA played fewer games a season than the NBA.
Answer: False. The ABA played an 84-game schedule from 1970 through 1976. In 1968 and 1969 they played a 78-game schedule.

5. True or False? The Nuggets have won titles in the ABA and in the NBA.
Answer: False. The Nuggets lost the last ABA Final in six games to the Nets in 1976. In 2023 they topped the Heat in five games to win their first NBA title.

6. True or False? Dallas won championships in both the ABA and the NBA.

Answer: False. The Dallas Chaparrals were one of the original ABA teams, beginning in 1967. After poor attendance, they moved to San Antonio for the 1973–74 season. Neither city won an ABA title. The NBA Mavericks secured a title in 2011.

7. What former ABA standout won the MVP of the 1980 All-Star Game?

A. George Gervin   B. Moses Malone   C. Julius Erving   D. Dan Issel

Answer: A. The "Ice Man" and Spurs shooting guard played a complete game, with his 34 points, 10 rebounds, and three steals helping the East to prevail 144–136.

8. What former ABA player was All-Star MVP the first year after the NBA-ABA merger?

A. George McGinnis   B. George Gervin   C. Rick Barry   D. Julius Erving

Answer: D. Erving and Bob McAdoo each scored 30 points for the East. In 38 minutes, McAdoo also secured 10 rebounds and Erving had 12 in 30 minutes. Erving took the award even though the West won 125–124.

9. True or False? The Indiana Pacers have lost more Finals than they have won.

Answer: False. They won three and lost three. The Indiana Pacers won three ABA Finals in 1970, 1972, and 1973. They lost ABA Finals in 1969 and 1975 and they lost an NBA Finals to the Lakers in six games in 2000.

10. What NBA legend coached the Utah Stars to a title in 1971?

Answer: Boston Celtic legend Bill Sharman led the Stars to a 57-27 mark in 1971. Then his troops beat the Colonels in seven in the Finals. The following year the Hall of Famer coached the Los Angeles Lakers to a 69-13 record and an NBA title.

11. Which of the following cities won NBA and ABA titles?

A. Indiana   B. New York   C. San Antonio   D. Utah

Answer: B. The New York Nets won ABA titles in 1974 and 1976. The Knicks won titles in 1970 and 1973.

12. What ABA star led the league in rebounding the most times?
A. Swen Nater   B. Artis Gilmore   C. Mel Daniels   D. Spencer Haywood
Answer: B. Gilmore led the league four of the ABA's nine seasons. HIs
highest average was 18.31 rebounds a game in 1973.

13. Who led the ABA in scoring the most years?
A. Spencer Haywood   B. Julius Erving   C. Charlie Scott   D. Dan Issel
Answer: B. Erving led the ABA in scoring in three of the last four years
of the league's existence.

ALL-STAR GAME

14. Name the MVP of the 1962 All-Star Game.
A. Bob Pettit   B. Bill Russell   C. Oscar Robertson   D. Wilt Chamberlain
Answer: D. The Warriors center posted an incredible 42 points and 24
rebounds, enough to propel the East to a 150–130 win.

15. Name the MVP of the 1977 All-Star Game.
A. Bob McAdoo   B. Paul Westphal   C. Julius Erving
D. Kareem Abdul-Jabbar   E. Bob Lanier
Answer: C. Erving took his new league by storm, posting 30 points,
12 rebounds, and four steals.

**16. Who earned the most votes for the 2008 All-Star Game in
New Orleans?**
A. LeBron James   B. Tim Duncan   C. Kevin Garnett   D. Dwyane Wade
Answer: C. The Celtic power forward drew 2,399,148 votes but did not
play due to injury. LeBron James walked off with the MVP hardware,
leading the East to a 134–128 victory with 27 points, nine assists, and
eight rebounds.

17. Who was the MVP of the 1955 All-Star contest?
A. Bob Cousy   B. Jim Pollard   C. Bill Sharman   D. Harry Gallatin
Answer: C. The Celtics' marksman Sharman netted 15 points in 18
minutes off the bench, earning the honors in the East's 100–91 victory at
Madison Square Garden.

18. Which game had the largest margin of victory in All-Star Game history?

A. 1959   B. 1963   C. 1966   D. 1971

Answer: C. The East won the game played in Cincinnati, 137–94. Adrian Smith, the Royals' star guard, was MVP with 24 points and eight rebounds. It was the Eastern Conference's fourth straight victory, as they won their 11th of the 16 games played.

19. When was the first All-Star Game played between the ABA and NBA?

A. 1970   B. 1971   C. 1972   D. 1973

Answer: B. The NBA won the first "Super Game" between the two pro leagues 125–120 at the Houston Astrodome on May 28, 1971. Walt Frazier logged 32 points and won the MVP of the game and a car.

20. Which of the following players won or tied for the MVP in three of the first 10 All-Star Games played?

A. Bob Cousy   B. George Mikan   C. Bill Sharman   D. Bob Pettit

Answer: D. In the 1956 game at Rochester War Memorial Coliseum, the Hawks forward led both teams in points with 20 and rebounds with 24 in the West's 108–94 victory over the East. Playing on his home court in St. Louis in 1958, Pettit logged 28 points and 26 rebounds, pacing both teams for the second time in three years in a losing effort, 130–118. In 1959, Pettit posted 25 points and 16 rebounds in Detroit to lead both squads and grab MVP honors for the third time in four seasons.

21. Besides Bob Pettit, who else won two All-Star Game MVPs in the 1950s?

A. Ed Macauley   B. George Mikan   C. Bill Sharman   D. Bob Cousy

Answer: D. In 1954 the Boston point guard scored 20 and grabbed 11 boards as the East grabbed a 98–93 overtime victory at Madison Square Garden in New York. The Lakers' Jim Pollard scored 23 for the West. The New York native did it again in 1957, grabbing MVP honors at the Boston Garden with 10 points (on just 4-of-14 shooting) and seven assists. Bob Pettit scored 21 points and grabbed 11 boards in the 109–97 defeat for the West.

Bob Pettit

22. Who was the leading scorer in the 1975 All-Star Game?
A. Kareem Abdul-Jabbar   B. Bob McAdoo   C. Walt Frazier
D. Rick Barry   E. Sidney Wicks
Answer: C. Playing without his longtime teammates Willis Reed and
Dave DeBusschere, but playing alongside his more recent mate Earl
Monroe, Walt Frazier logged 30 points in 35 minutes. He made 10 of 17
field goal attempts and 10 of 11 from the foul line. He also snatched five
rebounds and made four steals in leading the East to a 108–102 victory
at the Veterans Memorial Coliseum in Phoenix.

**23. Who led all scorers in the NBA's 50th-anniversary All-Star Game
in 1997 at the Gund Arena in Cleveland?**
A. Grant Hill   B. Glen Rice   C. Gary Payton   D. Latrell Sprewell
Answer: B. With the excitement of the league's 50th anniversary, the
Hornets small forward logged 26 points and snatched the MVP in a
132–120 victory for the East.

24. Who was the leading scorer in the 1974 All-Star Game?
A. Spencer Haywood   B. Bob Lanier   C. Gail Goodrich
D. Pete Maravich   E. Kareem Abdul-Jabbar
Answer: B. Lanier, a center for the Pistons, played a dogged 26 minutes
off the bench and scored 24 points and grabbed 10 rebounds as the
West thumped the East 134–123. Haywood, playing before his home
crowd in Seattle, scored 23 points and gathered 11 rebounds. Trail
Blazers forward Wicks added 16. The East was also paced by a bench
player, Dave DeBusschere, who tallied 16 points.

25. When was the first NBA All-Star Game played?
A. 1947   B. 1949   C. 1950   D. 1951
Answer: D. Played at the Boston Garden before an excited throng of
10,094 fans on March 2, 1951. It was fitting that a Celtic paced the attack
for the East. Forward "Easy" Ed Macauley scored 20 and was helped
by 19 from the Warriors' "Jumpin'" Joe Fulks and 15 from the Nationals'
Dolph Schayes. The East led by 11 at the half and coasted to a 111–94 win.

26. True or False? The East won the first two All-Star Games played.
Answer: True. Despite a contribution of 26 points and 15 rebounds
from Minneapolis Lakers center George Mikan, in the 1952 game the
East pulled away in the second half and rolled to a 108–91 win. Warriors
guard Paul Arizin matched Mikan with 26 and Celtic playmaker Bob
Cousy amassed 13 assists before 10,211 home fans at the Boston Garden.

27. When was the second All-Star Game played between the ABA and NBA?
A. 1972   B. 1973   C. 1974   D. 1975
Answer: A. The first neck and neck contest was followed by a closer one, with the NBA winning 106–104 on May 25, 1972, at the Nassau Coliseum in New York. With the ABA ahead by 19 points in the second quarter, they inexplicably sat Julius Erving until two minutes remained in the third with the NBA ahead 81–78. Center Bob Lanier scored 15 points and won the MVP.

28. What Celtic played in 13 consecutive All-Star Games from 1951 to 1963?
A. Ed Macauley   B. Bob Cousy   C. Bill Sharman   D. Bill Russell
Answer: B. Cousy played in the All-Star Game in each of his 13 pro seasons.

29. Who was the first All-Star MVP to win the honor on his home court and go on to win the championship that season?
A. Bob Cousy   B. Bob Pettit   C. Jerry West   D. Willis Reed
Answer: A. The East beat the West 109–97 at Boston Garden in 1957, as the Celtics guard posted 10 points and seven assists and won the MVP. The vote was questionable since Warriors center Neil Johnston recorded 19 points and nine rebounds. The Celtics beat the Hawks in the Finals, winning Game 7 in double overtime, as forward Tommy Heinsohn poured in 37 points.

30. Match the All-Stars with their uniform numbers.
1. Ed Macauley   2. Joe Fulks   3. Dolph Schayes   4. Bob Cousy
A. 4   B. 22   C. 14   D. 10
Answer: 1-B; 2-D; 3-A; 4-C.

31. Name the first San Diego Clipper to play in an All-Star Game.
A. World B. Free   B. Marvin Barnes   C. Bill Walton   D. Swen Nater
Answer: A. In a season in which he averaged 30.2 points per game, Free played in the 1980 All-Star Game at the Capital Center in Maryland. He logged 14 points for the West, but the East prevailed in overtime, 144–136, led by 34 points from George Gervin.

32. Who was the first Charlotte player to play in an All-Star Game?
A. Larry Johnson   B. Alonzo Mourning   C. Kemba Walker   D. Glen Rice
Answer: A. Johnson played in the 1993 All-Star Game.

33. Name the team whose players received three consecutive All-Star Game MVPs in the 1960s.
A. Celtics   B. Royals   C. Hawks   D. Lakers
Answer: B. Oscar Robertson, Jerry Lucas, and Adrian Smith took the honor from 1964 through 1966. In 1964 Robertson nearly posted a triple-double with 26 points, 14 rebounds, and eight assists in a 111–107 win at the Boston Garden. In 1965 it was Lucas's turn, as he recorded 25 points and 10 rebounds in a 124–123 squeaker at the St. Louis Arena. It was Smith off the bench for 24 points and eight rebounds in 26 minutes in a 137–94 triumph at the Cincinnati Gardens in 1966.

34. Who played in the most All-Star Games as a Hawk?
A. Bob Pettit   B. Dominique Wilkins   C. Cliff Hagan   D. Lou Hudson
Answer: A. Pettit played in 11 All-Star contests, making the team in all of his pro seasons.

35. Match the All-Stars with their uniform numbers.
1. Paul Arizin   2. Andy Phillip   3. Harry Gallatin   4. Red Rocha
A. 4   B. 10   C. 11   D. 19
Answer: 1-C; 2-D; 3-B; 4-A.

36. What Bulls made the All-Star Game in the team's inaugural season?
A. Bob Boozer   B. Jerry Sloan   C. Guy Rodgers   D. Chet Walker
Answer: B and C. The Bulls landed two players on the All-Star team in 1966–67, their first season. Jerry Sloan, a 6'5" guard and six-time All-Defensive Team recipient, made the squad. Nine-year guard Guy Rodgers, who posted 18 points and 11 rebounds per game that year, also made the team.

37. Who was the first Maverick to be selected as an All-Star?
A. Mark Aguirre   B. Rolando Blackman   C. James Donaldson
D. Jason Kidd
Answer: A. His first game was in 1984. He tallied 13 points in 13 minutes.

38. True or False? The only Mavericks All-Star from 2020 through 2022 was Luka Dončić.
Answer: True.

39. Who were the coaches in the 1952 All-Star Game?
A. Joe Lapchick   B. Al Cervi   C. Red Auerbach   D. John Kundla
Answer: B and D. Cervi, the 5'10" former Syracuse point guard, led the East to a 108–91 win. Kundla, who coached the Lakers' dynasty, piloted the West.

40. Match the All-Stars with their uniform numbers.
1. Max Zaslofsky   2. Dick McGuire   3. George Mikan   4. Jim Pollard
A. 15   B. 99   C. 17   D. 10
Answer: 1-D; 2-A; 3-B; 4-C.

41. When did the West win its first All-Star Game?
A. 1951   B. 1952   C. 1953   D. 1954
Answer: C. Behind game MVP George Mikan's 22 points and 16 rebounds, the West prevailed 79–75 in the Allen County War Memorial Coliseum in Fort Wayne, Indiana.

42. Who was the MVP of the first All-Star Game played in Madison Square Garden?
A. Bill Sharman   B. Ray Felix   C. Jim Pollard   D. Bob Cousy
Answer: D. Playing at the old Garden at 50th Street and Eighth Avenue before a throng of 16,487 fans in 1954, the Celtics' point guard poured in 20 points and grabbed 11 rebounds as the East won in overtime 98–93.

43. The 1976 game was played in Philadelphia for the bicentennial. What player was chosen MVP in a controversial decision?
A. Bob McAdoo   B. Dave Bing   C. Kareem Abdul-Jabbar
D. Dave Cowens
Answer: B. The Bullets guard had 16 points. McAdoo had 22 for the Braves. Cowens had 16 points and 16 rebounds. Abdul-Jabbar had 22 points and 15 rebounds.

44. What 1974 All-Star MVP led his team to a victory at the center position?
A. Kareem Abdul-Jabbar   B. Bob Lanier   C. Spencer Haywood
D. Nate Thurmond
Answer: B. The Pistons' 6'11" Lanier was stellar, hitting a crazy 11 of 15 shots for 24 points. He also grabbed 10 rebounds in a 134–123 victory.

45. Match the All-Stars with their uniform numbers.
1. Vern Mikkelsen   2. Bobby Wanzer   3. Slater Martin   4. Bob Davies
A. 9   B. 22   C. 11   D. 19
Answer: 1-D; 2-A; 3-B; 4-C.

46. Who was the MVP of the 1968 All-Star Game?
A. John Havlicek   B. Dave DeBusschere   C. Hal Greer   D. Bill Russell
Answer: C. The 76ers' diminutive point guard came off the bench for the Eastern Conference squad and scored 21 points in 17 minutes. Havlicek added 26 points off the bench in a 144–124 blowout at Madison Square Garden.

47. Who won his second All-Star Game MVP in the 2005 contest?
A. Shaquille O'Neal   B. Allen Iverson   C. Kobe Bryant   D. Kevin Garnett
Answer: B. He connected on only four of 14 shots, but his 10 assists and five steals aided the East in a 125–115 victory.

48. Who was the leading scorer in the 1993 All-Star Game?
A. David Robinson   B. Mark Price   C. Karl Malone   D. Michael Jordan
Answer: D. Jordan tallied 30, but the East lost in overtime 135–132. Teammates and co-MVPs Malone and John Stockton prevailed. Malone had 30 points and 10 rebounds and Stockton had 15 assists.

49. In 2023, what player set the record for points scored in an All-Star Game?
A. Damian Lillard   B. Jayson Tatum   C. Donovan Mitchell
D. Jaylen Brown
Answer: B. Jayson Tatum logged 55 points, breaking the record of 52 set by Anthony Davis in 2017. He led Team Giannis to a 184–175 victory over Team LeBron.

50. True or False? The leading vote getter won the MVP in the 2019 game.

Answer: False. LeBron James, now a Laker, drew 4,620,809 votes, but his teammate Kevin Durant tallied 31 points, seven assists, and seven rebounds in Team LeBron's 178–164 victory over Team Giannis.

51. True or False? The leading vote getter in the 2020 All-Star Game was also the MVP of the game.

Answer: False. LeBron James got 6,275,459 votes to lead the way. But the Clippers' Kawhi Leonard hoisted 30 points and grabbed seven rebounds as Team LeBron won a squeaker over Team Giannis 157–155.

52. Name the team with the most All-Star selections.

A. Lakers   B. Celtics   C. 76ers   D. Pistons

Answer: A. The Lakers have had 65 All-Stars. The Celtics are second with 60.

53. Who was the MVP of the 1967 game?

A. Rick Barry   B. Wilt Chamberlain   C. Elgin Baylor   D. Guy Rodgers

Answer: A. Playing for the Warriors, Barry scored 38 points. He accepted the trophy from Commissioner Walter Kennedy after a 135–120 West victory.

ALL-TIME GREATS

54. True or False? None of the top 10 players in minutes played in a game are in the Hall of Fame.
Answer: False. Wilt Chamberlain and Nate Thurmond each played 63 minutes in a game, Chamberlain in 1961 and again in 1969, and Thurmond in 1969. Both are in the Hall of Fame.

55. How many of the top 10 scoring games did Kobe Bryant record in 2006–7, the 60th anniversary of the league?
A. One   B. Four   C. Five   D. Six
Answer: D. Bryant scored a season-high 65. His five other top 10 season totals were between 52 and 60 points.

56. What two players are tied for most free throws made in a game?
A. Allen Iverson   B. Michael Jordan   C. Adrian Dantley
D. Wilt Chamberlain
Answer: C and D. Dantley made an astounding 28 of 29 free throws and scored 46 points against the Rockets in a 116–111 victory on January 4, 1984. Chamberlain made 28 of 32 free throws, and 36 of 63 field goals, in his 100-point game in a 169–147 win against the Knicks on March 2, 1962.

57. How many of the top 10 single-game scoring records belong to Warriors?
A. One   B. Three   C. Four   D. Six
Answer: D. All six belong to Wilt Chamberlain, who scored 100, 78, 73 three times, and 72.

58. How many of the top 10 marks for rebounds in a game belong to Wilt Chamberlain?
A. Three   B. Five   C. Six   D. Seven
Answer: C. Chamberlain set the record with 55 rebounds in a game in 1960 against Bill Russell and the Celtics, who had 59 rebounds as a team. Playing all 48 minutes, Chamberlain also scored 34 points, but the Celtics prevailed 132–129. Russell had the next three highest totals. Chamberlain also had 45 in a game and 43 four times.

59. True or False? No player ever had 20 offensive rebounds in a game.
Answer: False. With the Rockets, Moses Malone had 21 offensive rebounds on February 21, 1982, in a 117–100 win over the Sonics. Malone also had the second highest total with 19 in 1979.

60. Who owns most of the top 10 records for assists in a single game?
A. Scott Skiles   B. Bob Cousy   C. John Stockton   D Isiah Thomas
Answer: C. Stockton recorded 28, 27, and 26 assists in a single game between 1988 and 1991. Those are the fifth, seventh, and eighth highest marks of all time.

61. How many of the top 10 games in field goals attempted are owned by one player?
A. Four   B. Eight   C. Nine   D. Ten
Answer: C. Wilt Chamberlain owns nine of the top 10 marks for field goals attempted in a game. Laker Elgin Baylor took 55 shots in a triple-overtime contest on December 8, 1961. He made 22 and tallied 63 points, 31 rebounds, and seven assists. Wilt played in that contest and made 31 of his 62 attempts. He scored 78 points and secured 43 rebounds. Despite Wilt's heroic efforts, his Warriors lost 151–147.

62. Match the players with how long it took for them to win their first NBA championship.
1. Julius Erving   2. Michael Jordan   3. Earl Monroe   4. Walt Frazier
A. Three years   B. Six years   C. Seven years   D. Nine years
Answer: 1 and 2-C; 3-B; 4-A.

63. Of the 13 games in which a player has scored 70 or more points, how many of those games were posted by Wilt Chamberlain?

A. Two   B. Five   C. Six   D. Seven

Answer: C. Chamberlain posted six games of 70 or more points. He reached 70 three times in the 1961–62 season, including a high of 100 on March 2, 1962.

64. The NBA gave us an alphabetical list of the 75 greatest players in its 75th anniversary year. ESPN took the further step of ranking them. Which player didn't rank in the top five on their list?

A. Bill Russell   B. Magic Johnson   C. Wilt Chamberlain

D. Kareem Abdul-Jabbar

Answer: A. Russell was ranked sixth. In his 13 seasons, the Celtics won 11 championships.

65. Rank the great point guards with the number of championship teams they played on.

A. John Stockton   B. Oscar Robertson   C. Magic Johnson

D. Isiah Thomas   E. Stephen Curry

Answer: 1-C, five titles, 1980, 1982, 1985, 1987, 1988; 2-E, four, 2015, 2017, 2018, 2022; 3-D, two, 1989, 1990; 4-B, 1971; 5-A, none.

66. Which center was in the top 10 players ranked on the ESPN list of the top 75 players?

A. Tim Duncan   B. Shaquille O'Neal   C. Moses Malone

D. Hakeem Olajuwon

Answer: A. Duncan was ranked eighth on ESPN's list of the top 75 players. He played on five NBA champions.

ANNIVERSARIES

67. True or False? None of the following players got 60 points in any game during the NBA's 75th anniversary season.
A. Kyrie Irving   B. LeBron James   C. Trae Young
D. Karl-Anthony Towns
Answer: False. Towns tallied 60 and grabbed 17 rebounds on March 14, 2022, in a 149–139 win over the Spurs. On March 15 Irving scored 60 on 20-of-31 from the field and 8-of-12 from 3-point territory for a 150–108 blowout over the Magic.

68. Which of the following teams won a title 25 years after winning another title?
A. 1959 Celtics   B. 1967 76ers   C. 1985 Lakers   D. 1987 Lakers
Answer: A, C. After their second crown in 1959, the Celtics won a quarter-century later when they beat the Lakers in seven games in 1984. The 1985 Lakers topped the Celtics in six games. In 2010 they topped the Celtics in seven games.

69. Who scored the most points in a single game in the NBA's 25th anniversary year?
A. Dave Bing   B. Elvin Hayes   C. Walt Wesley   D. Kareem Abdul-Jabbar
Answer: A. The Pistons guard logged 54 in a losing effort against the Bulls on February 21, 1971. Abdul-Jabbar scored 53 twice that season.

70. Who grabbed 30 rebounds the most times in 1971, the 25th anniversary of the NBA?
A. Willis Reed   B. Elvin Hayes   C. Wilt Chamberlain   D. Gus Johnson
Answer: C. Chamberlain did it three times, with a high of 32. The others here did it twice. Hayes had the high total with 35.

71. True or False? None of the following players got 20 assists in any game during the NBA's 25th anniversary season.
A. Lenny Wilkens   B. Norm Van Lier   C. Larry Siegfried   D. Jerry West
Answer: False. Previously with the Celtics during five of their championship years, Rockets guard Siegfried got 21 assists on November 16, 1970, in a victory over the Trail Blazers, 136–118.

72. True or False? None of the following players scored 50 points during the NBA's 50th anniversary season.
A. Michael Jordan   B. Glen Rice   C. Hakeem Olajuwon   D. Allen Iverson
Answer: False. Jordan tallied 51 in an 88–87 victory over the Knicks on January 21, 1997. It was the highest total during the 50th anniversary season.

73. True or False? None of the following players got 20 assists during the NBA's 50th anniversary year.
A. Robert Pack   B. Nick Van Exel   C. Mark Jackson   D. John Stockton
Answer: False. Van Exel posted the highest total of the season with 23 on January 5, 1997. Pack and Jackson each had 22 in other games.

74. True or False? No player scored 50 points during the 1998–99 season 25 years ago.
Answer: True. Oddly, no one scored 50. Antonio McDyess, Allen Iverson, and Grant Hill tied for the highest score with 46.

75. Who had the highest scoring game 10 years ago in 2014?
A. LeBron James   B. Kevin Durant   C. Carmelo Anthony
D. Terrence Ross
Answer: C. Anthony tallied 62 for the Knicks in a 125–96 win over the Bobcats on January 24, 2014. He connected on 23 of 35 shots. Kevin Durant had five of the top 10 top scores ranging from 46 to 54 points.

76. Who scored the most points in a single game during the 1973–74 season, 50 years ago?
A. Fred Brown   B. Bob McAdoo   C. Rick Barry   D. Gail Goodrich
Answer: C. Barry was the only 60-point scorer in 1974, pouring in 64 for the Warriors against the Blazers in a 143–120 win in the penultimate game of the season on March 26, 1974. Barry also topped 50 points twice that season, giving him the fourth and fifth highest totals too.

77. True or False? None of the following players got 30 rebounds in a game during the 1973–74 season 50 years ago.

A. Elvin Hayes   B. Nate Thurmond   C. Jim Fox   D. George Johnson

Answer: False. A, C, and D hit the mark. The Wizards' Hayes registered a season best 32 boards in a 115–109 loss against the Hawks. Sonics center Jim Fox grabbed 30 and got 25 points and nine assists in a 129–105 win against the Lakers. Johnson, the Warriors' 6'11" center, only averaged 7.9 a game but grabbed 30 in a 112–107 loss to the Lakers.

78. True or False? No player had 20 assists during the 1998–99 season 25 years ago.

Answer: False. Playing for the Nets, Stephon Marbury logged 26 points and 20 assists against the Pacers in a 120–98 victory on April 25, 1999.

79. Which player led in minutes in the most games 50 years ago?

A. Austin Carr   B. Jo Jo White   C. Bob Love   D. Kareem Abdul-Jabbar

Answer: D. Ten players stayed on the floor for 53 minutes in a game in 1974. Abdul-Jabbar was the only player who did it more than once, accomplishing the feat three times. In one of the three overtime games, on March 12, Abdul-Jabbar posted 44 points, 12 rebounds, four steals, and four blocks.

80. True or False? No player had 25 assists during the 1973–74 season 50 years ago.

Answer: False. The Braves' diminutive guard Ernie DiGregorio got 25 assists on January 1, 1974, in a 120–119 road victory over the Blazers. He also had 20 points and nine rebounds.

81. Which Knick had his career high in points 50 years ago?

A. Dave DeBusschere   B. Earl Monroe   C. Walt Frazier   D. Willis Reed

Answer: C. Frazier connected on 20 of his 24 shots and scored 44 for the game in a 106–91 road win over the Lakers on November 2, 1973.

82. Which of the following teams won a title 10 years after they won their first title?

A. Lakers   B. Warriors   C. Celtics   D. Royals

Answer: None of them. The Lakers won in 1949 and were swept by the Celtics in 1959. The Warriors won in 1947 and didn't play in the Finals in 1957. The Celtics won in 1957 but lost in the conference finals to the 76ers in 1967. The Royals won in 1951 and didn't make the Finals as the Royals in 1961.

83. Which team won the championship in the NBA's 25th anniversary year?

A. Knicks   B. Bucks   C. Lakers   D. Celtics

Answer: B. The 1971 Bucks took the Bullets four straight in the silver anniversary season.

84. Which team won the championship in the NBA's 50th anniversary year?

A. Pistons   B. Rockets   C. Bulls   D. Spurs

Answer: C. In 1996 the Bulls won 72 and lost 10. In the Finals they beat the Sonics four games to two.

85. Which team won the championship in the NBA's 75th anniversary year?

A. Warriors   B. Bucks   C. Lakers   D. Raptors

Answer: B. The Bucks won in 2021, beating the Suns in six after falling behind two games to none.

86. What team was the champion in the NBA's 30th anniversary year?

A. Warriors   B. Celtics   C. Lakers   D. Knicks

Answer: B. The Celtics topped the Suns in six games in the 1976 Finals.

87. Name the team that won the championship in the NBA's 10th anniversary year.

A. Nationals   B. Celtics   C. Warriors   D. Pistons

Answer: C. The Philadelphia Warriors took the Fort Wayne Pistons in five games. Paul Arizin led the way with 27.6 points and eight rebounds per game. George Yardley was stellar for the Pistons in a losing cause, averaging 24.8 points and 15 rebounds.

AWARDS

88. Name the player whose number has been retired by all teams.
A. Wilt Chamberlain   B. Bill Russell   C. Michael Jordan
D. Kareem Abdul-Jabbar
Answer: B. Following Russell's death on July 31, 2022, the NBA decided that no player would ever wear #6 again.

89. Which of the following player(s) won Rookie of the Year and MVP in the same season?
A. Kareem Abdul-Jabbar   B. Wilt Chamberlain   C. Wes Unseld
D. Magic Johnson   E. Larry Bird
Answer: B and C. Chamberlain won both honors in 1960, when he averaged an astounding 37.6 points and 27 rebounds per game. Unseld, the Bullets' 6'7" center, grabbed both honors in 1969, when he posted 13.8 points and 18.2 rebounds a game.

90. Name the first Comeback Player of the Year.
A. Bernard King   B. Nate Archibald   C. Gus Williams   D. Paul Westphal
Answer: B. Archibald took the honor in 1980, when he averaged 14.1 points and 8.4 assists as the Celtics point guard. Seven years earlier he was the only player in NBA history to lead the league in points (34.0) and assists (11.4) while playing for the Kansas City–Omaha Kings.

91. Who was the last player to win back-to-back MVP Awards?
A. LeBron James   B. Giannis Antetokounmpo   C. James Harden
D. Nikola Jokić
Answer: D. The Nuggets' center took the award in 2021 and 2022.

92. Name the MVP of the 1976 Finals.

A. Jo Jo White   B. Dave Cowens   C. Charlie Scott   D. John Havlicek

Answer: A. White posted 21.7 points, 4.3 rebounds, and 5.8 assists per game. The Celtics beat the Suns in six games.

93. True or False? No one has ever won Defensive Player of the Year three or more times.

Answer: False. Dikembe Mutombo, Ben Wallace, and Rudy Gobert won it four times each. Dwight Howard won it three times.

94. Who was the last player to win three straight MVPs?

A. Magic Johnson   B. Kevin Durant   C. Larry Bird   D. Michael Jordan

Answer: C. He reeled off three straight from 1984 through 1986.

95. True or False? Three players won all the MVPs in the 1960s.

Answer: False. Four players won all 10 awards. Wilt Chamberlain won in 1960 and 1966 through 1968. Bill Russell also won four: 1961 through 1963 and 1965. The other two were won by Oscar Robertson (1964) and Wes Unseld (1969).

96. What player(s) won the Finals MVPs in the Knicks' 1970 and 1973 championships?

A. Willis Reed   B. Walt Frazier   C. Earl Monroe   D. Dave DeBusschere

Answer: A. In 1970 Reed limped out on the court and played 27 minutes against Wilt Chamberlain in Game 7. He averaged 23 points and 10 rebounds for the series. In 1973 the Knicks beat the Lakers in five games and Reed posted 16 points and nine rebounds per game.

97. Who won the game MVP of the 1977 All-Star Game?

A. Paul Westphal   B. George McGinnis   C. Kareem Abdul-Jabbar
D. Julius Erving

Answer: D. In the first All-Star Game following the NBA-ABA merger, Julius Erving heard boos as he accepted the MVP trophy from Commissioner Larry O'Brien. The crowd at Milwaukee Arena booed, thinking that the Suns' Paul Westphal should have been MVP. But Erving posted 30 points, 12 rebounds, three assists, and four steals, compared to Westphal's 20 points, one rebound, six assists, and three steals. The West won 125–124.

98. Who was the NBA Defensive Player of the Year in 2022?
A. Marcus Smart   B. Rudy Gobert   C. Mikal Bridges   D. Jrue Holiday
Answer: A. Smart received 37 first place votes from a panel of 100 sports media. He was the first guard to win the award since Gary Payton won in 1996.

99. Who won the All-Star Game MVP the most times?
A. Bob Cousy   B. Kobe Bryant   C. Oscar Robertson   D. Bob Pettit
Answer: B and D. Each won or shared the award four times. A Hawks forward who averaged 26 points and 16 rebounds per game for his career, Pettit won in 1956, 1958, shared it with Elgin Baylor in 1959, and won in 1962. Bryant won in 2002, 2007, shared it with Shaquille O'Neal in 2009, and won in 2011.

100. Which player won the MVP of the 1996 All-Star Game in a controversial decision?
A. Michael Jordan   B. Shaquille O'Neal   C. Anfernee Hardaway
D. David Robinson
Answer: A. Jordan scored 20 but his teammate O'Neal had 25 points and 10 rebounds in a 129–118 victory for the East.

101. True or False? Celtics players have won the most MVPs.
Answer: True. Celtics have won 10. The Lakers are second with eight.

102. Name the last coach to win Coach of the Year in the year his team won the championship.
A. Steve Kerr   B. Gregg Popovich   C. Nick Nurse   D. Mike Budenholzer
Answer: B. Popovich won the award in 2014 when his Spurs finished 62-20 and took the Heat 4–1 in the NBA Finals.

103. Name the player who was first to win Sixth Man of the Year in back-to-back seasons.
A. John Havlicek   B. Kevin McHale   C. Frank Ramsey
D. Detlef Schrempf
Answer: B. The Celtics' Hall of Fame forward won in 1984 and 1985. In both seasons he played more than 30 minutes off the bench.

104. Name the MVP of the 1975 Finals.
A. Wes Unseld   B. Phil Chenier   C. Kevin Porter   D. Rick Barry
Answer: D. Barry averaged 29.5 in the Warriors' four-game sweep of the Bullets.

105. Who was the first to win the Most Improved Player Award and also be inducted into the Hall of Fame?
A. Tracy McGrady   B. Jalen Rose   C. Jermaine O'Neal
D. Darrell Armstrong
Answer: A. McGrady won the award in 2001 and was inducted to the Hall in 2017.

106. Name the first player to win the Sixth Man Award.
A. Bobby Jones   B. John Havlicek   C. Kevin McHale   D. Frank Ramsey
Answer: A. Famous sixth men—including Celtics' Hall of Famers Frank Ramsey and John Havlicek—competed for decades before the NBA gave out an award for it. The 76ers' Hall of Fame forward Bobby Jones won it in 1983, the first year it was given.

107. Name the most recent player to win the Sixth Man of the Year Award in consecutive seasons.
A. Jamal Crawford   B. Lamar Odom   C. Bobby Jackson
D. Lou Williams
Answer: D. The 17-year veteran point guard for the Hawks has won the award thrice, most recently in 2018 and 2019.

108. Who won the All-Star Game MVP in 2007?
A. Kobe Bryant   B. Kevin Garnett   C. LeBron James   D. Vince Carter
Answer: A. Bryant hoisted the West on his shoulders in a 153–132 win as he posted 31 points, five rebounds, six assists, and six steals.

109. Who took home MVP honors in the 2021 All-Star Game?
A. Stephen Curry   B. LeBron James   C. Luka Dončić
D. Giannis Antetokounmpo
Answer: D. Giannis scored 35 in Team LeBron's 170–150 victory over Team Durant. Neither of the players the teams were named for saw action.

110. Who scored 50 points and won the MVP in the 2022 All-Star Game?
A. Joel Embiid   B. LeBron James   C. Stephen Curry   D. Devin Booker
Answer: C. He hit 16 of 27 from the 3-point line and one 2-pointer as Team LeBron eked out a 163–160 victory over Team Durant.

111. Which of the following players did not win the Defensive Player of the Year Award twice?

A. Michael Cooper   B. Mark Eaton   C. Dennis Rodman
D. Hakeem Olajuwon

Answer: A. The rail-thin 6'7" Laker guard won it only once, in 1988, when the Lakers won a second straight title.

112. Name the Most Valuable Player in the 2009 All-Star Game played in Phoenix.

A. Shaquille O'Neal   B. Tim Duncan   C. Kobe Bryant   D. LeBron James

Answer: A and C. The Lakers' guard and Suns center were reunited on the same side. Bryant tallied 27 points. Playing just 11 minutes off the bench, O'Neal scored 17 to help the West to a 146–119 blowout.

113. Three different players won two or more MVPs in the 1980s. Who are they?

A. Magic Johnson   B. Julius Erving   C. Moses Malone   D. Larry Bird

Answer: A, C, and D. Malone won in 1982 and 1983. Bird won from 1984 through 1986. Johnson won in 1987 and 1989.

114. Name the most recent Most Improved Player Award winner to later win an MVP.

Answer: Giannis Antetokounmpo was voted the most improved player in 2017, his fourth season, when he tallied 22.9 points and 8.8 rebounds per game.

115. Which of the following coaches did not win three NBA Coach of the Year Awards?

A. Larry Brown   B. Gregg Popovich   C. Pat Riley   D. Don Nelson

Answer: A. Brown is the only coach to win honors three times in the ABA. But he won just once in the NBA.

116. Name the first Knick to win Rookie of the Year honors.

A. Patrick Ewing   B. Carl Braun   C. Jim Barnes   D. Willis Reed

Answer: D. Drafted 10th overall in 1964, Reed, a 6'9" center and forward, played all 80 games and averaged 19.5 points and 14.7 rebounds per game. He beat out runner-up Luke Jackson for the award.

117. Name the most recent 76er to win Rookie of the Year honors.

A. Ben Simmons   B. Michael Carter-Williams   C. Luke Jackson
D. Allen Iverson
Answer: A. Simmons, a 6'10" point guard, beat out runner-up Donovan Mitchell in 2018. Simmons made an overall contribution, averaging 15.8 points, eight rebounds, and eight assists.

118. Who won his first of consecutive MVPs in 2019?

A. LeBron James   B. James Harden   C. Luka Dončić
D. Kawhi Leonard   E. Giannis Antetokounmpo
Answer: E. "The Greek Freak" averaged 27.7 points and 12.5 rebounds in 2019. He drew 78 percent of the first-place votes, winning easily over runner-up James Harden.

119. Who won the MVP in 1960?

A. Wilt Chamberlain   B. Bill Russell   C. Bob Pettit   D. Bob Cousy
E. Elgin Baylor
Answer: A. Chamberlain, in his rookie season, won the award with the other four here finishing two through five in the voting. Chamberlain averaged 37.6 points and 27 rebounds.

120. How many times did Red Auerbach win Coach of the Year in the first 10 years the award was given?

A. One   B. Five   C. Seven   D. Eight
Answer: A. Auerbach led the Celtics to four titles the first four years the award was bestowed, from 1963 to 1966. Despite that run of excellence, Red was awarded just once, when his troops finished 62-18 in 1965.

121. Rank the oldest players among the following to win Finals MVP Awards.

A. Michael Jordan   B. Kareem Abdul-Jabbar   C. Stephen Curry
D. Wilt Chamberlain
Answer: 1-B, 38, 1985 Finals; 2-D, 35 years, 8 months; 3-A, 35 years, three months; 4-C, 34 years, 3 months.

122. Who won the MVP of the 1979 Finals?

A. Dennis Johnson   B. Gus Williams   C. Jack Sikma   D. Fred Brown
Answer: A. Johnson was a force on offense and defense, leading the Sonics to a five-game victory over the Bullets. He averaged 22.6 points, six rebounds, and six assists. He also recorded 11 blocks and nine steals.

123. What coach won the Coach of the Year Award for the Grizzlies?
A. Lionel Hollins   B. Bob Hill   C. Hubie Brown   D. Taylor Jenkins
Answer: C. Brown earned the award in 2004, leading the Grizzlies to
their first 50-win season.

124. True or False? Bill Russell won the MVP of the 1969 Finals.
Answer: False. Though his Lakers lost in seven games to the Celtics in
the last series played by Russell and Sam Jones, Jerry West averaged
37.9 points and 7.4 assists and won the award for the 1969 series. His
high score was 53 points in Game 1.

**125. Name the three Sixth Man of the Year Award winners to play for
the Knicks.**
A. John Starks   B. Anthony Mason   C. J. R. Smith   D. Truck Robinson
Answer: A (1997), B (1995), and C (2013).

126. Name the first winner of the NBA Hustle Award.
A. Patrick Beverley   B. Amir Johnson   C. Marcus Smart
D. Montrezl Harrell   E. Thaddeus Young
Answer: A. Beverley won the award in 2017, the first year it was given. All
five of the players here have won, with Smart winning twice.

127. Name the MVP of the 1971 Finals.
A. Wes Unseld   B. Bob Dandridge   C. Kareem Abdul-Jabbar
D. Earl Monroe
Answer: C. Abdul-Jabbar was unstoppable in the four-game sweep of
the Bullets, averaging 27 points and 18.5 rebounds for the series.

**128. Name the Grizzlies' player who won the Defensive Player of the
Year Award.**
A. Ja Morant   B. Marc Gasol   C. Shane Battier   D. Rudy Gay
Answer: B. The center and Barcelona native won the award in 2013, as
the team posted a best ever 56-26 record.

**129. Which team is the last to win back-to-back Rookie of the Year
Awards?**
Answer: The Timberwolves did it back-to-back with Andrew Wiggins
winning in 2015 and Karl-Anthony Towns in 2016.

Tim Duncan

130. Name the most recent Rookie of the Year to make the Hall of Fame.
A. Vince Carter   B. Allen Iverson   C. Tim Duncan
D. Damon Stoudamire
Answer: C. Duncan earned Rookie of the Year honors in 1998 and was elected to the Hall of Fame in 2020.

131. True or False? One Grizzlies player won the MVP award.
Answer: False. No Grizzlies player ever won the award.

132. Name the first person who won the Executive of the Year Award who had already been elected to the Hall of Fame.
A. Eddie Donovan   B. Bob Ferry   C. Walter Brown   D. Red Auerbach
Answer: D. Red was the eighth person to win the Executive of the Year award when he won in 1980. He had been elected to the Hall of Fame 11 years earlier as a coach.

133. True or False? Miami has had two different MVPs in their history.
Answer: False. Only LeBron James has won the award in the 34-year history of the Heat. He won it in 2012 and 2013.

134. What guard was named to the NBA All-Defensive First Team nine consecutive times from 1994 through 2002?
A. Gary Payton   B. Mookie Blaylock   C. Kobe Bryant   D. Michael Jordan
Answer: A. "The Glove" won nine straight for the Sonics. He was named to the NBA 75th Anniversary Team in 2021.

135. What centers were named to the NBA All-Defensive First Team in their last season?
A. Bill Russell   B. Willis Reed   C. Wilt Chamberlain   D. Dave Cowens
Answer: A and C. Russell won the award in 1969, the first year it was given and his last title year with the Celtics. Chamberlain earned the honor in 1973 for his second straight season.

136. Who did not win a Finals MVP more than once?
A. Larry Bird   B. Magic Johnson   C. Isiah Thomas
D. Kareem Abdul-Jabbar
Answer: C. Thomas's lone MVP was for the Pistons' five-game victory over the Blazers in 1990, when he averaged 27 points, five rebounds, and seven assists.

137. True or False? One Knick has won the Most Improved Player.

Answer: True. Julius Randle won the award in 2021. He posted a career best 24.1 points and 10 rebounds and made the All-Star team.

138. True or False? One Hall of Famer won the Twyman-Stokes Award for teammate of the year.

Answer: True. Tim Duncan won the award in 2015, the third year it was given. The award is named after Jack Twyman and Maurice Stokes, who played together on the Rochester/Cincinnati Royals from 1955 to 1958, when Stokes's career was cut short by a head injury he suffered from a fall. Stokes later became paralyzed due to post-traumatic encephalopathy, a brain injury that damages the motor-control center. Twyman became Stokes's legal guardian and advocate until Stokes died in 1970.

139. Who won the most MVPs from 2000 through 2009?

A. Kobe Bryant   B. Steve Nash   C. Tim Duncan   D. Allen Iverson

Answer: B and C. Nash (2005 and 2006) and Duncan (2002 and 2003) won two each.

140. Name the player who has won back-to-back MVPs twice since 2000.

A. Stephen Curry   B. Tim Duncan   C. LeBron James   D. Kobe Bryant

Answer: C. "King James" did it twice: in 2009 and 2010 and 2012 and 2013.

141. Name the most recent player to win Finals MVPs with at least two different teams.

A. Kevin Durant   B. Kawhi Leonard   C. LeBron James
D. Shaquille O'Neal

Answer: C. James has done it with three teams: the Heat (2012 and 2013), the Cavaliers (2016), and the Lakers (2020).

BASKETBALL BY THE DECADE

142. Name the franchise that had three number one overall draft picks in the 1970s.
A. Pistons   B. Cavaliers   C. Bucks   D. Trail Blazers
Answer: D. The Blazers picked La Rue Martin first in 1972, Bill Walton in 1974, and Mychal Thompson in 1978.

143. Match the 1970s players with their nicknames.
1. Darryl Dawkins   2. Julius Erving   3. Eric Floyd   4. Walt Frazier
A. Clyde   B. Sleepy   C. Chocolate Thunder   D. The Doctor
Answer: 1-C; 2-D; 3-B; 4-A.

144. Match the 1950s players with their nicknames.
1. Nathaniel Clifton   2. Slater Martin   3. Vern Mikkelsen   4. Jim Pollard
A. Bones   B. The Great Dane   C. Dugie   D. Sweetwater
Answer: 1-D; 2-C; 3-B; 4-A.

145. Match the 1970s players with their nicknames.
1. Nate Archibald   2. Marvin Barnes   3. Dick Barnett   4. Bill Bradley
A. Fall-Back Baby   B. Mr. President   C. Tiny   D. Bad News
Answer: 1-C; 2-D; 3-A; 4-B.

146. Name the only team to have two number one overall draft picks in the 1980s.
A. Rockets   B. Spurs   C. Clippers   D. Knicks
Answer: A. The Rockets picked Ralph Sampson first in 1983 and Hakeem Olajuwon first in 1984.

147. Name the only team to have three number one overall draft picks in the 1960s.

A. Bucks   B. Rockets   C. Pistons   D. Knicks

Answer: D. The Knicks drew the first draft pick in 1963 and selected Art Heyman, picked Jim Barnes first in 1964, and took Cazzie Russell first in 1966.

BASKETBALL BY THE LETTERS

148. Who scored the most points for a player whose last name began with H?
Answer: Elvin Hayes scored 26,313 points.

149. Who scored the most points for a player whose last name began with I?
Answer: Dan Issel tallied 27,482 points.

150. Who scored the most points for a player whose last name began with E?
Answer: Alex English scored 25,613 points.

151. Who scored the most points for a player whose last name began with W?
Answer: Jerry West, 25,192 points.

152. Who scored the most points for a player whose last name began with A?
Answer: Kareem Abdul-Jabbar, 38,387 points.

153. Name the only player whose last name begins with the letter U who was named to the NBA's 75th Anniversary Team.
Answer: Wes Unseld (1946–2020), the 6'7" center for the Baltimore/Capital/Washington Bullets, who averaged 14 rebounds per game for his 13-year career. He was elected to the Hall of Fame in 1988.

154. True or False? No one whose last name begins with the letter I was picked for the NBA's 75th Anniversary Team.
Answer: False. Allen Iverson was picked. The 2016 Hall of Fame inductee was an 11-time All-Star and won the scoring title four times.

155. True or False? Julius Erving was the only player whose last name began with E to be selected to the NBA's 75th Anniversary Team.
Answer: False. Patrick Ewing, the "Hoya Destroya," played 17 seasons and was inducted to the Hall of Fame in 2008.

156. True or False? Only one player whose last name begins with F was selected for the NBA's 75th Anniversary Team.
Answer: True. Walt Frazier, a guard from Southern Illinois University who was inducted to the Hall of Fame in 1987, made the 75th Anniversary Team.

157. True or False? Only one player whose last name begins with K was picked for the NBA's 75th Anniversary Team.
Answer: False. No one on the 75th Anniversary Team has a last name beginning with K.

158. Name the two players whose last name begins with T to be picked for the NBA's 75th Anniversary Team.
Answer: Pistons guard Isiah Thomas and Warriors center Nate Thurmond.

159. True or False? Dirk Nowitzki was the only player whose last name began with N to be selected to the NBA's 75th Anniversary Team.
Answer: False. Steve Nash, known as "MVSteve," played 18 years, won the MVP twice, and was elected to the Hall of Fame in 2018.

160. How many players whose last name begins with H were selected to the NBA's 75th Anniversary Team?
A. One   B. Two   C. Three   D. Four
Answer: C. Elvin Hayes, John Havlicek, and James Harden were all selected.

161. Which of the following players scored the most points for a player whose last name began with G?
A. Kevin Garnett   B. George Gervin   C. Artis Gilmore   D. Hal Greer
Answer: B. Gervin scored 26,595 points.

162. Who scored the most points for a player whose last name began with B?
Answer: Kobe Bryant scored 33,643 points.

163. Who scored the most ABA points for a player whose last name began with D?
Answer: Louie Dampier scored 13,726 points.

164. Who gathered the most rebounds for a player whose last name began with D?
Answer: Tim Duncan, 15,091.

165. Who gathered the most rebounds for a player whose last name began with T?
Answer: Nate Thurmond grabbed 14,464 rebounds.

166. True or False? There is no player whose last name begins with Z in the Hall of Fame.
Answer: True, though Fred Zollner is in the Hall as a contributor since he was a key figure in the merger between the Basketball Association of America and the National Basketball Leagues to form the NBA in 1949.

167. True or False? There is no player whose name begins with Y who is in the Hall of Fame.
Answer: False. Small forward George Yardley played seven years with Fort Wayne, Detroit, and Syracuse and led the league in scoring in 1957.

BASKETBALL BY THE NUMBERS

168. Who is the most recent player to lead the league in assists per game in five different seasons?
A. Russell Westbrook   B. Steve Nash   C. Chris Paul
D. Rajon Rondo
Answer: C. Paul got his fifth assist title in 2022. Nash got his fifth in 2011.

169. Which of the following players led the league in assists in 1995?
A. Rod Strickland   B. Tim Hardaway   C. John Stockton
D. Kenny Anderson
Answer: C. Stockton led the circuit with 12.3 assists per game. The Jazz guard was the only player to register double-digit assists.

170. Rank the following players for single-season records in 3-point goals.
A. Stephen Curry   B. James Harden   C. Paul George   D. Buddy Hield
E. Klay Thompson
Answer: 1-A, 402 3-pointers in 2016 (of the top 10 single-season totals, Curry also owns the record for the third through fifth best seasons and the tenth best); 2-B, 378, fourth best in 2019 (and seventh best); 3-E, 301, sixth best in 2023; 4-C, eighth best with 292 in 2019; 5-D, ninth best with 282 in 2023.

171. Who made 60 percent of his field goals twice in the NBA Finals?
A. Shaquille O'Neal   B. Artis Gilmore   C. Wilt Chamberlain
D. Kareem Abdul-Jabbar
Answer: D. He did it in 1971 against the Bullets (60.5) and 1985 against the Celtics (60.4).

172. Who posted 21 points and 15 assists to win the All-Star Game MVP in 1984?
A. Larry Bird   B. Magic Johnson   C. Isiah Thomas
Answer: C. Thomas also stole the ball four times in the 154–145 victory. He topped Julius Erving in the voting, who posted 34 points and eight rebounds. He also topped Magic Johnson, who nearly got a triple-double with 15 points, 22 assists, and nine rebounds.

173. Name the Hornets' all-time assist leader.
A. Muggsy Bogues   B. Kemba Walker   C. David Wesley
D. Raymond Felton
Answer: A. The 5'3" guard had 5,557 assists, ahead of Walker by 2,249 assists for the team record.

174. Who holds the record for most rebounds in a season?
Answer: Wilt Chamberlain gathered 2,149 rebounds in 1961, which averages to 27.2 per game. He owns the top seven totals of all time.

175. True or False? Only Alex English scored 20,000 points as a Nugget.
Answer: True. English scored 21,645 points.

176. Name the player who drew the most votes for the 2011 All-Star Game and also won the MVP.
A. Kevin Durant   B. LeBron James   C. Dwyane Wade   D. Kobe Bryant
Answer: D. Bryant received 2,380,016 votes and then proceeded to tear up the court with 37 points and 14 rebounds in a 148–143 victory for the West.

177. Name the three starters who combined for 85 points in the 2012 All-Star Game.
A. Kevin Durant   B. Kobe Bryant   C. Blake Griffin   D. LeBron James
Answer: A, B, and C. The frontcourt starters for the West were led by Durant, who tallied 36 points (James had the same number for the East) and won the MVP.

178. True or False? Only one player averaged three or more blocks per game for his Nets career.
Answer: True. Shawn Bradley, the 7'6" center from Germany, averaged 3.8 blocks during his two seasons with the Nets.

179. True or False? Only one player averaged 20 points or better for his career with the Hornets.
Answer: False. Glen Rice averaged 23.5 points per game, Alonzo Mourning averaged 21.3, and Jamal Mashburn put up 20.6.

180. True or False? Joe Harris holds the Nets' record for 3-point field goals in a season.
Answer: False. D'Angelo Russell made 234 in 2019 for the team record.

181. Who hold the Bulls' season record for assists per game?
A. Derrick Rose   B. Guy Rodgers   C. Michael Jordan   D. Ennis Whatley
Answer: B. Rodgers, the former Warrior who was the point guard when Chamberlain averaged 50.4 points in 1962, averaged a record 11.2 assists for the Bulls in 1967.

182. Who holds the mark for most points scored in a season?
Answer: Wilt Chamberlain scored 4,029 points in 1962 for the record. The closest player, Michael Jordan, is nearly 1,000 behind at 3,041 in 1987.

183. True or False? Only Wilt Chamberlain snagged 50 rebounds in a game.
Answer: False. Before Chamberlain recorded 55 rebounds in a losing effort against the Celtics in November of 1960, Bill Russell grabbed 51 against the Syracuse Nationals in February of 1960.

184. True or False? Stephen Curry holds the record for free throws made in a quarter.
Answer: False. Anthony Davis hit 18 free throws in the third quarter against the Grizzlies on October 29, 2019. The Lakers won 120–91.

185. True or False? Michael Jordan attempted the most free throws in a quarter.
Answer: False. A month after his NBA debut, Ben Simmons set the mark when he attempted 24 in the fourth quarter against the Wizards on November 29, 2017. He also set the rookie record for attempts in a game with 29. But he made just 15 in a 118–113 victory over the Wizards.

186. Name the last player to score 2,500 points in a season.
A. Russell Westbrook   B. LeBron James   C. James Harden
D. Stephen Curry
Answer: C. Then with Houston, Harden logged 2,818 points in the 2019 season, when he averaged a personal best 36.1 per game.

187. True or False? More than one player has scored more than 20,000 points and 20,000 rebounds.
Answer: False. Only Wilt Chamberlain has accomplished the feat.

188. What two players combined to win five consecutive scoring titles from 2001 to 2005?
Answer: Allen Iverson (2001, 31.1 ppg; 2002, 31.4; 2005, 30.7) and Tracy McGrady (2003, 32.1; 2004, 28).

189. True or False? No player ever won 10 rebounding titles in a row.
Answer: True. Wilt Chamberlain won 11 rebounding titles overall in 14 years but never 10 in a row.

190. What two players tied for the record for free throws made in one half?
A. Jerry West   B. Rick Barry   C. Michael Jordan   D. Devin Booker
Answer: C and D. Jordan made 20 of 23 charity tosses in the first half and scored 39 against the Heat in a 105–100 win on December 30, 1992. Booker made 20 free throws in the second half and 24 of 26 overall and scored 70 points on March 24, 2017. The Suns lost to the Celtics 130–120.

191. Since 1980, what players have won five consecutive rebounding titles?
A. Andre Drummond   B. Moses Malone   C. Dennis Rodman
D. Dwight Howard
Answer: B and C. Malone won five straight from 1981 through 1985. Rodman ran off eight straight from 1991 through 1998.

192. True or False? Several players have recorded 1,000 assists in a season.
Answer: True. John Stockton did it seven times, while Isiah Thomas and Kevin Porter did it once each.

193. Who made the most free throws in a game without missing?
A. James Harden   B. Rick Barry   C. Mark Price   D. Stephen Curry
Answer: A. Playing for the Rockets, Harden dropped 24 without a miss against the Spurs on December 3, 2019.

194. Name the leading scorer in the 1986 All-Star Game.
A. Larry Bird   B. Moses Malone   C. James Worthy   D. Isiah Thomas
Answer: D. "Zeke" won his second MVP in three years, gathering 30 points, 10 assists, and five steals in a 139–132 East victory.

195. Who won five assist titles in a row?
A. Steve Nash   B. Magic Johnson   C. Bob Cousy   D. John Stockton
Answer: C and D. Cousy won eight in a row from 1953 through 1960. Stockton won nine straight from 1988 through 1996.

196. True or False? No one has averaged four blocks per game in a season since 2000.
Answer: True. The last player to average four blocks was Dikembe Mutombo, who averaged 4.49 blocks in 1996.

197. To qualify for an NBA scoring title, how many of his team's games must a player compete in?
A. 70 percent   B. 75 percent   C. 80 percent   D. 85 percent
Answer: A. The player must play at least 58 of the team's games in an 82-game schedule.

198. To qualify for an NBA field goal percentage title, how many field goals must he attempt?
A. 250   B. 300   C. 350   D. 400
Answer: B. A player must take 300 shots, which is less than four per game in an 82-game schedule.

199. True or False? The Nuggets never won 60 or more games in back-to-back seasons.
Answer: False. They won 65 in 1975 and 60 in 1976.

200. What two players share the mark for steals in a game?
A. Walt Frazier   B. Larry Kenon   C. Kendall Gill   D. John Stockton
Answer: B and C. Both had 11 steals in a game. Playing for the Spurs, Kenon did it against the K.C. Kings on December 26, 1976. Competing for the Nets, Gill did it against the Heat on April 3, 1999.

201. Name the player who scored 40 in the 1988 All-Star Game.
A. Dominique Wilkins   B. Michael Jordan   C. Magic Johnson
D. Moses Malone
Answer: B. Playing at Chicago Stadium, Jordan was all over. He hit 17 of 23 shots in 29 minutes. He also had eight rebounds, four blocks, and four steals.

202. True or False? All five of the following players have 35,000 points or more.
A. LeBron James   B. Dirk Nowitzki   C. Kareem Abdul-Jabbar
D. Karl Malone   E. Kobe Bryant
Answer: False. Dirk Nowitzki and Kobe Bryant do not have 35,000 points.

203. To qualify for an NBA 3-point percentage title, how many shots must a player attempt?
A. 82   B. 100   C. 164   D. 246
Answer: A. Attempt one 3-pointer per game and you qualify for the title.

204. Name the Mavericks' career leader in assists per game and steals per game?
A. Jason Kidd   B. Steve Nash   C. Luka Dončić   D. Michael Finley
Answer: A. He averaged 8.4 assists and 1.9 steals as a Maverick.

205. Who played the most seasons with one team?
A. Bob Cousy   B. Dirk Nowitzki   C. Bob Pettit   D. John Stockton
Answer: B. "The German Race Car" debuted in 1999 and played his last game in 2019, all 21 seasons with the Dallas Mavericks.

206. Who led the league in deflections per game in 2022?
A. Delon Wright   B. Nikola Jokić   C. Jimmy Butler   D. Jrue Holiday
Answer: B. In the "hustle" category, it was the Nuggets' star who deflected four balls per game.

207. Rank the all-time leaders in points.

A. Karl Malone   B. Kareem Abdul-Jabbar   C. Kobe Bryant
D. LeBron James   E. Michael Jordan

Answer: Two of the five never played in college: LeBron James and Kobe Bryant. James and Bryant made their NBA debuts at 18 years of age. By contrast, Abdul-Jabbar finished college and didn't debut until he was 22 years and four months old. So, when people talk of James passing Abdul-Jabbar in points, they never mention that he had four extra years to amass points, since he never attended college. 1-D, 38,652; 2-B, 38,387; 3-A, 36,928; 4-C, 33,643; 5-E, 32,292.

208. Who posted a triple-double in the 1994 All-Star Game?

A. Kenny Anderson   B. Mark Price   C. Scottie Pippen   D. John Stockton

Answer: C. With Jordan off playing baseball, it was Pippen's year to thrive. He won MVP honors, posting 29 points, 11 rebounds, 11 assists, and had four steals in a 127–118 win for the East.

209. How many field goals per game did Wilt Chamberlain average during his record-setting 1961–62 season?

A. 15   B. 17   C. 20   D. 21

Answer: C. Wilt made a record 1,597 field goals in 80 games for an average of 20 made per game.

210. Who tallied the most points in the West's 196–173 win in the 2016 All-Star Game?

A. Stephen Curry   B. Russell Westbrook   C. Anthony Davis
D. Paul George

Answer: D. George scored a game-high 41, but Westbrook snatched his second straight MVP with 31 as the West scored 50 or more in three of four quarters.

211. What record did Stephen Curry set in Game 1 of the 2022 Finals?

A. He hit 12 3-pointers in the game.   B. He hit nine 3-pointers in a half.   C. He hit six 3-pointers in the first quarter.
Answer: C.

212. True or False? No one has averaged three steals per game since 2000.

Answer: True. It's been more than 30 years since anyone averaged three steals per game. Alvin Robertson stole 3.04 per game in 1991.

213. Which player holds the season record for minutes per game since 2000?
A. Allen Iverson   B. Michael Jordan   C. Cuttino Mobley
D. Antoine Walker
Answer: A. The diminutive Philadelphia guard averaged an astounding 43.7 minutes per game over the 2001–2 season. In fact, Iverson holds the top four yearly marks since 2000.

214. Rank the following players in career NBA points.
A. Kareem Abdul-Jabbar   B. Karl Malone   C. Dirk Nowitzki
D. Michael Jordan   E. Wilt Chamberlain
Answer: 1-A, 38,387 points; 2-B, 37,062; 3-D, 32,292; 4-C, 31,560; 5-E, 31,419.

215. True or False? Russell Westbrook leads all active players in games with 50 points and 10 assists.
Answer: False. James Harden has eight such games. Westbrook has three.

216. How many players had 19 or more points for the West in the 2003 All-Star Game?
A. One   B. Three   C. Five   D. Six
Answer: C. Led by Kevin Garnett who posted a monstrous 37 points and nine rebounds and earned MVP honors, the West needed two overtimes to win 155–145.

217. Who holds the ABA record for minutes per game?
A. Spencer Haywood   B. Gerald Govan   C. Rick Barry
D. Connie Hawkins
Answer: A. The 6′8″ Silver City, Mississippi, native averaged a staggering 45.73 minutes per game as a rookie during the 1969–70 season when he played for the Denver Rockets.

218. True or False? Michael Jordan has the most seasons with 25 or more points per game in the NBA.
Answer: False. LeBron James has 19 seasons scoring 25 or more.

219. Name the last player to average 20 rebounds per game for a season?

A. Bob Pettit   B. Dennis Rodman   C. Jerry Lucas   D. Wilt Chamberlain

Answer: D. It was 1969, over a half-century ago, that the "Big Dipper" grabbed 20 per game off the glass. Wilt averaged 21.14 boards per game. It was his 10th consecutive year grabbing 20 per game.

220. How many players have posted three or more consecutive scoring titles?

A. One   B. Two   C. Four   D. Six   E. Eight

Answer: E. The eight are George Mikan, Neil Johnston, Wilt Chamberlain, Bob McAdoo, Michael Jordan, George Gervin, Kevin Durant, and James Harden.

221. Match the players with their original jersey number.

1. Bob Cousy   2. Wilt Chamberlain   3. John Havlicek   4. Bob Pettit
5. Julius Erving

A. 13   B. 17   C. 9   D. 14   E. 32

Answer: 1-D; 2-A; 3-B; 4-C; 5-E.

222. Name the player(s) who hold the record for most free throws made in a game.

A. Adrian Dantley   B. Bob McAdoo   C. Wilt Chamberlain
D. George Gervin

Answer: A and C. Oddly, the Warriors' Wilt Chamberlain, one of the poorest free throw shooters, hit 28 of 32 in his 100-point game on March 2, 1962 against the Knicks, The Jazz's Dantley made 28 of 29 on January 4, 1984 against the Rockets.

223. Match the player with his uniform number.

1. Stephen Curry   2. Joel Embiid   3. Kevin Durant   4. Russell Westbrook

A. 21   B. 0   C. 35   D. 30

Answer: 1-D; 2-A; 3-C; 4-B.

BASKETBALL AND LITERATURE

224. Match the basketball classic with the year it was published.
1. *A Season on the Brink*   2. *Tall Tales*   3. *The Breaks of the Game*
4. *Total Basketball: The Ultimate Basketball Encyclopedia*
A. 1992   B. 2003   C. 1981   D. 1986
Answer: 1-D; 2-A; 3-C; 4-B.

BASKETBALL BY POSITION

225. What guard holds the Celtics' mark for assists per game over a season?
A. Bob Cousy   B. Sherman Douglas   C. Rajon Rondo
D. Tiny Archibald
Answer: C. Rajon owns the team's top four marks, with his best coming in 2012 with 11.7 per game.

226. True or False? No guard has averaged 13 assists for a season.
Answer: False. John Stockton leads all guards, having averaged 13 assists five times. Isiah Thomas, Magic Johnson, and Kevin Porter did it once each.

227. Name the center who broke Kareem Abdul-Jabbar's career mark for blocks during the 1995–96 season.
A. Patrick Ewing   B. Hakeem Olajuwon   C. Robert Parish
D. David Robinson
Answer: B. Olajuwon broke Abdul-Jabbar's mark of 3,189 blocks. He has held the record since with 3,830 blocks. The record excludes Bill Russell and Wilt Chamberlain, since blocks have only been recorded since 1974.

228. True or False? Rajon Rondo leads all active guards (and players) in 20-assist games.
Answer: True. Sixteen-year guard Rondo has nine games with 20 or more assists. Ahead of him are John Stockton with 34 and Magic Johnson with 22. (Statistics are kept since the 1982–83 season.)

229. What forward holds the Hornets record for minutes per game over a season?
A. Anthony Mason   B. Larry Johnson   C. Gerald Wallace   D. Glen Rice
Answer: A. Mason played 43.1 minutes per game during the 1997 season with the Hornets.

230. Name the forward who held the career record for offensive rebounds before Moses Malone broke the record during the 1980–81 season.
A. Elvin Hayes   B. Paul Silas   C. Charles Barkley   D. Buck Williams
Answer: B. Silas had 2,025 offensive rebounds when Malone broke his record. Malone has owned the record since with 6,731 offensive boards.

231. True or False? There are two Hall of Famers who attended the University of Texas at El Paso and they are both guards.
Answer: True. Point guard Nate Archibald was inducted to the Hall in 1991. Tim Hardaway, also a point guard, was inducted in 2022.

232. What guard won MVP honors in the 2014 All-Star Game?
A. Kyrie Irving   B. John Wall   C. Stephen Curry   D. Tony Parker
Answer: A. The Cleveland point guard led the East to a 163–155 win. The teams combined to score 40 or more points in five quarters. Irving contributed 31 points and 14 assists.

233. Who made the most free throws of any center?
A. Wilt Chamberlain   B. Kareem Abdul-Jabbar   C. Moses Malone
D. Hakeem Olajuwon
Answer: C. Malone made 9,018 free throws, over 200 more than any other center.

234. True or False? Center Wilt Chamberlain has the most points and rebounds added all-time.
Answer: False. Center Kareem Abdul-Jabbar had 38,387 points and 17,440 rebounds for a total of 55,827. Chamberlain is second with 31,419 points and 23,924 rebounds for a total of 55,343.

235. True or False? Kareem Abdul-Jabbar, Wilt Chamberlain, and Karl Malone are the only frontcourters (and players) to post 30,000 points and 10,000 rebounds.
Answer: False. Small forward LeBron James has 38,652 points and 11,498 rebounds. Center and forward Dirk Nowitzki posted 31,560 points and 11,489 rebounds.

236. What guard won the All-Star Game MVP in the 2015 game?
A. Stephen Curry   B. Chris Paul   C. Damian Lillard
D. Russell Westbrook
Answer: D. The West prevailed 163–158. Westbrook tallied 41 points in just 25 minutes.

237. Which guard won the All-Star Game MVP in 2010?
A. LeBron James   B. Dwyane Wade   C. Steve Nash
D. Chauncey Billups
Answer: B. Combining with his teammate James for the starting East backcourt, the duo tallied 53 points. Wade had 28 points, and 11 assists, six rebounds, and five steals.

238. What guard came off the bench to win the MVP of the 1981 All-Star Game?
A. Michael Ray Richardson   B. Otis Birdsong   C. Tiny Archibald
D. Dennis Johnson
Answer: C. The Celtic guard scored only nine points, but he also logged nine assists and made three steals in a 123–120 triumph for the East. Several months later Archibald would win his only title.

239. What frontcourt star won the 2004 All-Star Game MVP?
A. Dirk Nowitzki   B. Shaquille O'Neal   C. Ben Wallace   D. Tim Duncan
Answer: B. O'Neal had 24 points and 11 rebounds off the bench to lead the West to a 136–132 win.

240. Match the guard with their nickname.
1. Vernal Coles   2. Bob Cousy   3. Jamal Crawford   4. Stephen Curry
A. Mr. And-One   B. Baby-Faced Assassin   C. Bimbo   D. The Houdini of the Hardwood
Answer: 1-C; 2-D; 3-A; 4-B.

241. Match the guard with their nickname.

1. Fred Brown   2.   Chauncey Billups   3. Vince Carter   4. Sam Cassell

A. Mr. Big Shot   B. Downtown   C. Air Canada   D. The Space Man

Answer: 1-B; 2-A; 3-C; 4-D.

242. What two centers shared MVP honors in the first All-Star Game of the new millennium?

A. Alonzo Mourning   B. Tim Duncan   C. David Robinson

D. Shaquille O'Neal

Answer: B and D. The duo combined for 46 points, 23 rebounds, and four blocks to pace the West to a 137–126 victory.

CHAMPIONSHIP NICKNAMES

243. Match the players from the 44th NBA Finals between the 1989–90 championship Detroit Pistons and the Portland Trail Blazers with their nicknames.
1. James Edwards   2. Mark Aguirre   3. Terry Porter   4. Buck Williams
A. Ajax   B. Gandhi   C. Buddha   D. Elephant Drawers
Answer: 1-C; 2-D; 3-B; 4-A.

244. Match the players from the 45th NBA Finals between the 1990–91 championship Chicago Bulls and the Los Angeles Lakers with their nicknames.
1. Scottie Pippen   2. Horace Grant   3. Michael Jordan   4. Sam Perkins
A. Big Smooth   B. The Enforcer   C. His Airness   D. Robin
Answer: 1-D; 2-B; 3-C; 4-A.

245. Match the players from the 46th NBA Finals between the 1991–92 championship Chicago Bulls and the Portland Trail Blazers with their nicknames.
1. Bill Cartwright   2. Jerome Kersey   3. B. J. Armstrong   4. Stacey King
A. The Kid   B. Romeo   C. Pearl   D. Teach
Answer: 1-D; 2-B; 3-A; 4-C.

246. Match the players from the 47th NBA Finals between the 1992-93 championship Chicago Bulls and the Phoenix Suns with their nicknames.
1. Scott Williams   2. Trent Tucker   3. Charles Barkley   4. Mark West
A. Doc   B. Tank   C. The Hammer   D. Bread Truck
Answer: 1-B; 2-A; 3-D; 4-C.

247. Match the players from the 48th NBA Finals between the 1993–94 championship Houston Rockets and the New York Knicks with their nicknames.

1. Hakeem Olajuwon   2. Vernon Maxwell   3. Kenny Smith
4. Patrick Ewing

A. Hawk   B. The Dream   C. Hoya Destroya   D. The Jet

Answer: 1-B; 2-A; 3-D; 4-C.

COACHES

248. Name the coach of the 76ers when they won their last title.
A. Matt Guokas   B. Billy Cunningham   C. Gene Shue   D. Jim Lynam
Answer: B. Cunningham was in his sixth season as the Sixers coach when they won 65, lost 17, and swept the Lakers in the 1983 Finals.

249. Which coaches had lifetime winning percentages of .600 or better?
A. Red Auerbach   B. Danny Ainge   C. Rick Adelman   D. Larry Bird
Answer: A, B, and D. Auerbach finished with a percentage of .661 and led the Celtics to nine NBA titles from 1957 through 1966. In three years with the Pacers, Bird led his charges to a .687 mark. Ainge had a .602 mark in four years at the helm.

250. Name the Hall of Fame coach who was a point guard on the championship Rochester Royals.
A. Bob Davies   B. Dick McGuire   C. Red Holzman   D. Arnie Risen
Answer: C. A City College graduate, Red played 68 games with the 1951 Royals, averaging seven points and two assists per contest. As a coach, he led the Knicks to the 1970 and 1973 NBA championships.

251. Name the first coach of the Hornets.
A. Gene Littles   B. Dick Harter   C. Allan Bristow   D. Dave Cowens
Answer: B. Harter coached them to a 20-62 mark in 1989, their first season.

252. Which coach led the Celtics to a title?
A. Jim O'Brien   B. John Carroll   C. Brad Stevens   D. Doc Rivers
Answer: D. Rivers has coached for 24 years, including nine with the
Celtics, and has won one NBA title. He led them to a title in 2008, when
they beat the Lakers in a six-game Finals.

253. What former player was the Bulls' first coach?
A. Red Kerr   B. Scotty Robertson   C. Jerry Sloan
Answer: A. A three-time All-Star who averaged double-digits in
rebounds for eight of 12 seasons, Kerr coached the Bulls to consecutive
losing records in 1967 and 1968. The 6'9" forward also played on the
1955 Syracuse Nationals who won an NBA championship.

254. Name the coach of the 1977 championship Trail Blazers.
A. Lenny Wilkens   B. Jack Ramsay   C. Jack McCloskey
D. Rick Adelman
Answer: B. Ramsay coached the Blazers for nine years and won a title
with them in his first season.

**255. True or False? Since 2000, no coach has won Coach of the Year
three or more times.**
Answer: False. Gregg Popovich won the award in 2003, 2012, and 2014.
He coaches the Spurs, who won the championship in 2012 and 2014.

**256. Name the first coach to win a championship in the ABA and in
the NBA.**
A. Larry Brown   B. Alex Hannum   C. Hubie Brown   D. Red Auerbach
Answer: B. Hannum piloted two renowned NBA teams to success. He led
the 1958 Hawks past the defending champion Celtics in six games. Nine
years later he coached a more famous team: the 1967 76ers, who won
a record 68 games and beat the Celtics in six again in the Finals. Two
seasons later he won with the Oakland Oaks of the ABA in 1969.

**257. True or False? The last Knicks coach to win Coach of the Year
was Pat Riley.**
Answer: False. Tom Thibodeau won the award in 2020–21 in leading
the Knicks to a 41-31 mark and a fourth-place finish in the Eastern
Conference. In the playoffs the Knicks lost to the Hawks in the Eastern
Conference first round.

258. True or False? No Magic coach has ever earned Coach of the Year honors.
Answer: False. Doc Rivers coached the Magic to a 41-41 mark in the 2000 season. Oddly, their record was far worse in 2000 than under Chuck Daly during the previous season. Daly led them to a 33-17 mark but didn't win an award.

259. Name the coaches of the 1956 All-Star Game.
A. Charles Eckman   B. John Kundla   C. Al Cervi   D. George Senesky
Answer: A and D. Piloting the Fort Wayne Pistons to the playoffs in three of four years, Eckman held the reigns for the 1956 contest played at the Rochester Memorial Coliseum as the West thumped the East 108–94 behind Bob Pettit's MVP performance of 20 points and 24 rebounds. Warriors coach Senesky coached the East. He led his team to a league title in 1956.

260. True or False? Only one Black coach has won two or more NBA titles.
Answer: False. Bill Russell was a player-coach for the Celtics and won titles in 1968 and 1969. K. C. Jones won titles in 1984 and 1986.

261. Match the coaches with the first teams they coached.
1. Bill Fitch   2. Red Holzman   3. Billy Cunningham   4. Bill Sharman
A. Cleveland Cavaliers   B. Philadelphia 76ers   C. San Francisco Warriors   D. Milwaukee Hawks
Answer: 1-A; 2-D; 3-B; 4-C.

262. Who coached the Hawks to their only world championship?
A. Harry Gallatin   B. Alex Hannum   C. Cliff Hagan   D. Red Holzman
Answer: B. In just his second season coaching St. Louis in 1958, the Hawks were just 41-31 during the season. But Hannum led his charges to their second straight Finals and a world title as they toppled the Celtics in six.

263. Name the two coaches in the first All-Star Game.
A John Kundla   B Red Auerbach   C Joe Lapchick   D Al Cervi
Answer: A and C. In the 1951 contest Kundla, the Lakers coach, led the West and Knicks skipper Lapchick led the East to a 111–94 win.

264. True or False? Only two coaches won more than five championships.
Answer: True. Phil Jackson won 11 and Red Auerbach won nine.

265. True or False? None of the following coaches won 1,000 games.
A. Mike Brown   B. Larry Brown   C. Hubie Brown   D. Brett Brown
Answer: False. In 26 years on the sidelines in the ABA and NBA, Larry Brown won 1,098 games while losing 904. He led the 2004 Pistons to an NBA title.

266. True or False? No coach in NBA history coached 30 or more years.
Answer: False. Two did. Lenny Wilkens coached 32 years and Don Nelson 31. Wilkens led the Sonics to a title in 1979.

267. True or False? Miami has never had a Coach of the Year winner.
Answer: False. Pat Riley won the award in 1997 when he led the Heat to a 61-21 record. After winning the first two rounds of playoffs against the Magic and the Knicks, the Heat lost to the Bulls four games to one. No Heat coach has won the award in the 25 years since then.

268. Name the coach who won more ABA titles than any other.
A. Jack Ramsay   B. Slick Leonard   C. Hubie Brown   D. Larry Brown
Answer: B. Slick Leonard led the ABA Pacers to four Finals in six years between 1970 and 1975 and the Pacers won three of them, in 1970, 1972, and 1973.

269. Name the last Hall of Fame player to win Coach of the Year.
A. Byron Scott   B. Larry Brown   C. Larry Bird   D. Sam Mitchell
Answer: C. In 1998 Bird led his Indiana charges to a 58-24 mark and to the Eastern Conference finals.

COLLEGE

270. True or False? No player from the University of Massachusetts made the Hall of Fame. (All references to the Hall of Fame in this section are to the [pro] Naismith Memorial Basketball Hall of Fame in Springfield, Massachusetts, not the College Basketball Hall of Fame in Kansas City, Missouri.)
Answer: False. Of the nine NBA and ABA players who attended the university, Julius Erving made it in 1993.

271. Match the players with their colleges.
1. Pearl Washington   2. Walt Frazier   3. Rick Barry   4. Elvin Hayes
A. Southern Illinois   B. Houston   C. Miami (FL)   D. Syracuse
Answer: 1-D; 2-A; 3-C; 4-B.

272. True or False? Of those who attended Purdue and went to the NBA and ABA, two or more made the Hall of Fame.
Answer: False. None of the 40 made the Hall of Fame.

273. True or False? One player who attended Colorado State made the Hall of Fame.
Answer: False, though Colorado State produced excellent NBA players such as Jason Smith and Bob Rule, a 6'9" center for the SuperSonics who averaged over 20 points his first four years in the league.

274. True or False? One attendee of Loyola Marymount is in the Hall of Fame.
Answer: True. Drafted by the San Diego Rockets in 1968, Rick Adelman, who played point guard, attained greater fame as a coach for 23 years, including leading the Trail Blazers to the Finals in 1990 and 1992. He won 1,042 games and lost 789 (.582).

275. True or False? No players from Bowling Green State University (OH) made the Hall of Fame.
Answer: False. Of the 16 NBA and ABA players to attend Bowling Green, only center Nate Thurmond made the Hall of Fame in 1985. Known as the "Chairman of the Boards," he was the Warriors' third pick overall in the 1963 draft. A defensive wunderkind, Thurmond played 15 seasons and averaged 15 points and 15 rebounds and was a seven-time All-Star. He was on the NBA's 75th Anniversary Team.

276. True or False? More than one graduate of Detroit Mercy (formerly the University of Detroit) made the Hall of Fame.
Answer: True. Of the 23 NBA and ABA players who graduated from the school, Dave DeBusschere and Spencer Haywood were inducted. DeBusschere was inducted in 1983 and Haywood in 2015.

277. True or False? No player from West Texas A&M University made the Hall of Fame.
Answer: False. "Little Mo" Cheeks, who amassed 7,392 assists in his NBA career, was inducted into the Hall of Fame in 2018.

278. True or False? Only one of the 66 NBA and ABA players who attended Michigan State made the Hall of Fame.
Answer: True. Inducted in 2002, only Magic Johnson represents Michigan State in the Springfield Hall.

279. Rank the following colleges by their number of players who went to the Hall of Fame.
1. Notre Dame   2. Providence   3. Maryland   4. Cincinnati
A. One   B. Two   C. None   D. Three
Answer: 1-A, Adrian Dantley; 2-B, Lenny Wilkens, John Thompson; 3-C; 4-B, Oscar Robertson, Jack Twyman.

280. Of the 35 NBA and ABA players who played at Iowa, how many made the Hall of Fame?
A. None   B. One   C. Five   D. Seven
Answer: B. Don Nelson played 14 years in the NBA but he was inducted into the Hall of Fame as a coach in 2012. He coached 31 seasons from 1977 to 2010.

281. True or False? One graduate of the University of Wyoming is in the Hall of Fame.
Answer: False. Of the 25 NBA and ABA players who graduated Wyoming, none made the Hall of Fame.

282. True or False? No Hall of Famers came from the University of Pittsburgh.
Answer: True. Of the 23 players who played in either the NBA or ABA from the University of Pittsburgh, not one made it to the Hall of Fame.

283. Match the players with their colleges.
1. Moses Malone   2. George McGinnis   3. World B. Free
4. Vinnie Johnson   5. Dennis Rodman
A. Baylor   B. Guilford College   C. Indiana   D. Southeastern Oklahoma State University   E. None
Answer: 1-E; 2-C; 3-B; 4-A; 5-D.

284. True or False? Paul Arizin is the only Hall of Famer to graduate Villanova.
Answer: True. Philadelphia native "Pitchin' Paul" was drafted third overall by the Warriors in 1950. Due to a two-year commitment to the Marines, he played just 10 NBA seasons and averaged above 20 points in nine of them. He led the league in scoring twice (1952 and 1957) and led the Warriors to a title in 1956 when he averaged 27.7 points and eight rebounds to top the Fort Wayne Pistons in five games. He was inducted into the Hall of Fame in 1978.

285. True or False? No Marquette graduate is in the basketball Hall of Fame.
Answer: False. Dwyane Wade was elected in 2023.

286. True or False? No St. Bonaventure graduate made the basketball Hall of Fame.
Answer: False. Buffalo native Bob Lanier was inducted in 1992. The Pistons center with the feathery touch averaged more than 20 points in eight consecutive seasons from 1972 through 1979. He was an eight-time All-Star.

287. True or False? No basketball player from Providence College made the Hall of Fame as a player.
Answer: False. Brooklyn-born guard Lenny Wilkens was inducted as a player in 1989 and as a coach in 1998. The nine-time All-Star is third all-time with 1,332 coaching wins. He was also chosen for the NBA 75th Anniversary Team.

288. True or False? No one from Grambling State University made the Hall of Fame.
Answer: False. Of the 12 NBA and ABA players who played for Grambling, Willis Reed, who graduated in 1964, played 10 years in the NBA and was inducted to the Hall in 1982.

289. True or False? No player from the University of New Mexico is in the basketball Hall of Fame.
Answer: False. The Pacers' Mel Daniels was voted to the Hall of Fame in 2012. "Big D" was a 6'9" stellar center for the Pacers, and posted 24 points and 16.5 rebounds a game for the 1969 team. Two years later he averaged 21 points and 18 rebounds. He won the MVP both seasons.

290. True or False? No player from Saint Joseph's College made the basketball Hall of Fame.
Answer: True. Of the 22 NBA and ABA players who attended Saint Joseph's, none made the Hall of Fame.

291. True or False? No New York University graduate ever made the Hall of Fame.
Answer: False. Celtics small forward Tom "Satch" Sanders, who played on eight championship teams between 1961 and 1973, was inducted as a contributor in 2011. Syracuse power forward Dolph Schayes, who played on the Nats' title team in 1955, was inducted in 1973.

292. Which player was picked first overall in the 2000 draft?

A. Darius Miles   B. Jamal Crawford   C. Mike Miller   D. Kenyon Martin

Answer: D. New Jersey selected the 6'9" forward first overall.

293. True or False? No Saint Louis University player went to the Hall of Fame.

Answer: False. Of the 17 NBA and ABA players who attended Saint Louis, Ed Macauley, who debuted in 1949 and was inducted in 1960, was the only one who made the Hall of Fame.

294. How many of the 56 NBA and ABA players who played at St. John's made the Hall of Fame?

A. One   B. Three   C. Seven   D. Nine

Answer: B. Al McGuire, a guard who debuted in the NBA in 1951, was inducted as a coach in 1992. Al's brother Dick McGuire, a point guard whose NBA debut was in 1949, made the Hall of Fame in 1993. Chris Mullin, a small forward who debuted with the Warriors in 1985, made the Hall of Fame in 2011.

295. How many Hall of Famers attended Notre Dame?

A. None   B. One   C. Six   D. Seven

Answer: B. Of the 62 NBA and ABA players to attend Notre Dame, Adrian Dantley, inducted in 2008, is the only Notre Dame grad.

296. True or False? Ray Allen is the only player attending the University of Connecticut who made the Hall of Fame.

Answer: True. Drafted fifth overall in 1997, Allen played 18 NBA seasons as a shooting guard and was voted to the NBA 75th Anniversary Team.

297. How many Hall of Famers went to the University of Tennessee?

A. None   B. One   C. Six   D. Eight

Answer: B. Of the 45 NBA and ABA players who went to Tennessee, only Bernard King, inducted in 2013, is in the Hall of Fame.

298. How many players from the University of Southern California are in the Hall of Fame?
A. One   B. Two   C. Three   D. Nine
Answer: C. Of the 47 NBA and ABA players to attend USC, three made the Hall of Fame. Player and coach Bill Sharman was inducted as a player in 1976 and a coach in 2004. Player and coach Alex Hannum was inducted in 1998. Player and coach Paul Westphal was inducted as a player in 2019.

299. True or False? No players from Pepperdine made the Hall of Fame.
Answer: False. Guard Dennis Johnson played 14 seasons and was a five-time All-Star, played on three championship teams, and was a Finals MVP. He graduated from Pepperdine in 1976.

300. What USC grad coached the Hawks to their only world championship?
A. Harry Gallatin   B. Alex Hannum   C. Cliff Hagan   D. Red Holzman
Answer: B. In just his second season coaching St. Louis in 1958, the Hawks were just 41-31 during the season. But Hannum led his charges to their second straight Finals and a world title as they toppled the Celtics in six.

301. True or False? None of the 20 NBA and ABA players who attended California State Long Beach reached the basketball Hall of Fame.
Answer: True.

302. Besides Indiana, what team in 1976 won 30 or more and lost none?
A. Louisiana State University   B. Georgetown   C. Rutgers   D. Michigan
Answer: C. The Rutgers Scarlet Knights were 31-0 but Michigan solved them in an 86–70 loss. Two days later, they lost the third-place game to UCLA, 106–92. Indiana won it all, finishing 32-0.

303. True or False? No Dartmouth player ever made an NBA All-Star team.
Answer: False. Rudy LaRusso, a 6'7" power forward, played 10 years for the Lakers and Warriors between 1960 and 1969 and was a five-time All-Star.

304. True or False? Just one Hall of Famer came from Holy Cross.
Answer: False. Playmaker Bob Cousy was drafted by the Celtics in 1950 and forward Tommy Heinsohn was drafted in 1956. Both played at Holy Cross.

305. True or False? Milligan College grad Del Harris coached both Rockets' Finals in the 1980s.
Answer: False. Harris coached the 1981 squad and Bill Fitch, who had won a title coaching the Celtics over the Rockets in 1981, coached the 1986 squad that lost to the Celtics.

306. True or False? One player from Brigham Young University made the Hall of Fame.
Answer: False. None of the 25 NBA and ABA players from BYU made the Hall of Fame.

307. True or False? No player who attended Truman State University made the Hall of Fame.
Answer: False. Of the four NBA and ABA players who attended Truman, power forward Harry "The Horse" Gallatin is the lone Hall of Famer, getting inducted in 1991.

308. True or False? No one from Oregon State made the Hall of Fame.
Answer: False. Gary "The Glove" Payton was the lone attendee of Oregon State to make the Hall of Fame. The nine-time All-Star and a nine-time All-Defensive Award winner was inducted in 2013.

309. Which of the following Hall of Famers graduated Florida State?
A. Wes Unseld   B. Dave Cowens   C. Jo Jo White   D. Kevin Garnett
Answer: B. Cowens is the only Hall of Famer from 46 Florida State players who made the pros.

310. Of the five greatest NBA rebounders of all time, what college did the only one of those drafted first go to?
Answer: Kareem Abdul-Jabbar, known as Lew Alcindor at the time he was drafted, ranks fourth with 17,440 rebounds. The Bucks picked the UCLA center first overall in the 1969 draft. The other top five rebounders were Wilt Chamberlain, Bill Russell, Karl Malone, and Artis Gilmore, none of whom were selected first overall.

311. True or False? No NBA All-Star ever played at Weber State.
Answer: False. Portland point guard Damian Lillard is a seven-time NBA All-Star.

312. True or False? No one from Seton Hall University made the Hall of Fame.
Answer: False. Of the 31 NBA and ABA players who attended Seton Hall, only Bobby Wanzer made the Hall. A shooting guard who played for the 1951 Royals, Wanzer was inducted in 1987.

313. Two Duke University players were chosen in the top 20 of the 1986 draft. Who were they?
A. Kenny Walker   B. Chuck Person   C. Johnny Dawkins   D. Mark Alarie
Answer: C and D. Dawkins, a point guard picked 10th overall, had a nine-year NBA career. Picked 16th, Alarie was a power forward for five NBA seasons.

314. True or False? One player from the Hall of Fame attended Long Island University.
Answer: False. None of the 22 NBA and ABA players who attended LIU made the Hall.

315. True or False? No player from Columbia University made the Hall of Fame.
Answer: True. Of the five players who played in the NBA or ABA, none made the Hall of Fame. Forward Jim McMillian, who played nine seasons, including with the 1972 Lakers that won 33 games in a row and the title, had the best NBA career of any Columbia grad.

316. True or False? None of the following players spent four years at college.
A. Christian Laettner   B. Kareem Abdul-Jabbar   C. Larry Bird
D. Michael Jordan
Answer: False. The only player who didn't was Michael Jordan. Jordan played three years at the University of North Carolina, from 1982 through 1984.

317. True or False? At least one player from Hamline University made the Hall of Fame.

Answer: True. Drafted in 1949, Lakers power forward Vern Mikkelsen, who was a six-time All-Star and played on four Lakers' title teams, made the Hall of Fame in 1995.

318. Which team holds the longest winning streak in college history?

A. Texas   B. UCLA (1966–1968)   C. UNLV   D. San Francisco
E. UCLA (1971–1974)

Answer: E. The Bruins, led by Bill Walton, won 88 straight games from 1971 to 1974. Notre Dame started and ended the streak. They beat UCLA 89–82 in 1971 to start the streak. In 1974 they trailed 70–59 but finished with a 12–0 run to win 71–70.

319. True or False? At least one player from the University of Idaho made the Hall of Fame.

Answer: True. Of four NBA and ABA Idaho players who went to the NBA, Gus Johnson, a power forward who played at Idaho and debuted in 1963, played nine of his 10 seasons with the Baltimore Bullets. He was inducted in 2010.

320. True or False? Of six Iona University players who played in the NBA, none made the Hall of Fame.

Answer: False. Richie Guerin, a shooting guard who debuted in 1956 and played eight of his 14 seasons with the Knicks, is the lone Iona player in the Hall of Fame. He was inducted in 2013.

321. How many Duke players were drafted among the top 14 in 1999?

A. One   B. Two   C. Three   D. Four

Answer: D. Elton Brand was picked first overall. Trajan Langdon was selected 11th, Corey Maggette was 13th, and William Avery was 14th.

322. Kareem Abdul-Jabbar (then known as Lew Alcindor) played 12 NCAA tournament games with UCLA from 1967 to 1969 and won all 12. Rank his highest scoring tournament games.

A. Wyoming   B. Pacific   C. Purdue   D. North Carolina

Answer: 1-B, 38 (1967); 2-C, 37 (1969); 3-D, 34 (1968); 4-A, 29 (1967). The Purdue game was his last college contest. He hit 15 of 20 shots, scored 37, and hauled down 20 rebounds in a 92–72 drubbing of the Boilermakers for the 1969 National Championship.

323. True or False? One player from Centenary made the Hall of Fame.
Answer: True. Of the four NBA and ABA players who attended Centenary, center Robert Parish was the eighth pick overall in the 1976 draft. He played 21 seasons and was inducted into the Hall in 2003.

324. True or False? None of the 11 NBA and ABA players from Marshall is in the Hall of Fame.
Answer: False. Hal Greer, a guard who debuted in 1958 and was a seven-time All-Star, was inducted in 1982.

325. How many graduates of Niagara University made the Hall of Fame?
A. None   B. One   C. Two   D. Three
Answer: C. Larry Costello was inducted as a contributor in 2022. He coached the Bucks to the 1971 title and led them to the Finals again in 1974. Just 5'9", Calvin Murphy nonetheless scored 20 points per game five times in his career. He was inducted to the Hall of Fame in 1993.

326. True or False? Two Hall of Famers who played for the Rockets attended the University of Houston.
Answer: True. The two alumni are Clyde Drexler, who made the Hall of Fame in 2004, and Hakeem Olajuwon, who was inducted in 2008.

327. True or False? No Princeton University graduate is in the Basketball Hall of Fame.
Answer: False. Bill Bradley, who graduated Princeton in 1966 and played 10 years with the Knicks, including their title teams in 1970 and 1973, made the Hall of Fame in 1983.

328. True or False? No St. Francis University player made the Hall of Fame.
Answer: False. Of the five St. Francis players who played in the NBA or ABA, only Maurice Stokes, drafted by the Royals second overall in the 1955 draft and a three-time All-Star, is in the Hall. He was inducted in 2004.

329. True or False? None of the eight NBA and ABA players who attended the University of Hawaii made the Hall of Fame.
Answer: True.

330. True or False? One player who attended Miami of Florida made the Hall of Fame.

Answer: True. Rick Barry, drafted in 1965, was the only one of 16 NBA and ABA players from Miami of Florida to make the Hall of Fame. He played on the 1969 Oakland Oaks who won an ABA title and was the Finals MVP on the 1975 Warriors that swept the Bullets.

331. How many players from Louisiana State University made the Hall of Fame?

A. None   B. One   C. Two   D. Three

Answer: D. Of the 52 NBA and ABA players who attended Louisiana State, the three who made the Hall are Pete Maravich, drafted in 1970; Shaquille O'Neal, 1992; and Bob Pettit, 1954.

332. True or False? Two players from the University of Minnesota made the Hall of Fame.

Answer: True. Kevin McHale was inducted in 1999 and Lou Hudson was inducted in 2022.

333. True or False? No player from Santa Clara University made the Hall of Fame.

Answer: False. Of 15 NBA and ABA players who attended Santa Clara, Steve Nash is the lone Hall of Famer. The eight-time All-Star and five-time assist leader made it to the Hall in 2018.

334. What is the most points Kareem Abdul-Jabbar (then known as Lew Alcindor) scored in a college game?

A. 48   B. 57   C. 61   D. 65

Answer: C. He logged 61 against Washington State on February 25, 1967. UCLA won 100–78, bringing their record to 23-0.

WINNING AND LOSING

335. True or False? The Nets have a losing record against all of the following teams, against whom they have played 200 or more games.
A. Knicks   B. Celtics   C. Pacers   D. Wizards
Answer: False. They have a record of 107-103 (.510) against the Knicks.

336. Against what team have the Celtics won the most games?
A. Warriors   B. Bulls   C. Knicks   D. Hawks
Answer: C. The Celtics have won 300 and lost 189 against the Knicks for an impressive .613 winning percentage.

337. True or False? The Bulls have not won 60 percent of their games against any teams they have played 200 or more times.
Answer: True. Their best won-lost record is 132-98 (.574) against Cleveland.

338. True or False? Of the following teams, the Hornets have had their best record against the Knicks.
A. Knicks   B. Timberwolves   C. Bucks   D. 76ers
Answer: False. The Hornets have posted a winning record against almost all these teams, but they have a losing mark of 57-64 (.471) against the Knicks.

339. In what year did the Celtics and Lakers playoff rivalry begin?

Answer: The rivalry started in 1959 as the Minneapolis Lakers lost four straight to the Celtics. It lasted to 2010, spanning 52 years. The bicoastal rivalry commenced in 1962. The Lakers edged ahead three games to two and faced a Game 7 in Boston. With seconds left in regulation, a Frank Selvy seven-foot jumper rimmed out. The Celtics won 110–107 in overtime and wiped out a combined 76 points from Elgin Baylor (41) and Jerry West (35). Bill Russell had 30 points and 40 rebounds, as the Lakers lost the battle of the boards 82–65.

340. Against what teams do the Hornets have a winning record?

A. Celtics   B. Pistons   C. 76ers   D. Knicks   E. Wizards

Answer: B, 64 wins, 61 losses; C, 59-57; and E, 68-57. It's a challenge for expansion teams to compile winning records against non-expansion teams. But the Hornets have accomplished it.

341. Against which of the following teams do the Nuggets have their highest winning percentage?

A. Bucks   B. Clippers   C. Nets   D. Warriors

Answer: A. The Nuggets have dominated the Bucks, winning 64 and losing 39 (.621).

CONTEMPORARY RECORDS

342. True or False? Only two active players have scored 50 or more points 10 times.
Answer: False. There are three: James Harden, 23 times; Damian Lillard, 15 times; Stephen Curry, 12 times.

343. Name the most recent player with 30 rebounds in a game.
A. Andre Drummond   B. Enes Freedom   C. Rudy Gobert
D. Hassan Whiteside
Answer: B. The Blazers' Enes Freedom snatched 30 boards in 37 minutes in a 118–103 win over Detroit on April 10, 2021. Of his 30 rebounds, 12 were offensive and he scored 24 points in the game.

344. Name the only player to appear on six consecutive NBA All-Defensive Teams from 2017 through 2022.
A. Rudy Gobert   B. Jrue Holiday   C. Draymond Green
D. Ben Simmons
Answer: A. The 7'1" center from France, who won the rebounding and field goal percentage titles in 2022, was voted to each of those All-Defensive teams.

345. Name the first player to earn the Defensive Player of the Year Award three times.
A. Dennis Rodman   B. Kareem Abdul-Jabbar   C. Bill Walton
D. Dikembe Mutombo
Answer: D. Dikembe Mutombo won it in 1997, 1998, and 2001.

346. Name the two teams that played in the highest scoring game in NBA history.

A. Nuggets and Warriors   B. 76ers and Celtics
C. 76ers and Warriors   D. Pistons and Nuggets

Answer: D. On December 13, 1983, the Pistons edged the Nuggets in triple overtime, 186–184. Two Nuggets—Kiki Vandeweghe and Alex English—combined for 98 points. It wasn't enough. Isiah Thomas had 47 points and 17 assists and John Long added 41 for the Pistons.

347. True or False? None of the following teams has had two players who scored 70 or more points in a game.

A. Celtics   B. Lakers   C. Nuggets   D. Cavaliers

Answer: False. Elgin Baylor scored 71 and hauled in 25 rebounds for the Lakers in a 123–108 drubbing of the Knicks at Madison Square Garden on November 15, 1960. Kobe Bryant connected on 28 of 46 shots, including seven of 13 3-pointers, to log 81 in a 122–104 dusting of the Raptors on January 22, 2006. Bryant's historic tally was second only to Chamberlain's 100 points in 1962.

348. Who has the most 3-pointers by a player in Game 7 of the Finals?

Answer: Draymond Green and Shane Battier are tied with six 3s in Game 7 of a Finals. Green got his in a losing cause in Game 7 in 2016, as Cleveland beat the Warriors 93–89 to win their first title. Battier did it for Miami versus San Antonio in 2013.

349. Who has the most 60-point games among active players?

A. Damian Lillard   B. Kyrie Irving   C. James Harden
D. Karl-Anthony Towns

Answer: A. Lillard has posted five and Harden is second with four.

350. True or False? James Harden made the most 3-point field goals without a miss.

Answer: False. While playing for the Knicks, Latrell Sprewell made nine against the Clippers without a miss on February 4, 2003. Ben Gordon also made nine without a miss, once in 2006 and again in 2012.

351. Which two players are tied for most 3-pointers missed in a game?
A. James Harden   B. Stephen Curry   C. Reggie Miller
D. Damon Stoudamire
Answer: A and D. Each missed 16 3-pointers in a game, with Stoudamire doing it in 2005. Harden has missed 16 six times since 2019.

352. True or False? The record for most consecutive 3-point field goals made to start a game is 10.
Answer: True. Ty Lawson did it for the Nuggets against the Timberwolves in 2011 and Klay Thompson did it for the Warriors against the Lakers in 2019.

353. Which player(s) made the most 3-point field goals in a half?
A. Chandler Parsons   B. Klay Thompson   C. Stephen Curry
D. Steve Kerr
Answer: A and B. Playing for the Rockets against the Grizzlies, Parsons hit 10 on January 24, 2014. Thompson hit his 10 for the Warriors against the Bulls on October 29, 2018.

354. Name the only team with three losing streaks of 20 or more games.
A. Mavericks   B. Knicks   C. 76ers   D. Clippers   E. Cavaliers
Answer: C. Over the course of two seasons in 2015 and 2016, the 76ers lost a record 28 straight. That snapped their previous record in the 2011 season where they lost 26 straight. In 1973 they dropped 20 straight.

355. What team holds the record for most consecutive postseason losses?
A. Grizzlies   B. Knicks   C. Bobcats   D. Pistons
Answer: D. The Pistons have an active streak of 14 straight postseason losses that began on May 28, 2008, in a 106–102 loss to the Celtics.

356. Name the last player to score 70 in a game.
A. James Harden   B. Damian Lillard   C. Klay Thompson
D. Devin Booker   E. Donovan Mitchell
Answer: B. The Blazers guard dropped 71 on the Rockets on February 26, 2023. The Blazers won in overtime 131–114. He also had six rebounds and six assists.

357. What players have the most consecutive 30-point games since 2000?

A. Tracy McGrady   B. Kobe Bryant   C. Kevin Durant
D. Shaquille O'Neal   E. James Harden

Answer: 1-E, 32 consecutive 30-point games, running from December 2018 through February 2019. 2-B, 16, between January and February 2002. 3-A, 14, between March and April 2003; 4-C, 12 games, January 2014; 5-D, 11 games, between March and April 2001.

358. True or False? Luka Dončić set a record for most 30-point games to start a season.

Answer: False. His nine consecutive 30-point games to begin the 2022–23 season was second only to Chamberlain's mark of 23 straight to begin the 1962–63 season. The Magic stopped Dončić's streak on November 10 when they held him to 24 points.

359. Name the active player with the most career rebounds.

A. DeAndre Jordan   B. LeBron James   C. Dwight Howard
D. Andre Drummond

Answer: B. LeBron James has 10,667 rebounds, which is more than 13,000 behind Wilt Chamberlain's record of 23,924.

360. True or False? No active player has 2,000 blocks.

Answer: True. Serge Ibaka is closest with 1,759.

361. What active player has the most career 3-pointers?

A. Stephen Curry   B. James Harden   C. Damian Lillard
D. LeBron James

Answer: A. Curry has 3,390 3-pointers, putting him more than 600 ahead of Harden, who has 2,774.

362. Who broke Artis Gilmore's record for turnovers in a season in 2016?

A. Russell Westbrook   B. LeBron James   C. Trae Young
D. James Harden

Answer: D. Harden had 374 turnovers, breaking Gilmore's record of 366 that had stood for 38 years. Harden then shattered his own record the following year with 464, which is nearly five per game.

Stephen Curry

363. True or False? Magic Johnson has posted the most games with 30 points and 10 assists (since the 1982–83 season).
Answer: False. Johnson is in fourth place with 55 such games since records have been kept. But James Harden leads the way with 101, followed by LeBron James with 96, and Russell Westbrook with 83.

364. Which player is the active leader in career assists?
A. Russell Westbrook   B. Rajon Rondo   C. LeBron James   D. Chris Paul
Answer: D. Paul has 11,501 assists, more than 4,000 behind the career mark set by John Stockton with 15,806.

DEBUTS

365. Match the Hall of Fame Celtics with their NBA debuts.
1. Ed Macauley   2. Bob Cousy   3. Bill Sharman   4. Bill Russell
A. November 1, 1949   B. October 31, 1950   C. November 1, 1950
D. December 22, 1956
Answer: 1-A; 2-C; 3-B; 4-D.

366. Match the Hall of Famers with their debuts.
1. Oscar Robertson   2. Jerry West   3. Tommy Heinsohn
4. Jerry Lucas   5. Wilt Chamberlain
A. October 24, 1959   B. October 19, 1960   C. October 27, 1956
D. October 16, 1963
Answer: 1 and 2-A; 3-C; 4-D; 5-A.

367. Match the Hall of Famers with their debuts.
1. Elgin Baylor   2. John Havlicek   3. Frank Ramsey   4. Sam Jones
A. October 22, 1962   B. October 30, 1954   C. October 22, 1957
D. October 22, 1959
Answer: 1-C; 2-A; 3-B; 4-D.

368. Match the Hall of Famers with their debuts.
1. Neil Johnston   2. Dick McGuire   3. K. C. Jones   4. Bob Pettit
A. November 3, 1951   B. November 1, 1949   C. October 30, 1954
D. November 1, 1958
Answer: 1-A; 2-B; 3-D; 4-C.

369. Match the Hall of Famers with their debuts.
1. Earl Monroe   2. Walt Frazier   3. Walt Bellamy   4. Wayne Embry
A. October 18, 1967   B. October 19, 1961   C. October 22, 1958
D. October 28, 1967
Answer: 1-A; 2-D; 3-B; 4-C.

370. Match the Hall of Famers with their debuts.
1. Elvin Hayes   2. Wes Unseld   3. Dennis Johnson   4. Bill Bradley
A. October 16, 1968   B. December 9, 1967   C. October 24, 1976
D. October 17, 1968
Answer: 1-A; 2-D; 3-C; 4-B.

371. Match the Hall of Famers with their debuts.
1. George Mikan   2. Andy Phillip   3. Manu Ginóbili   4. Bob Davies
A. November 6, 1948   B. November 13, 1947   C. November 4, 1948
D. October 29, 2002
Answer: 1-C; 2-B; 3-D; 4-A.

372. Match the Hall of Famers with their debuts.
1. Dolph Schayes   2. Tom Gola   3. Jim Pollard   4. Joe Fulks
A. November 17, 1955   B. November 3, 1949   C. November 7, 1946
D. November 4, 1948
Answer: 1-B; 2-A; 3-C; 4-D.

373. Match the Hall of Famers with their debuts.
1. Cliff Hagan   2. Paul Arizin   3. Willis Reed   4. Hal Greer
A. November 4, 1950   B. October 17, 1964   C. October 19, 1958
D. November 3, 1956
Answer: 1-A; 2-D; 3-B; 4-C.

374. Match the Hall of Famers with their debuts.
1. Slater Martin   2. Jack Twyman   3. Dave DeBusschere   4. Nate
Thurmond
A. November 5, 1955   B. October 19, 1962   C. November 2, 1949
D. October 19, 1963
Answer: 1-C; 2-A; 3-B; 4-D.

375. Match the Hall of Famers with their debuts.
1. Al Cervi   2. Tom Heinsohn   3. Billy Cunningham   4. Bobby Wanzer
A. October 27, 1956   B. October 16, 1965   C. November 3, 1949
D. November 6, 1948
Answer: 1-C; 2-A; 3-B; 4-D.

376. Match the Hall of Famers with their debuts.
1. Pete Maravich   2. Rick Barry   3. Tracy McGrady   4. Clyde Lovellette
A. October 31, 1987   B. October 30, 1953   C. October 7, 1970
D. October 15, 1965
Answer: 1-C; 2-D; 3-A; 4-B.

377. Match the Hall of Famers with their debuts.
1. Lenny Wilkens   2. Dave Bing   3. Harry Gallatin   4. Dave Cowens
A. October 13, 1970   B. October 22, 1960   C. October 15, 1966
D. October 20, 1948
Answer: 1-B; 2-C; 3-D; 4-A.

378. Match the Hall of Famers with their debuts.
1. Tiny Archibald   2. Bob Lanier   3. Connie Hawkins   4. Calvin Murphy
A. October 13, 1970   B. October 14, 1970   C. October 16, 1969
Answer: 1 and 2-B; 3-C; 4-A.

379. Match the Hall of Famers with their debuts.
1. Julius Erving   2. Dan Issel   3. Artis Gilmore
A. October 15, 1971   B. October 16, 1971   C. October 15, 1970
Answer: 1-A, ABA; 2-C, ABA; 3-B, ABA.

380. Match the Hall of Famers with their debuts.
1. Buddy Jeannette   2. Vern Mikkelsen   3. Kareem Abdul-Jabbar
4. George Yardley
A. November 1, 1953   B. November 2, 1949   C. October 18, 1969
D. November 12, 1947
Answer: 1-D; 2-B; 3-C; 4-A.

381. Match the Hall of Famers with their debuts.

1. David Thompson   2. Gail Goodrich   3. George Gervin

4. Bailey Howell

A. October 15, 1965   B. October 22, 1976   C. October 18, 1959

D. January 26, 1973

Answer: 1-B; 2-A; 3-D; 4-C.

382. Match the Hall of Famers with their debuts.

1. Alex English   2. Arnie Risen   3. Larry Bird   4. John Thompson

A. October 12, 1979   B. October 17, 1964   C. October 21, 1976

D. October 6, 1948

Answer: 1-C; 2-D; 3-A; 4-B.

383. Match the Hall of Famers with their debuts.

1. Kevin McHale   2. Isiah Thomas   3. Bob McAdoo   4. Moses Malone

A. October 10, 1980   B. October 10, 1972   C. October 30, 1981

D. October 18, 1974

Answer: 1-A; 2-C; 3-B; 4-D, ABA.

384. Match the Hall of Famers with their debuts.

1. Dražen Petrović   2. Magic Johnson   3. James Worthy

4. Robert Parish

A. October 12, 1979   B. November 3, 1989   C. October 22, 1976

D. October 29, 1982

Answer: 1-B; 2-A; 3-D; 4-C.

385. Match the Hall of Famers with their debuts.

1. Maurice Stokes   2. Joe Dumars   3. Dominique Wilkins

4. Charles Barkley

A. October 25, 1985   B. October 29, 1982   C. November 5, 1955

D. October 26, 1984

Answer: 1-C; 2-A; 3-B; 4-D.

386. Match the Hall of Famers with their debuts.

1. Patrick Ewing   2. Hakeem Olajuwon   3. Adrian Dantley

4. John Stockton

A. October 27, 1984   B. October 26, 1985   C. October 26, 1984

D. October 21, 1976

Answer: 1-B; 2-A; 3-D; 4-A.

387. Match the Hall of Famers with their debuts.
1. David Robinson   2. Michael Jordan   3. Scottie Pippen   4. Karl Malone
A. October 26, 1984   B. November 4, 1989   C. November 7, 1987
D. October 25, 1985
Answer: 1-B; 2-A; 3-C; 4-D.

388. Match the Hall of Famers with their debuts.
1. Gus Johnson   2. Dennis Rodman   3. Chris Mullin   4. Jamaal Wilkes
A. October 16, 1963   B. October 18, 1974   C. October 31, 1986
D. November 6, 1985
Answer: 1-A; 2-C; 3-D; 4-B.

389. Match the Hall of Famers with their debuts.
1. Reggie Miller   2. Mel Daniels   3. Ralph Sampson   4. Chet Walker
A. October 22, 1967   B. November 6, 1987   C. October 20, 1962
D. October 29, 1983
Answer: 1-B; 2-A, ABA; 3-D; 4-C.

390. Match the Hall of Famers with their debuts.
1. Gary Payton   2. Bernard King   3. Richie Guerin   4. Roger Brown
A. October 27, 1956   B. November 3, 1990   C. October 18, 1977
D. October 14, 1967
Answer: 1-B; 2-C; 3-A; 4-D.

391. Match the Hall of Famers with their debuts.
1. Guy Rodgers   2. Alonzo Mourning   3. Mitch Richmond
4. Jo Jo White
A. November 13, 1992   B. November 5, 1988   C. November 14, 1989
D. December 11, 1958
Answer: 1-D; 2-A; 3-B; 4-C.

392. Match the Hall of Famers with their debuts.
1. Šarūnas Marčiulionis   2. Spencer Haywood   3. Louie Dampier
4. Shaquille O'Neal
A. January 4, 1971   B. October 20, 1967   C. November 3, 1989
D. November 6, 1992
Answer: 1-C; 2-A; 3-B; 4-D.

393. Match the Hall of Famers with their debuts.
1. Yao Ming   2. Allen Iverson   3. Zelmo Beaty   4. Tracy McGrady
A. November 1, 1996   B. October 30, 2002   C. October 20, 1962
D. October 31, 1997
Answer: 1-B; 2-A; 3-C; 4-D.

394. Match the Hall of Famers with their debuts.
1. George McGinnis   2. Charlie Scott   3. Dino Radja   4. Steve Nash
A. October 17, 1970   B. November 5, 1993   C. October 24, 1975
D. November 1, 1996
Answer: 1-C; 2-A; 3-B; 4-D.

395. Match the Hall of Famers with their debuts.
1. Jason Kidd   2. Grant Hill   3. Maurice Cheeks   4. Ray Allen
A. November 4, 1994   B. October 13, 1978   C. November 5, 1995
D. November 1, 1996
Answer: 1-C; 2-A; 3-B; 4-D.

396. Match the Hall of Famers with their debuts.
1. Paul Westphal   2. Jack Sikma   3. Sidney Moncrief   4. Bobby Jones
A. October 12, 1979   B. October 11, 1972   C. October 19, 1977
D. October 22, 1976
Answer: 1-B; 2-C; 3-A; 4-D.

397. Match the Hall of Famers with their debuts.
1. Vlade Divac   2. Chuck Cooper   3. Carl Braun   4. Al Attles
A. November 13, 1947   B. November 1, 1950   C. October 28, 1960
D. November 3, 1989
Answer: 1-D; 2-B; 3-A; 4-C.

398. True or False? Michael Jordan was the highest scoring Bull in his debut.
Answer: False. Jordan tallied 16 points, seven rebounds, six assists, four blocks, and two steals in his first game on October 26, 1984. He hit just five of 16 shots, a poor 31 percent. His teammate Orlando Woolridge led in scoring with 28 points, as the Bulls beat the Bullets 109–93.

399. Match the Hall of Famers with their debuts.
1. Rudy Tomjanovich   2. Kevin Garnett   3. Tim Duncan   4. Kobe Bryant
A. November 3, 1996   B. October 13, 1970   C. November 3, 1995
D. October 31, 1997
Answer: 1-B; 2-C; 3-D; 4-A.

400. Match the Hall of Famers with their debuts.
1. Chris Webber   2. Ralph Sampson   3. Paul Pierce   4. Toni Kukoč
A. October 29, 1983   B. February 5, 1999   C. November 9, 1993
D. November 5, 1993
Answer: 1-C; 2-A; 3-B; 4-D.

401. Match the Hall of Famers with their debuts.
1. Bobby Dandridge   2. Chris Bosh   3. Lou Hudson   4. Tim Hardaway
A. October 15, 1966   B. November 3, 1989   C. October 18, 1969
D. October 29, 2003
Answer: 1-C; 2-D; 3-A; 4-B.

402. Match the overall first draft picks with the year of their debut.
1. Kyrie Irving   2. Anthony Davis   3. John Wall   4. Andrew Wiggins
A. 2012   B. 2014   C. 2011   D. 2010
Answer: 1-C; 2-A; 3-D; 4-B.

403. What player(s) hold the records for points and rebounds in an NBA debut?
A. Wilt Chamberlain   B. Maurice Stokes   C. John Drew   D. Bill Walton
Answer: A. On October 24, 1959, Chamberlain scored 43 points and grabbed 28 rebounds to lead the Warriors to a 118–109 win over the Knicks at Madison Square Garden. It's the most points and rebounds a player has ever recorded in his NBA debut. Wilt played the entire 48 minutes and connected on 17 of 27 field goal attempts and hit nine of 15 free throws. Small forward Kenny Sears led the way with 35 points and 15 rebounds for the Knicks.

DID YOU KNOW?

404. Who advocated the 24-second clock be adopted in 1954?
Answer: A native of Miglianico, Italy, and the owner of the Syracuse Nationals, Danny Biasone advocated the clock's use. He and general manager Leo Ferris thought that a well-paced game would mean each team taking around 60 shots a game. A total of 120 possessions of 24 seconds each would equal the 2,880 seconds of a game. Biasone was inducted into the Hall of Fame in 2000.

405. How many players in NBA history have 200 triple-doubles?
A. None   B. Two   C. Three   D. Four
Answer: A. The leader is Russell Westbrook with 198.

406. Name the twins drafted in 1965 who were both All-Stars.
Answer: Tom Van Arsdale and Dick Van Arsdale, both born in Indianapolis and both attending Indiana University, were also both three-time All-Stars. One difference was that Dick was selected to the All-Defensive Team three times, but Tom wasn't.

407. What two teams played before the largest regular-season crowd in NBA history?
A. Celtics–Lakers   B. Celtics–76ers   C. Bulls–Hawks   D. Bulls–Lakers
Answer: C. Playing one of his last regular-season games before his second retirement, Jordan and the Bulls played before 62,046 fans at the Georgia Dome on March 27, 1998. The Bulls prevailed 89–74.

408. Who is the Nuggets' career leader in points per game?
A. Larry Jones   B. Alex English   C. Carmelo Anthony   D. Allen Iverson
Answer: B. English averaged 25.9 for his Nuggets' career, the highest in the team's history.

409. True or False? Only one player has scored 3,000 points in a season.
Answer: False. Wilt Chamberlain did it three times and Michael Jordan did it once.

410. Who won the regular-season and Finals MVP in 1970, as well as the All-Star Game MVP?
A. Wes Unseld   B. Walt Frazier   C. Jerry West   D. Willis Reed
Answer: D. Reed scored 21 and gathered 11 rebounds in the East's 142–135 win in the All-Star Game.

411. Who was the first coach in NBA history to be awarded Coach of the Year?
A. Red Auerbach   B. Alex Hannum   C. Dolph Schayes   D. Harry Gallatin
Answer: D. Harry "The Horse" led the St. Louis Hawks to a 48-32 mark in 1963, his first year on the sidelines. He then led them to a 6-5 playoff mark, but they were ousted by the Lakers 4–3 in the Western Division finals.

412. Name the first Black player drafted in the NBA.
A. Chuck Cooper   B. Nat Clifton   C. Earl Lloyd
Answer: A. Cooper was drafted by the Celtics in 1950.

413. How many Knicks fouled out when Wilt Chamberlain scored 100 against them on March 2, 1962?
A. One   B. Three   C. Five   D. Seven
Answer: A. The 6'10" center Darrall Imhoff, who started the game guarding Wilt, fouled out.

414. What other records did Chamberlain set the night he scored 100 points?

Answer: On March 2, 1962, when Chamberlain logged 100 points in a 169–147 victory against the Knicks in Hershey, Pennsylvania, he set eight NBA records: most field goals in a game, 36; most field goal attempts, 63; most free throws in a game, 28; most field goals in a half, 22; most points in a game, 100; most field goal attempts in a half, 37; most field goal attempts in a quarter, 21; most points in a half, 50.

415. True or False? No player has ever led the league in blocks and rebounds in the same season.

Answer: False. Of course, blocks were not kept as a statistic until 1974, otherwise Bill Russell, Wilt Chamberlain, and Kareem Abdul-Jabbar would likely have done it. Playing for the Magic, Dwight Howard won both titles twice, in 2009 (13.8 rebounds and 2.9 blocks) and 2010 (13.2 rebounds and 2.8 blocks).

416. Who played every minute in the 1973 Finals?

A. Walt Frazier   B. Jerry West   C. Gail Goodrich   D. Wilt Chamberlain

Answer: D. Playing his 14th and last NBA season, the 36-year-old center played all 240 minutes in the Finals, which the Knicks won 4–1. In a time before the minute police cared about "load management," Chamberlain didn't take a breather. He averaged 11.6 points and 18.6 rebounds. Frazier wasn't far behind, averaging 46 minutes for the Finals.

417. Wilt Chamberlain scored 70 or more six times. How many times did everyone else combined score 70?

Answer: Everyone else combined did it seven times. Kobe Bryant scored 81; David Thompson, 73; Elgin Baylor, 71: David Robinson; 71, Donovan Mitchell, 71; Damian Lillard, 71; and Devin Booker, 70.

418. What is Wilt Chamberlain's record for consecutive 30-point games?

A. 22 games   B. 36 games   C. 65 games   D. 71 games

Answer: C. Chamberlain scored 30 or more for 65 straight games from November 4, 1961, through February 22, 1962.

419. What player on the inaugural Cavaliers team in 1970 had a father who was a basketball Hall of Famer?

Answer: Larry Mikan, whose father was Hall of Fame Minneapolis center George Mikan.

420. True or False? A player has grabbed 2,000 rebounds in a season more than once.

Answer: True. Chamberlain grabbed 2,149 in 1961 and 2,052 in 1962.

421. True or False? No Mavericks player ever averaged double digits in rebounds per game in a season.

Answer: False. Four have. James Donaldson, 11.9 rebounds per game in 1987; Roy Tarpley, 11.8 in 1988; Tyson Chandler, 11.5 in 2015; Popeye Jones, 10.6 in 1995.

422. When is the last time that LeBron James played 79 games in a season?

A. 2016   B. 2017   C. 2018   D. 2019

Answer: C. Since 2018, James have averaged just 56 games in a season. Workload management, now practiced by many sports teams, seeks to reduce the risk of injury and optimize performance by resting fatigued players.

423. Who was the oldest player to score 40 points in a game?

A. Vince Carter   B. Michael Jordan   C. Dirk Nowitzki
D. Jamal Crawford

Answer: B. Jordan turned the trick on February 21, 2003, when he tallied 43 against the Nets while playing for the Wizards. He was 40 years and four days old.

424. Who is the oldest player to tally 50 points in a game?

A. Michael Jordan   B. Karl Malone   C. Kareem Abdul-Jabbar
D. Jamal Crawford

Answer: D. Crawford was 39 years and 21 days old when he posted 51 while playing for the Suns against the Mavericks on the last day of the season on April 9, 2019. He hit 18 of 30 field goal attempts, including seven of 13 from 3-point range. Dallas prevailed 120–109.

425. Who was the oldest player to score 60 in a game?

A. Elgin Baylor   B. Wilt Chamberlain   C. Kobe Bryant   D. Karl Malone

Answer: Bryant was 37 years and 234 days old when he scored 60 for the Lakers against the Jazz on April 13, 2016, the last day of the season. Bryant made 22 of 50 field goals, though just six of 21 from 3-point range. The Lakers beat the Jazz 101–96 to finish the season 17-65.

426. Which players had 400 or more blocks in a season?
A. Mark Eaton   B. Manute Bol   C. Artis Gilmore   D. Elmore Smith
Answer: A and C. The Utah center owns the record with 456 in 1985.
Gilmore had 422 blocks for the Kentucky Colonels in 1972.

427. Who was the oldest player to lead the league in scoring?
A. Kobe Bryant   B. LeBron James   C. Michael Jordan   D. Karl Malone
Answer: C. Jordan was 35 years and 60 days old (on April 18, 1998)
when he led the league with an average of 28.7 points per game in 1998.

**428. Name the player drafted in 1966 who had a father and an uncle
play in the NBA.**
A. Whitey Skoog   B. Larry Mikan   C. Bud Grant   D. Jim Brewer
Answer: B. Mikan was drafted 36th overall by the Lakers. His father
George Mikan was a legendary center for the Lakers. His uncle Ed Mikan,
also a center, was drafted by the Stags in in 1948. His brother Terry
Mikan was drafted 104th overall by the Knicks in 1974, but never played
a pro game.

429. Who played the most seasons in NBA history?
A. Vince Carter   B. Kareem Abdul-Jabbar   C. Robert Parish
D. Kevin Garnett
Answer: A. Carter played an astounding 22 seasons with eight different
teams.

430. What player born in the Bahamas had two sons play in the NBA?
Answer: Mychal Thompson, who played center and forward for 12
seasons, including two title teams with the Lakers in 1987 and 1988, is
the father of Klay Thompson and Mychel Thompson.

431. Who were the NBA world champions in 1968?
A. 76ers   B. Warriors   C. Celtics   D. Lakers
Answer: C. The Celts won their 10th title in 12 years, topping the Lakers
in six games. Jerry West led all scorers with 31.3 points per game.

432. Who set the mark for most free throws attempted in a game?
A. Jerry West   B. Wilt Chamberlain   C. Oscar Robertson
D. Dwight Howard
Answer: D. The Magic center attempted 39 twice. The first time was
against the Warriors on January 12, 2012. He made just 21 but scored 45
points and gathered 23 rebounds as the Magic won 117–109. The next
occasion was against the Lakers on March 12, 2013. Howard hit 25 of 39
and finished with 39 points and 16 rebounds as the Lakers won 106–97.

433. Who attempted the most free throws in one half?
A. Andre Drummond   B. Dwight Howard   C. Donovan Mitchell
D. Michael Jordan
Answer: A. Amazingly, the Pistons center took 28 free throws in the
second half and made 11 against the Rockets on January 20, 2016.
The Pistons won 123–114.

**434. When Reggie Miller took over the career mark for 3-pointers in
1998, whose record did he break?**
A. Dan Majerle   B. Vernon Maxwell   C. Dale Ellis   D. Dennis Scott
Answer: C. The Seattle small forward had 1,461 when Miller passed him.
Miller then held the record for 13 years.

435. Which team had the largest margin of victory in a game?
A. Grizzlies   B. Lakers   C. Pacers   D. Cavaliers
Answer: A. Amazingly, the Grizzlies topped the Thunder by 73 points on
December 2, 2021. The final tally was 152–79, as Jaren Jackson led nine
players in double digits with 27 points.

**436. How many players were picked ahead of Wilt Chamberlain in the
1959 draft?**
A. None   B. One   C. Two   D. Three
Answer: C. Chamberlain, from the University of Kansas, was picked
third behind Bob Boozer from Kansas State and Bailey Howell from
Mississippi State.

437. Who is the youngest player to debut in the NBA?
A. LeBron James   B. Kobe Bryant   C. Andrew Bynum
D. Tracy McGrady
Answer: C. Just 18 years and six days old, Bynum debuted with the
Lakers against the Nuggets on November 2, 2005. Coming off the
bench in a 99–97 win, the center played five minutes without scoring.

438. In which season did Kyrie Irving win a championship?
A. Second   B. Third   C. Fourth   D. Fifth
Answer: D. For the regular season he averaged 19.6 points per game. In
the 2016 Finals against the Warriors, he upped that to 29.4 and hit the
game-winning shot over Stephen Curry in Game 7.

439. What player drafted in 1961 had a brother drafted the year before?
A. Tom Meschery   B. Ray Scott   C. Tom Stith   D. Don Kojis
Answer: C. A native of Queens, New York, and a 6'5" small forward out
of St. Bonaventure University, Tom, chosen second overall, was the
younger brother of Sam, a 6'3" guard chosen 56th overall in the 1960
draft. Both went to high school at St. Francis Prep in Queens.

440. Who hit the first 3-point shot in NBA history?
A. Kevin Grevey   B. Dennis Johnson   C. Chris Ford   D. M. L. Carr
Answer: C. Ford hit his shot on October 12, 1979, with three minutes and
48 seconds left in the second quarter. Grevey's shot was made later.

441. Which player has won the most rebounding titles since 2000?
A. Dikembe Mutombo   B. DeAndre Jordan   C. Andre Drummond
D. Kevin Garnett   E. Dwight Howard
Answer: E. A husky 6'10" native of Atlanta, Howard copped five
rebounding titles in six seasons, between 2008 and 2013. The first four
came with the Magic and the last with the Lakers.

DRAFT

442. Jason Kidd and Grant Hill were selected second and third respectively in the 1994 draft. Which of the two made the Hall of Fame first?

Answer: Neither. Both were inducted in 2018. Kidd was Rookie of the Year, a 10-time All-Star, and is second all-time behind only John Stockton with 12,091 assists.

443. Name the lowest draft pick among the top five scorers of all time.

Answer: It's a tie. Karl Malone, the third highest scorer of all time with 36,928 points, was drafted 13th overall by the Jazz in the 1985 draft. Kobe Bryant, the fourth highest scorer of all time with 33,643 points, was drafted 13th by the Hornets in the 1996 draft.

444. Name the player drafted in the top 10 in 1952 who made the Hall of Fame.

A. Joe Dean   B. Dick Groat   C. Bill Stauffer   D. Clyde Lovellette
Answer: D. Drafted 10th overall, the 6′9″ center, who was a four-time All-Star and three-time NBA champ, made the Hall of Fame in 1988.

445. Which of the following players from the 1985 draft played the most seasons?

A. Karl Malone   B. Chris Mullin   C. Charles Oakley   D. Patrick Ewing
Answer: A and C. Malone and Oakley each played 19 years.

446. Name the player picked first in the 1971 draft.
A. Elmore Smith   B. Sidney Wicks   C. Austin Carr   D. Ken Durrett
Answer: C. The shooting guard out of Notre Dame soon became "Mr. Cavalier" in Cleveland, as he played nine of his 11 seasons there. In his first three seasons he averaged over 20 points.

447. Name the future Hall of Famer who was not picked in the top 10 in the 1972 draft.
A. Julius Erving   B. Tom Riker   C. Bob McAdoo   D. Paul Westphal
Answer: A. Amazing to tell, but Dr. J. was chosen 12th in the draft, behind Riker and eight other non–Hall of Famers.

448. What player was overlooked until the third round and 39th pick overall in the 1972 draft but went on to win four assist titles?
A. Dave Twardzik   B. Jim Price   C. Kevin Porter   D. Chris Ford
Answer: C. The 6-foot guard who played 11 seasons peaked with 13.4 assists for the Pistons in 1979.

449. How many players drafted in the top five in the 1949 BAA draft made the Hall of Fame?
A. None   B. One   C. Two   D. Three
Answer: D. Ed Macauley, drafted second, inducted in 1960; Dick McGuire, third, 1993; Vern Mikkelsen, fourth, 1995.

450. Name the player drafted in the top 10 of the 1957 draft who went to the Hall of Fame.
A. Sam Jones   B. Bob Pettit   C. Elgin Baylor   D. Si Green
Answer: A. Jones was drafted 10th. After a 12-year career in which the Celtics won 10 titles, he retired in 1969 and was inducted to the Hall of Fame in 1984.

451. True or False? The Hornets have had one number one pick in the draft since 1988.
Answer: True. They drafted Larry Johnson first out of Nevada–Las Vegas in 1991.

452. How many Hall of Famers were among the top 10 picks in the 1981 draft?

A. None   B. One   C. Two   D. Three

Answer: B. The would-be Hall of Famer who was drafted second from Indiana University was the great small guard Isiah Thomas, who at 6'1" tall was a 12-time All-Star, two-time NBA champ, and Finals MVP in 1990.

453. Name the last player to be drafted first overall by the Hawks.

A. Luka Dončić   B. Al Horford   C. Marvin Williams
D. David Thompson   E. Pete Maravich

Answer: D. Though drafted by the Hawks, Thompson didn't play for them but was drafted by the ABA's Virginia Squires two weeks later and started his career in the ABA with Denver in 1975.

454. True or False? Jason Kidd was the Mavericks' highest draft pick in the last 40 years.

Answer: True. Kidd was the second overall pick in 1994. He is the highest pick for the Mavericks since 1981, their second ever draft, when Mark Aguirre was picked first.

455. Rank the order of the following picks in the 1970 draft.

A. Dave Cowens   B. Rudy Tomjanovich   C. Bob Lanier
D. Pete Maravich

Answer: 1-C, center; 2-B, power forward; 3-D, guard; 4-A, center.

456. Name the last player to be drafted first overall by the Celtics.

A. Jayson Tatum   B. Len Bias   C. Chuck Share   D. Bob Cousy

Answer: C. The 6'11" center from Bowling Green was not just the Celtics' first and only number one pick in 1950, but the first player ever drafted in the NBA.

457. Name the player picked first in the 1961 draft.

A. Tom Stith   B. Ray Scott   C. Walt Bellamy   D. Larry Siegfried

Answer: C. One of the true underrated players of all time, Bellamy, drafted by the Chicago Packers, enjoyed a stellar NBA career. In an otherworldly rookie season, the 6'11" center averaged 31.6 points and 19 rebounds while shooting a league best .519 from the field.

458. How many top 10 picks from the 1951 draft made it to the Basketball Hall of Fame?

A. None   B. Two   C. Three   D. Four

Answer: A. No players from the 1951 draft made the Hall.

459. Name the first player drafted number one to later be inducted into the Hall of Fame.

A. Chuck Share   B. Si Green   C. Elgin Baylor   D. Oscar Robertson

Answer: C. Drafted first overall out of Seattle University in 1958, Baylor was elected to the Hall of Fame in 1977.

460. Name the last team to have consecutive number one draft picks.

A. Timberwolves   B. Knicks   C. 76ers   D. Pelicans

Answer: C. The Sixers drafted Ben Simmons first in 2016 and Markelle Fultz first in 2017.

461. Name the year that LeBron James was drafted.

A. 2002   B. 2003   C. 2004   D. 2005

Answer: B. James was selected first. His future teammates Carmelo Anthony (third), Chris Bosh (fourth), and Dwyane Wade (fifth) were also picked in the 2003 draft.

LeBron James

462. Which draft produced five Hall of Famers in the top 10 picks?
A. 1962   B. 1963   C. 1964   D. 1965
Answer: D. Bill Bradley (second), Rick Barry (fourth), Jerry Sloan (sixth), Billy Cunningham (seventh), and Gail Goodrich (10th) all were drafted in 1965.

463. True or False? The Nuggets never landed a number one draft pick.
Answer: True. In 46 drafts since 1977 they have never gotten a number one pick.

464. True or False? No players drafted in the top 10 in 1991 made the Hall of Fame.
Answer: False. Dikembe Mutombo was drafted fifth overall. A three-time block champion and two-time rebounding champion, the eight-time All-Star was inducted to the Hall of Fame in 2015.

465. True or False? The Nets have never had the number one pick in the draft.
Answer: False. Their most recent number one pick was Kenyon Martin, who they drafted in 2000. In 1990 they drafted Derrick Coleman first.

466. Who was the lowest draft pick in 1947 to make the Hall of Fame?
A. Jim Pollard   B. Red Rocha   C. Andy Phillip   D. Harry Gallatin
Answer: A. Pollard was 61st overall in the first BAA draft in 1947. Named "The Kangaroo Kid," the 6'4" small forward played on five title teams for the Minneapolis Lakers and was elected to the Hall of Fame in 1978.

467. In what draft were Andre Drummond, Damian Lillard, and Anthony Davis all picked in the top 10?
A. 2010   B. 2011   C. 2012   D. 2013
Answer: C. Davis, who led Kentucky to a title as a freshman in 2012, was selected first overall.

468. True or False? No players drafted in the top 10 of the 1971 draft made the Hall of Fame.
Answer: True.

469. Which of these players picked in the top 10 in the NBA Draft made the Hall of Fame?
A. Cliff Hagan   B. Walter Dukes   C. Frank Ramsey   D. Ray Felix
Answer: C. Ramsey, the Celtics' original sixth man, was picked eighth and inducted in 1982. Hagan made the Hall of Fame in 1978 but was picked 20th in the 1953 draft.

470. True or False? Elvin Hayes was picked ahead of Wes Unseld in the 1968 draft.
Answer: True. The Rockets picked Hayes first overall, and the Bullets picked Unseld second.

471. True or False? The Bulls have had only one number one draft pick in the last 25 years.
Answer: False. They've had two. Derrick Rose was their number one pick out of Memphis in 2008. Elton Brand, from Duke, was their number one in 1999.

472. What player from the 1961 draft played on five championship teams?
A. Tom Stith   B. Larry Siegfried   C. Walt Bellamy   D. Don Kojis
Answer: B. Picked third in the draft, the guard and Ohio State graduate was selected by the Royals third overall and then signed as a free agent with the Celtics. His seven seasons with the Celtics (1964–1970) included titles in 1964, 1965, 1966, 1968, and 1969.

473. Rank the following players one through four in the 1969 draft.
A. Terry Driscoll   B. Kareem Abdul-Jabbar   C. Neal Walk
D. Lucius Allen
Answer: 1-B, center; 2-C, center; 3-D, point guard; 4-A, power forward.

474. In which of the following years did the number one draft pick make the Hall of Fame?
A. 1947   B. 1948   C. 1953   D. 1955
Answer: D. In 1955 LaSalle guard Tom Gola was drafted first by the Warriors, played 10 years, and was elected to the Hall of Fame.

475. In which of the following years did the number one draft pick make the Hall of Fame?

A. 1956   B. 1957   C. 1958   D. 1959

Answer: C. Elgin Baylor was selected first by the Minneapolis Lakers in the 1958 draft from Seattle University.

476. Who was picked first overall in the 2022 draft?

A. Jalen Green   B. Evan Mobley   C. Cade Cunningham
D. Scottie Barnes

Answer: C. The point guard from Oklahoma State was drafted number one overall in 2022.

477. In what year(s) did the number one draft pick make the Hall of Fame?

A. 1960   B. 1961   C. 1962   D. 1963

Answer: A, B, and C. A: Oscar Robertson and Jerry West were drafted first and second in the 1960 draft. B: Walt Bellamy was drafted first by the Chicago Packers in the 1961 draft. C: Dave DeBusschere and Jerry Lucas went first and second in the 1962 draft.

478. In what year(s) did the number one draft pick make the Hall of Fame?

A. 1964   B. 1965   C. 1966   D. 1967

Answer: B. The Knicks picked Princeton legend Bill Bradley first in the 1965 draft. In his 10-year career he was a two-time champion with the Knicks.

479. In what year(s) did the number one draft pick make the Hall of Fame?

A. 1968   B. 1969   C. 1970   D. 1971

Answer: A, B, and C. A. Elvin Hayes and Wes Unseld were selected first and second in the 1968 draft. B. Kareem Abdul-Jabbar was picked first in the 1969 draft. C. Bob Lanier went first in the 1970 draft.

480. How many of the 31 NBA and ABA players drafted from the University of Utah made the Hall of Fame?

A. None   B. One   C. Two   D. Three

Answer: A. Some very good players emerged from Utah, such as 20,000-point scorer Tom Chambers and Mike Newlin. But the school produced no Hall of Famers.

481. Match the following stars with the year they were drafted.
1. Charles Barkley   2. Larry Bird   3. Tim Duncan   4. Tony Parker
5. Magic Johnson
A. 1984   B. 1978   C. 2001   D. 1997   E. 1979
Answer: 1-A; 2-B; 3-D; 4-C; 5-E.

DUBIOUS DISTINCTIONS

482. Name the players who averaged four or more turnovers a game for the most seasons.
A. James Harden   B. LeBron James   C. Russell Westbrook
Answer: A and C. Each had four or more turnovers a game for seven seasons.

483. Name the players who averaged 5.5 or more turnovers a game for a season.
A. Russell Westbrook   B. LeBron James   C. James Harden
D. Kobe Bryant
Answer: C and D. Harden is the true record holder, since he averaged 5.7 per game over an 81-game season in 2017. Bryant did it in 2014 but played just six games that year.

484. What Boston team lost three straight games in the Finals?
A. 1958   B. 1967   C. 1985   D. 2022
Answer: D. After leading the Warriors 2–1 in the 2022 Finals, the Celtics dropped three straight games. It was the first Celtic team to lose three straight games in the Finals.

485. What team has gone the longest without a title?
A. Suns   B. Clippers   C. Kings   D. Jazz
Answer: C. The Kings last won as the Rochester Royals in 1951.

486. Who attempted the most free throws in a game without making one?

A. Wilt Chamberlain   B. Chris Dudley   C. Shaquille O'Neal
D. Dwight Howard

Answer: C. On his way to a second straight title with the Lakers, O'Neal missed all 11 attempts against the Sonics on December 8, 2000. The Lakers lost 103–95.

487. Who missed the most free throws in a game?

A. Dwight Howard   B. Wilt Chamberlain   C. Shaquille O'Neal
D. Andre Drummond

Answer: D. The Pistons center clanged 23 when he made just 13 of 36 attempts against the Rockets on January 20, 2016. The Pistons won 123–114.

488. How many times were Shaq's teams swept before he first won a title?

A. Two   B. Three   C. Four   D. Five

Answer: D. Shaq and the Magic were swept by the Pacers in 1994, the Rockets in 1995, and the Bulls in 1996. With the Lakers he was swept by the Jazz in 1998 and the Spurs in 1999. He won three consecutive titles with the Lakers from 2000 through 2002.

489. Name the teams that are below .500 all-time.

A. Warriors   B. Celtics   C. Nets   D. Spurs

Answer: A and C. The Golden State Warriors (1971–2023), who first played in Philadelphia (1946–1962) and then in San Francisco (1962–1971) have a record of 2,923 wins and 3,098 losses (.485). Only the Philadelphia Warriors (558-554, .506) were above .500. The Nets, who played as the New Jersey Americans in the ABA (1967–68), in New York in the ABA (1968–76) and NBA (1976–77), then in New Jersey (1978–2012) and in Brooklyn (2012–present), have won 1,996 and lost 2,534 (.441).

490. What team committed the most turnovers in a game?

A. Spurs   B. Bobcats   C. Suns   D. Warriors

Answer: D. The San Francisco Warriors turned it over 45 times against the Celtics in a 134–112 loss on March 9, 1971.

491. True or False? No active players have 4,000 turnovers.

Answer: False. LeBron James has 4,966 turnovers and Russell Westbrook has 4,443.

492. Name the oldest player to debut in NBA history.

A. Wayne Embry   B. Nat Hickey   C. Kenny Sailors   D. Red Rocha

Answer: B. A 5'11" guard and forward from Hoboken, New Jersey, Hickey, who coached the Providence Steamrollers, activated himself as a player and made his debut on January 27, 1948. He was 45 years and 362 days old. He missed all five of his field goal attempts and made two of three from the charity stripe for two points, the only two points in his career. His coaching record for the 1947–48 season was 4-25.

493. Name the team(s) that have the longest losing streak in NBA history.

A. Grizzlies   B. 76ers   C. Knicks   D. Cavaliers

Answer: B and D. Two teams share the record for futility. After the departure of LeBron James, the Cavs lost 26 straight during the 2010–11 season. The 2013–14 Sixers, not the 9-73 Sixers of 1973, also lost 26 in a row.

494. Rank the following coaches by most losses.

A. Bill Fitch   B. Don Nelson   C. Lenny Wilkens   D. Dick Motta

Answer: 1-C, Wilkens lost 1,332 games. 2-A, 1,106; 3-B, 1,063; 4-D, 1,017. The first three are in the Hall of Fame.

495. What team holds the record for worst winning percentage in a single season?

A. Bobcats   B. 76ers   C. Cavaliers   D. Royals

Answer: A. The Cats finished 7-59 in 2012 during a lockout season. Their .106 percentage was worse than the 9-73 Sixers in 1973 (.110).

496. Name the two players who attempted the most field goals in a playoff game without making one.
A. John Starks   B. Tim Hardaway   C. Chick Reiser   D. Dennis Johnson
Answer: C and D. Baltimore Bullets guard Chick Reiser missed all 14 of his shots in Game 1 against the Philadelphia Warriors on April 10, 1948. Missing was contagious, as the Bullets made just 19 of 103 shots (.184) and lost 71–60. The Bullets rallied to win their first championship. Thirty years later, on June 7, 1978, Sonics guard and future Hall of Famer Dennis Johnson helped the cause of the Bullets, missing all 14 shots in a Game 7 105–99 loss.

497. Who holds the mark for most field goal attempts in a game while making none?
A. Allen Iverson   B. Chris Dudley   C. Tim Hardaway   D. John Starks
Answer: C. The Warriors' Hardaway missed all 17 of his shots against the Timberwolves on December 27, 1991.

498. Name the player who missed the most field goal attempts in a single game.
A. Joe Fulks   B. George Mikan   C. Kobe Bryant   D. Wilt Chamberlain
Answer: A. The Warriors' 6'5" power forward made 13 shots and missed 42 against the Providence Steamrollers on March 18, 1948. On other nights Fulks shot 4-for-31, 6-for-38, 5-for-31, 7-for-36, 7-for-40, and 8-for-46.

499. Name the only players to get 20 points and 20 rebounds in consecutive playoff games and still lose.
A. Shaquille O'Neal   B. Kareem Abdul-Jabbar   C. Giannis Antetokounmpo   D. Wilt Chamberlain   E. Bill Russell
Answer: C, D, and E. Former MVP Antetokounmpo did it against the Celtics in the Eastern Conference semifinals in 2022 and the Bucks lost both. He thus joined Chamberlain and Russell as the only players to post 20-20 games consecutively in the postseason and lose both.

500. Name the team with the most 60-loss seasons.
A. Clippers   B. Grizzlies   C. Timberwolves   D. Warriors
Answer: A. The Clippers have 11 seasons with 60 or more losses.

501. Who committed the most fouls in a season?
A. Draymond Green   B. Dennis Rodman   C. Darryl Dawkins
D. Wilt Chamberlain
Answer: C. The 6'11" breaker of backboards, "Sir Slam" committed
386 fouls the 1984 season, which is almost five fouls per game.
Dawkins played 81 games and 2,417 minutes, barely 30 minutes per
game.

502. Name the team with the most losses in a season.
A. Clippers   B. Knicks   C. 76ers   D. Nets
Answer: C. The 76ers hold first and second place. They dropped 73
games in 1973 and lost 72 in 2016. No other team has lost more than 71.

**503. What player had the highest points per game over his career
without winning a scoring title?**
A. Jerry West   B. Walt Bellamy   C. Bob Pettit   D. Elgin Baylor
Answer: D. Though he averaged 27.36 points over his brilliant career
with the Lakers, Baylor never won a scoring title in his 14-year career.

**504. What team scored 48 points in a quarter in a game during the
2022–23 season but still lost?**
Answer: The Knicks scored 48 points in the first quarter of a game on
November 13, 2022, but still lost to the Thunder at Madison Square
Garden 145–135. After taking the opening quarter 48–36, the Knicks
were outscored 109–87 over the remaining three quarters.

**505. Who has the highest points per game by a player who wasn't an
All-Star that season?**
A. Adrian Dantley   B. George Mikan   C. Bob Rule   D. Bradley Beal
Answer: A. In 1983 the Jazz forward averaged 30.7 points but did not
make the All-Star team.

**506. Which expansion team has gone the longest without winning
a title?**
A. SuperSonics/Thunder   B. Suns   C. Clippers   D. Hornets
E. Trail Blazers
Answer: B. The Suns began in the 1968–69 season. They have failed to
win an NBA title in 55 years.

507. True or False? The record number for most 3-pointers attempted in a game without making one is 12.
Answer: True. Brook Lopez, playing for the Bucks, missed all 12 against the Suns without a make on November 23, 2018.

508. Who played for the most teams in one season?
A. Ish Smith   B. Vince Carter   C. Bobby Jones   D. Jamal Crawford
Answer: C. A small forward, Jones played for five teams during the 2007–8 season: the Nuggets, Grizzlies, Rockets, Heat, and Spurs.

509. True or False? The most teams played for by one player is 11.
Answer: False. Point guard Ish Smith, who is 34, has played for 13 teams in his 13-year NBA career. The teams are the Rockets, Grizzlies, Warriors, Magic, Bucks, Suns, Thunder, 76ers, Pelicans, Pistons, Wizards, Hornets, and Nuggets.

510. What two teams have lost a seventh game by the most points?
A. Nets   B. Magic   C. Suns   D. Bombers   E. Stags
Answer: C and D. The 2022 Suns lost to the Mavericks 123–90 in the conference semifinals, the 33-point margin being the most in a loss since the St. Louis Bombers lost to the Philadelphia Warriors in the 1948 BAA semifinals by 39 points, 85–46.

511. Rank the all-time leaders in turnovers.
A. John Stockton   B. Karl Malone   C. Russell Westbrook
D. LeBron James   E. Moses Malone
Answer: Turnovers have been recorded since 1977–78 in the NBA and 1967–68 in the ABA. 1-D, 4,966 turnovers; 2-B, 4,524; 3-E, 4,443; 4-E, 4,264; 5-A, 4,244.

512. How many different teams that LeBron James played for were eliminated from the playoffs?
A. Two   B. Three   C. Four   D. Five
Answer: B. Cleveland, Miami, and Los Angeles were all eliminated.

513. The Brooklyn Nets played 226 regular-season games from 2020 to 2022. How many of those games did Kyrie Irving play in?
Answer: Just 103. He missed many home games since he would not receive the COVID-19 vaccine.

514. Name the only two teams in NBA history to win 64 games and not make it to the conference finals.

A. Suns   B. Mavericks   C. Warriors   D. 76ers

Answer: A and B. The Suns finished a league-best 64-18 but lost the Western Conference semifinals to the Mavericks four games to two in 2022. The 2007 Mavs were 67-15 and were the top seed in the Western Conference but lost in the first round to the Warriors four games to two.

515. How many times have Chris Paul's teams led 2–0 in the playoffs but still lost?

A. Two   B. Three   C. Four   D. Five

Answer: D. In 2008 Paul's Hornets led the Spurs 2–0 and lost in seven games in the Western Conference semifinals. With the Clippers in 2013, Paul lost to the Grizzlies in the first round 4–2 after leading 2–0. In 2016 Paul's Clippers lost to the Blazers in the first round after a 2–0 lead. In 2021 Paul, with the Suns, held a 2–0 lead in the Finals against the Bucks but lost the next four. In 2022 Paul's Suns lost to the Mavericks in six after leading 2–0 in the Western Conference semifinals.

516. Name the opposing center(s) in Wilt Chamberlain's 100-point game.

A. Walt Bellamy   B. Darrall Imhoff   C. Willie Naulls   D. Nate Thurmond   E. Cleveland Buckner

Answer: B and E. In a statistical oddity, the 6'9" Buckner scored 33 points in 33 minutes. The 33 points were the highest total in Buckner's two-year, 68-game career. At 6'10", Imhoff played 20 minutes. The Warriors beat the Knicks 169–147.

517. Name two guards who are tied for most turnovers in a game.

A. John Drew   B. Stephen Curry   C. Jason Kidd   D. John Starks

Answer: A and C. Drew turned over the ball 14 times for the Hawks against the Nets on March 1, 1977. Kidd matched Drew for futility 23 years later, turning it over 14 times against the Knicks on November 17, 2000.

518. Which team lost the most home games in an NBA season?

A. 76ers   B. Hornets   C. Knicks   D. Mavericks

Answer: D. The 1994 Mavs finished 13-69, one of the worst records in NBA history. They lost 35 of those games at home, finishing with a 6-35 mark. They were one better on the road, with a 7-34 mark.

519. Which teams have won a championship in the last 40 years?
A. Knicks   B. Wizards   C. 76ers   D. Pacers
Answer: C. In 1983 the Sixers swept the Lakers in the Finals, led by Most Valuable Player Moses Malone. For the Finals he averaged 25.8 points and 18 rebounds. The Knicks haven't won since 1973. The Wizards last won in 1978. The Pacers haven't won in the NBA and last won in 1972 in the ABA.

520. What team scored the fewest points in a game during the shot clock era?
A. Knicks   B. Nationals   C. Hawks   D. Bulls
Answer: D. The game was played against the Heat on April 19, 1999, post–shot clock and post-Jordan. Playing at home, the Bulls scored just eight points in the first quarter. They hit just 18 of 77 field goal attempts (.234) and lost 82–49.

521. What two players share the record for turnovers in an NBA Finals?
A. Jason Kidd   B. LeBron James   C. Magic Johnson   D. James Harden
Answer: B and C. Magic Johnson committed 31 turnovers in the 1984 Finals and James equaled that total in the 2016 Finals.

522. What player fouled out the most times in one Finals series?
A. Stephen Curry   B. Draymond Green   C. Kyle Lowry   D. Marc Gasol
Answer: B. Green fouled out three times in the 2016 Finals when his Warriors fell to the Cavs in seven games.

523. How many games did Zion Williamson play in his first four years?
A. 56   B. 72   C. 85   D. 114
Answer: D. He played in just 114 games in four years, dealing with a series of injuries.

524. Name the player who is the worst free throw shooter in NBA history.
A. Shaquille O'Neal   B. Chris Dudley   C. DeAndre Jordan
D. Ben Wallace
Answer: D. Free throws weren't free for "Big Ben." Air balls were such a common occurrence that it was often considered an achievement if one of his free tosses struck iron or the backboard. Over his 16-year career he made just 41.4 percent of his charity tosses.

ECONOMICS

525. Which of the following Hall of Famers earned the highest salary in 1947?
A. George Mikan   B. Bob Davies   C. Jim Pollard
Answer: B. Davies, the Rochester Royals guard, earned $12,500, having inked a four-year, $50,000 deal. With a five-year, $60,000 contract, Minneapolis center Mikan earned $12,000. Pollard, Mikan's teammate, also earned $12,000.

526. How much money did Kyrie Irving lose in salary for not playing home games during the 2021–22 season?
Answer: For the games missed, Irving lost about $15,580,000 in salary.

527. How much did Wilt Chamberlain make in his rookie season in the NBA?
A. $22,000   B. $25,000   C. $30,000   D. $35,000
Answer: C. It was the highest salary in the league in the 1959–60 season.

528. How much did Wilt Chamberlain get paid for being a Globetrotter a year before his NBA season?
Answer: $50,000.

FAMOUS FIRSTS AND OTHER RECORDS

529. In what year did Wilt Chamberlain break the record for points in one game?
A. 1960   B. 1961   C. 1962   D. 1963
Answer: B. It was December 8, 1961, when Wilt was playing for the Warriors and scored 78 in a triple-overtime win against the Lakers to break Elgin Baylor's 71-point game in 1960.

530. Name the first player to be awarded Defensive Player of the Year.
A. Dennis Rodman   B. Sidney Moncrief   C. Mark Eaton
D. Alvin Robertson
Answer: B. The Bucks guard won the first two seasons the award was given in 1983 and 1984.

531. Name the first player to score 35,000 points.
A. Wilt Chamberlain   B. Moses Malone   C. Kareem Abdul-Jabbar
D. Michael Jordan
Answer: C. Abdul-Jabbar passed the 35,000 milestone in 1986, his 17th season, when he turned 39 years old but still averaged 25.3 points per game.

532. Name the first player to win three consecutive scoring titles.
Answer: The Lakers' George Mikan led the league in scoring from 1949 through 1951.

533. Name the first player to lead the NBA in scoring.
A. George Mikan   B. Joe Fulks   C. Neil Johnston   D. George Yardley
Answer: B. A 6'5" Philadelphia Warriors power forward "Jumpin' Joe"
led the circuit in each of the NBA's first two seasons. In the 1946–47
season his 23.2 points per game helped his team to a 35-25 mark and a
defeat of the Chicago Stags four games to one in the first championship
season.

**534. True or False? Only one player has ever averaged three steals per
game more than once in the NBA.**
Answer: True. Spurs guard Alvin Robertson averaged three or more
steals four times.

**535. Name the first player(s) in NBA history to average 30 points in
a game.**
A. Bob Pettit   B. George Yardley   C. Elgin Baylor   D. Jack Twyman
E. Wilt Chamberlain
Answer: D and E. It took 14 years, but the Royals forward Twyman and
Chamberlain were the first to post 30-plus points, both doing it in 1960.
Chamberlain, then playing his rookie season for the Warriors, averaged
37.6 points. Twyman scored 31.17.

536. Where was the first NBA game played?
A. Boston   B. New York   C. Toronto   D. Philadelphia
Answer: C. The first match was contested at the home of the Toronto
hockey team, Maple Leaf Gardens. A scheduled hockey game pre-
empted the NBA game, so the New York Knicks–Toronto Huskies game
got moved up to November 1, 1946. The Knicks prevailed in this pre–shot
clock era contest 68–66 before a crowd of 7,090.

**537. True or False? Wilt Chamberlain was the first player to reach
20,000 points.**
Answer: False. Bob Pettit, the St. Louis Hawks' 6'9" forward, broke the
20,000-point barrier during the 1964–65 campaign, his 11th and last
season in the NBA.

538. Name the first player to reach 10,000 points.
A. Joe Fulks   B. Max Zaslofsky   C. George Mikan   D. Ed Macauley
Answer: C. Mikan reached 10,000 points during the 1955–56 season and
finished with 10,156.

539. Name the 40-point scoring duos that tallied the most points in a playoff game.
A. Anthony Davis and Jrue Holiday
B. Sleepy Floyd and Hakeem Olajwuon
C. LeBron James and Kyrie Irving   D. Elgin Baylor and Jerry West
Answer: A. Davis scored 47 and Holiday 41 for the Pelicans in a 131–123 win against the Blazers for a four-game sweep of the Western Conference first round on April 21, 2018. Their total of 88 edged Baylor and West who scored 85.

540. True or False? Wilt Chamberlain was the first 20-20-20 player in history.
Answer: True. Chamberlain posted 25 points, 22 rebounds, and 21 assists on February 4, 1968.

541. Which New York Knick scored the first basket in NBA history?
A. Bud Palmer   B. Sonny Hertzberg   C. Ossie Schectman
D. Ralph Kaplowitz
Answer: C. It was a Friday night, November 1, 1946. Schectman, a 6-foot guard who had played for Long Island University, scored the first bucket on a layup.

542. True or False? Russell Westbrook posted the fastest triple-double ever in a game.
Answer: False. The Nuggets' 6'10" center Nikola Jokić did it in 14 minutes against the Bucks on February 15, 2018. He broke Jim Tucker's previous record of 17 minutes in 1955.

543. True or False? Nate Thurmond is the first player to have a quadruple-double in NBA history.
Answer: True. Playing in his first game with the Bulls after joining them in a September 1974 trade, the 6'11" center had 22 points, 14 rebounds, 13 assists, and 12 blocks. Thurmond had the benefit of an overtime period as the Bulls beat the Hawks 120–115.

544. Name the first Nuggets player to make the Hall of Fame.
A. David Thompson   B. Dan Issel   C. Alex English
D. Spencer Haywood
Answer: B. Issel, who scored over 27,482 points, made the Hall of Fame in 1993.

545. Name the duo who hold the record for minutes played in a playoff game.

A. Red Rocha   B. Paul Seymour   C. Bob Cousy   D. Wilt Chamberlain

Answer: A and B. Appropriately nicknamed "The Thin Man" at 6'9",
185 pounds, Rocha, who played center for the Nationals, played 67 of
a possible 68 minutes in a four-overtime loss to the Celtics in Game
2 of the 1953 Eastern Division semifinals. Seymour, a guard, matched
his teammate and the two combined for 37 points and 19 rebounds.
It wasn't enough to offset Bob Cousy's 50 points (a record 30 on free
throws) as the Celts won 111–105 to sweep the two-game series.

FINAL ACT

546. Which player won an NBA championship in his last game?
A. Shaquille O'Neal   B. Tim Duncan   C. David Robinson
D. Tim Hardaway
Answer: C. Robinson posted 13 points and 17 rebounds and walked off
with a second title in his last game as the Spurs topped the Nets in
Game 6 of the 2003 Finals on June 15, 2003.

547. Which future Hall of Famer scored 20 in his last game?
A. Shaquille O'Neal   B. Patrick Ewing   C. Gary Payton
D. Dirk Nowitzki
Answer: D. The 7-foot German center posted 20 points and 10 rebounds,
a loss against the Spurs on April 10, 2019.

548. Who scored 60 points in their final NBA game?
A. Wilt Chamberlain   B. Kobe Bryant   C. Dominique Wilkins
D. George Gervin
Answer: B. He took 50 shots to do it, but on April 13, 2016, he dropped
60 in a comeback victory against the Jazz. Addressing the crowd after
the game he said, "Mamba Out."

**549. What Hall of Famer scored just six points in his last game but led
his team to a Finals victory?**
A. Willis Reed   B. John Havlicek   C. Karl Malone   D. Bill Russell
Answer: D. He also snatched 21 rebounds on May 5, 1969, his last game
as a player and a coach, which the Celtics won 108–106 over the Lakers
for his record 11th title.

550. This guard, a former champion, dropped 25 points, 11 rebounds, and 10 assists in his last game.
A. Jason Kidd   B. Isiah Thomas   C. Dwyane Wade   D. Magic Johnson
Answer: C. It came in a losing cause against the Brooklyn Nets on April 10, 2019, but it was a triple-double to close out the season.

551. What forward scored 27 in his last game, including four 3-pointers, in 2005?
A. Reggie Miller   B. Larry Bird   C. Paul Pierce   D. Kevin Garnett
Answer: A. Miller did it in Game 6 of the second round of playoffs against the Pistons in 2005. He hit 11 of 16 field goals but it wasn't enough to stop the Pistons.

552. What center tallied 23 points and 21 rebounds in his last game?
A. Nate Thurmond   B. Kareem Abdul-Jabbar   C. Dave Cowens
D. Wilt Chamberlain
Answer: D. He also played 48 minutes, bowing out with great pride in a Game 5 loss in the 1973 Finals, as the Knicks topped the Lakers for the second time in four years.

553. Who ended their career with 15 points, four rebounds, and four assists in 2003?
A. John Stockton   B. Charles Barkley   C. Michael Jordan
D. Allen Iverson
Answer: C. In a loss to the 76ers on April 16, 2003, Jordan played 28 minutes and left the court for the final time.

554. Did any of the following players fail to score a point in their last game?
A. Patrick Ewing   B. Gary Payton   C. Shaquille O'Neal   D. Walt Frazier
Answer: B and C. Playing for the Heat, Payton played 18 minutes of a playoff game against the Bulls and didn't score. The Bulls swept that series in 2007. O'Neal played just three minutes without scoring in a playoff loss for the Celtics against the Heat on May 9, 2011.

FINALS

555. When did the Minneapolis Lakers win their last title?
A. 1952   B. 1953   C. 1954   D. 1955
Answer: C. The Lakers' dynasty rolled to a stop in 1954, as they captured their fifth title in six years. It took seven games to beat Syracuse. They won the final game at the Minneapolis Auditorium as "The Kangaroo Kid," small forward Jim Pollard, led all scorers with 21 points in the 87–80 victory. Center George Mikan had the highest series average with 18.

556. Who led all scorers in Game 6 of the 1958 Finals?
A. Bill Russell   B. Tommy Heinsohn   C. Bob Pettit   D. Bob Cousy
Answer: C. Pettit netted 50 in the elimination game as they beat the Celtics to win their first and only title. The Boston starting five accounted for 90 points, with Bill Sharman (26) and Tommy Heinsohn (23) leading the way. Sharman's layup closed the gap to one point, but the Hawks dribbled out the clock to win 110–109.

557. When was the first time the Celtics beat the Los Angeles Lakers in the Finals?
A. 1962   B. 1965   C. 1966   D. 1968
Answer: A. The Lakers led three games to two but lost Game 6 in Los Angeles and Game 7 in Boston. The Celtics had beaten the Minneapolis Lakers four games straight in 1959.

558. What player had 42 points, 15 rebounds, and seven assists in the last game of an NBA Finals?

A. Walt Frazier   B. Bob Pettit   C. Bill Russell   D. Magic Johnson
E. Larry Bird

Answer: D. With Kareem Abdul-Jabbar suffering a high ankle sprain in Game 5 of the 1980 Finals, Johnson jumped center against the Sixers. The rookie logged one of the most impressive performances ever in a clinching game and was awarded MVP of the series. The Lakers won 123–107, their first of five titles in the 1980s.

559. Name the MVP of the 1981 Finals.

A. Larry Bird   B. Moses Malone   C. Cedric Maxwell   D. Robert Reid

Answer: C. Houston had tied the Celtics at two games apiece, but the Celtics staged a 109–80 blowout in Game 5 as Maxwell scored 28 and hit the boards for 15 rebounds. They won by 11 in Game 6. Maxwell shot 57 percent for the series and averaged 17.7 points and 9.5 rebounds.

560. Name the player who won the Finals MVP in 1982.

A. Andrew Toney   B. Magic Johnson   C. Kareem Abdul-Jabbar
D. Julius Erving

Answer: B. For the second time in three years, the Lakers eliminated the Sixers in six. Johnson also grabbed MVP hardware for the second time, averaging 16 points, 10.8 rebounds, and eight assists. He also drained 53 percent of his shots.

561. Who led the 1974 Finals in scoring in a losing effort?

A. Dave Cowens   B. Jo Jo White   C. Kareem Abdul Jabbar
D. Bob Dandridge

Answer: C. Abdul-Jabbar averaged 32 points and 12 rebounds, but the Celtics won in seven games.

562. True or False? The Heat have had two different Finals MVPs.

Answer: True. Dwyane Wade won the Finals MVP in 2006. The Mavericks led 2–0 in the series, but Wade led the Heat to a 4–2 victory as he averaged 34.7 points and 7.8 rebounds. LeBron James won consecutive Finals MVPs in 2012 and 2013.

563. Name the last year that a team won the Finals after losing to the same team the year before.
A. 2014   B. 2015   C. 2016   D. 2017
Answer: D. The Warriors lost to the Cavaliers in six games in 2016 and then beat them in five in 2017.

564. Name the scoring and rebounding leader of the 1983 Finals.
A. Julius Erving   B. Kareem Abdul-Jabbar   C. Moses Malone
D. Jamaal Wilkes
Answer: C. The Sixers avenged their loss to the Lakers of the previous season, sweeping their left-coast rivals in four games. Having Moses in the pivot made the difference. Malone posted 25.8 points and 18 rebounds per contest. Malone was awarded the Finals MVP and Julius Erving finally got his title, after coming up short from 1977 through 1982.

565. Who competed in the 1960 NBA Finals?
A. Celtics-Lakers   B. Celtics-Hawks   C. 76ers-Hawks   D. 76ers-Lakers
Answer: B. The Celtics prevailed in seven games. They won the final contest in Boston by a convincing 122–103 tally. No Finals MVP was awarded in 1960 but Bill Russell, who scored 22 points and grabbed 35 rebounds in Game 7, would have been a likely candidate, as the Celtics topped the Hawks for the second time in four years. Russell averaged 16.7 points and 24.9 rebounds over the series.

566. Match the players with their statistics in clinching games of the Finals.
1. Bob Pettit   2. Walt Frazier   3. Magic Johnson   4. Bill Russell
A. 36 points, 19 assists, 7 rebounds   B. 30 points, 40 rebounds
C. 50 points, 19 rebounds   D. 42 points, 15 rebounds, 7 assists
Answer: 1-C, 1958; 2-A, 1970; 3-D, 1980; 4-B, 1962.

567. Name the last center to twice win a Finals MVP.
A. David Robinson   B. Shaquille O'Neal   C. Kareem Abdul-Jabbar
D. Hakeem Olajuwon
Answer: B. O'Neal won the Finals MVP three consecutive years: 2000–2002.

568. True or False? In their four-game sweep of the Lakers in 1983, the 76ers won each game by four points or more.

Answer: True. They won Game 3 by 15 points but won by 10 or less in the other three.

569. True or False? The 76ers were the only team to sweep a Finals series in the 1980s.

Answer: False. Aside from the 76ers' sweep of the Lakers in 1983, the Pistons swept the Lakers in 1989.

570. True or False? Julius Erving is the only ABA player to win two playoff MVPs.

Answer: True. Erving won his two in leading the New York Nets to ABA championships in 1974 and 1976. In 1974 he averaged 27.9 points and 9.6 rebounds in the playoffs. In 1976 he got better, posting 34.7 points and 12.6 rebounds.

571. Who hit two free throws and stole the ball to give Syracuse its first title?

A. George King   B. Paul Seymour   C. Dolph Schayes   D. Red Kerr

Answer: A. With 12 seconds remaining in Game 7 against the Pistons, the Nationals guard hit a free throw for a 92–91 lead and then stole the ball to secure the Nats' only title. They trailed three games to two but won the last two games at home, at the Onondaga Memorial Coliseum.

572. True or False? The Dallas Mavericks have won two championships.

Answer: False. The Mavericks won one title, which was in 2011 when they beat the Heat in six games.

573. Besides the Lakers, name the other team to win more than one championship over the league's first 10 seasons.

A. Celtics   B. Nationals   C. Warriors   D. Royals   E. Bullets

Answer: C. Behind league-leading (and playoff-leading) scorer Joe Fulks, the Warriors copped the BAA title in 1947, beating the Chicago Stags in five games. In 1956, the circuit's 10th season, the Warriors were at it again, dusting the Pistons in the Finals by the same 4–1 tally.

574. Name the leading scorer and rebounder in the 1964 Finals.
A. John Havlicek   B. Nate Thurmond   C. Wilt Chamberlain
D. Bill Russell
Answer: C. Wilt's 30 points and 27 rebounds in the last game weren't enough to keep his San Francisco Warriors from losing in five games. For the series he averaged 29.2 points and 27.6 rebounds. Even the 13 rebounds contributed by power forward and center Nate Thurmond couldn't stave off the Celtics, who won their sixth consecutive title.

575. Who hit the last second shot to give the Lakers a Game 1 victory in the 1950 Finals?
A. Jim Pollard   B. George Mikan   C. Vern Mikkelsen   D. Bob Harrison
Answer: D. The 6'1" guard hit a 30-footer to give Minneapolis a 68–66 Game 1 road victory over Syracuse.

576. True or False? Walt Frazier was the leading scorer in the 1970 Finals.
Answer: False. Lakers guard Jerry West averaged 31.3 over seven games in a losing cause against the Knicks.

577. True or False? The Suns have won more Finals than they have lost.
Answer: False. The Suns have played in three NBA Finals in 1976, 1993, and 2021. They lost all three in six games.

578. True or False? Only four teams made it to two or more Finals in the 1980s.
Answer: False. Five did. The Sixers (three), Rockets (two), Pistons (two), Celtics (five), and Lakers (eight) all made it to two or more.

579. Name the team that competed in its second NBA Finals in 1986.
A. Sixers   B. Rockets   C. Bucks   D. Pistons
Answer: B. The Rockets' season ended on the parquet floor in Boston, where the Celtics prevailed in six games.

580. How many Finals sweeps have there been since 1993?
A. One   B. Two   C. Four   D. Five
Answer: C. 1995, Rockets swept the Magic; 2002, Lakers swept the Nets; 2007, Spurs swept the Cavaliers; 2018, Warriors swept the Cavaliers.

581. Name the leading scorer in the 1968 Finals.
A. John Havlicek   B. Jerry West   C. Bailey Howell   D. Elgin Baylor
Answer: B. West averaged 31.3 points and 5.7 assists for the Finals. But the Celtics, who watched their streak of eight consecutive titles end at the hands of the 76ers in 1967, wanted their title back. They led 70–50 at halftime in Game 6 and coasted to a 124–109 victory for the title. Havlicek averaged 27 points for the series and logged 40 points, 10 rebounds, and seven assists in the decisive game.

582. Rank the following teams by most championships.
A. Bulls   B. Warriors   C. Lakers   D. Celtics
Answer: 1-C and D, 17 championships. 3-B, seven; 4-A, six.

583. Name the leading scorer in the 1972 Finals.
A. Gail Goodrich   B. Jerry West   C. Walt Frazier
Answer: A. Goodrich averaged 25.6 points, as the Lakers thumped the Knicks in five games. The Lakers' starting five averaged 96 points for the series. The Knicks won the first game in Los Angeles 114–92 but were then drubbed four straight.

584. How did Patrick Ewing fare against Hakeem Olajuwon in the 1994 Finals?
Answer: Not well. In a battle of Hall of Fame centers, Olajuwon averaged 26.9 points, 9.1 rebounds, and 3.6 assists on 50 percent shooting. Ewing averaged 18.9 points, 12.4 rebounds, and 1.7 assists on 36 percent shooting. He did have 4.3 blocks per game to Olajuwon's 3.9. The Rockets overcame a 3-2 deficit to win in seven.

585. What two future Hall of Famers played for the Bullets in the 1975 Finals?
A. Phil Chenier   B. Wes Unseld   C. Elvin Hayes   D. Jamaal Wilkes
Answer: B and C. The frontline stalwarts of the Bullets weren't enough to stave off a Finals sweep. Rick Barry led the Warriors with 29 points per game. The Warriors average margin of victory was just four points. Game 1 was typical of the Bullets' frustrations. They jumped out to a 16-point lead at home, only to be throttled 61–41 in the second half. The Warriors won two of the remaining three by a single point.

586. Which Bullets averaged 20 points in the 1978 Finals?
A. Elvin Hayes   B. Wes Unseld   C. Bob Dandridge
D. Kevin Grevey   E. None
Answer: E. Hayes and Dandridge each averaged 19. Dandridge had been a major contributor to the 1971 Bucks that won the NBA title. Now the 6'6" small forward was completing the Bullets' frontline muscle. The SuperSonics led three games to two, thanks to their balanced attack of Dennis Johnson, Gus Williams, and Fred Brown. The Bullets beat the Sonics by 35 points in Game 6 and a bench boost from Charles Johnson and Mitch Kupchak helped them to a 105–99 victory in Game 7.

587. True or False? The leading scorer of the 2014 Finals was also the MVP.
Answer: False. The Spurs shot an amazing 53 percent as a team. MVP Kawhi Leonard shot 61 percent and was second in scoring (17.8) to Tony Parker (18).

588. Name the Hall of Fame center who dominated the 1951 Finals.
A. George Mikan   B. Connie Simmons   C. Arnie Risen
D. Dolph Schayes
Answer: C. It was an all–New York final and surely the strangest in the first decade of the NBA. Taking advantage of their home court advantage, the Rochester Royals raced to a 3-0 lead. But the Knicks won the next three. With the deciding game at the Edgerton Park Sports Arena in Rochester, the Royals prevailed 79–75 as the 6'9" Risen posted 24 points and 13 rebounds. He averaged 21.7 points and 14.3 rebounds for the series.

589. True or False? The Trail Blazers have won the same number of Finals that they lost.
Answer: False. They won one and lost two. In 1977 they topped the 76ers in six. In 1990 they faced the defending champion Pistons, who beat them in five games. In 1992 they faced another defending champion, the Bulls, who topped them in six games.

590. Which of the following Warriors was neither suspended nor fouled out of a game in the 2015 or 2016 Finals?

A. Draymond Green   B. Stephen Curry   C. Klay Thompson
D. Harrison Barnes

Answer: D. Harrison Barnes, who played in every game of both Finals, and averaged 8.8 points per game in 2015 and 9.3 in 2016.

591. True or False? Hakeem Olajuwon was the leading scorer in the 1986 Finals.

Answer: False. Kevin McHale averaged 25.8 points to Olajuwon's 24.7 in the Celtics' six-game victory.

592. What team beat the defending champion Warriors in the 1948 Finals?

A. Celtics   B. Bullets   C. Pistons   D. Lakers

Answer: B. The Bullets overcame 23.5 points per game from Warriors power forward and future Hall of Famer Jumpin' Joe Fulks. The Baltimore Bullets got key contributions from Connie Simmons, Paul Hoffman, Kleggie Hermsen, and Buddy Jeannette to dethrone the champs in six games.

593. Who did the Celtics beat for their eighth straight title in 1966?

A. Hawks   B. Lakers   C. Warriors   D. Pistons

Answer: B. The Celtics jumped out to a three games to one lead, but the Lakers clawed back to tie the series. In Game 7, at the Boston Garden, the Lakers made a furious fourth-quarter push, scoring 33 to the Celtics' 19. But they fell two points short, losing 95–93. Jerry West scored 36, but Bill Russell tallied 25 points and 32 rebounds.

594. Who holds the record for the highest points per game in a Finals series?

Answer: Michael Jordan averaged 41 in the 1993 Finals, just ahead of Rick Barry's 40.8 in 1976.

595. Who holds the record for most rebounds per game in the Finals?

Answer: Bill Russell averaged 29.5 rebounds in the 1959 Finals.

596. Who holds the record for career assists in NBA Finals?

Answer: Magic Johnson averaged 11.7 assists over his career in the Finals.

Michael Jordan

597. Name the team since 1980 that won eight of nine games in consecutive Finals.

A. 76ers   B. Bulls   C. Lakers   D. Pistons

Answer: D. The Pistons swept the Lakers in the 1989 Finals and then cooled the Blazers four games to one in the 1990 Finals.

598. Name the player who hit the shot with one second remaining to send Game 5 of the 1976 Finals into a third overtime.

A. Curtis Perry   B. Ricky Sobers   C. Gar Heard   D. Jo Jo White
E. Dave Cowens

Answer: C. John Havlicek's running one-hander with a second remaining in the second overtime gave the Celtics a one-point lead. Suns guard Paul Westphal called a timeout which his team didn't have, so a technical foul resulted, and Jo Jo White hit a free throw. The Suns had the ball at halfcourt now. Heard caught an inbound pass and hoisted a 20-footer as time ran out. The ball went in and tied the game at 112. The Celtics won in overtime 128–126 and the Celtics went on to win Game 6 for the title.

FUN

599. Name four players who would be eligible for an "All-Color" team.
Answer: Johnny Green, Fred Brown, Jo Jo White, Tarik Black.

600. Name five players eligible for an "All-Boxing" team.
Answer: George Dempsey, Walt Frazier, Justin Wright Foreman, Tyson Chandler, Kawhi Leonard.

601. Name five players eligible for an "All-City" team.
Answer: Allan Houston, Brandon Boston Jr., Trenton Hassell, Dallas Comegys, London Perrantes.

602. Name five players eligible for an "All-Fish" team.
Answer: Paris Bass, Blue Edwards, Jerry Dover, David Sole, Cat Barber.

603. Name five players eligible for an "All-Literary" team.
Answer: Mark Pope, Kaniel Dickens, Brian Shaw, Dick Fitzgerald, Kevin Joyce.

604. Name five players who would qualify for an "All–Baseball Diamond" team.
Answer: Travia Mays, Aaron Gordon, Ernie Cobb, DaJuan Wagner, Derrick Rose.

605. Name four players who would be eligible for an "All–Trees and Flowers" team.
Answer: Tree Rollins, Charles Oakley, Jalen Rose, Derrick Rose.

606. Name five players who would be eligible for an "All-College" team.

Answer: Elgin Baylor, Bill Bradley, Bradley Beal, Byron Houston, David Duke Jr.

607. Name three players who would be eligible for an "All-Foods" team.

Answer: Cornbread Maxwell, DeJuan Wheat, Tacko Fall.

608. Name five players who would be eligible for an "All-Occupations" team.

Answer: Vin Baker, Donnie Butcher, Jimmy Butler, Bob Carpenter, Karl "The Mailman" Malone.

609. Name five players who would be eligible for an "All-Music" team.

Answer: Keith Starr, Harrison Barnes, Raymond Townsend, Harold Pressley, Dylan Windler.

610. Name four players who would be eligible for an "All-Presidents" team.

Answer: Joe Kennedy, Clinton Wheeler, Norm Nixon, Magic Johnson.

611. Name three NBA players, coaches, or officials who would be eligible for an "All-Temperament" team.

Answer: Happy Hairston, David Stern, Jack Smiley.

612. Name four players who would be eligible for an "All-Birds" team.

Answer: Jay Vincent, Tarik Black, Brian Cardinal, Duck Williams.

613. Name three players who would be eligible for an "All–Body Parts" team.

Answer: Foots Walker, Luther Head, Jeff Foote.

614. Name four players who would be eligible for an "All-Kings" team.

Answer: Charles Barkley, Andy Phillip, George McGinnis, Xavier Henry.

615. Name four players who would be eligible for an "All-Jewelry" team.

Answer: Pearl Washington, Diamond Stone, Elvin Ivory, Jasper Wilson.

616. Name four players who would be eligible for an "All-Royalty" team.

Answer: Earl Monroe, Walter Dukes, Bernard King, Tayshaun Prince.

617. Name four players who would qualify for an "All-Female" team.

Answer: Jalen Rose, Kelly Tripucka, Dominique Wilkins, Pat Cummings.

GEOGRAPHY

618. Match the cities with the team names from the 1946–47 season.
1. Providence 2. St. Louis 3. Cleveland 4. Detroit
A. Falcons B. Rebels C. Bombers D. Steamrollers
Answer: 1-D; 2-C; 3-B; 4-A.

619. Match the cities with their team names from the 1948–49 season.
1. Baltimore 2. Rochester 3. Fort Wayne 4. Indianapolis
A. Pistons B. Jets C. Bullets D. Royals
Answer: 1-C; 2-D; 3-A; 4-B.

620. Match the cities with their team names between the 1950 and 1952 seasons.
1. Waterloo 2. Indianapolis 3. Denver 4. Milwaukee
A. Olympians B. Hawks C. Nuggets
Answer: 1-B; 2-A; 3-C; 4-B.

621. Match the teams with their original city.
1. Kings 2. 76ers 3. Thunder 4. Pelicans
A. New Orleans/Oklahoma City B. Seattle C. Syracuse D. Rochester
Answer: 1-D; 2-C; 3-B; 4-A.

622. In what city did Wilt Chamberlain score 100 points?
A. New York B. San Francisco C. Philadelphia D. Hershey
Answer: D. It was March 2, 1962, in a game against the Knicks, in Hershey, Pennsylvania, where the Warriors played some of their home games. He made 36 field goals and 28 free throws.

623. Which city didn't the Clippers play their home games in?
A. Sacramento   B. San Diego   C. Los Angeles   D. Buffalo
Answer: A.

624. Match the teams with their original city.
1. Nets   2. Hawks   3. Wizards   4. Pistons
A. Fort Wayne   B. Baltimore   C. Tri-Cities   D. Teaneck, New Jersey
Answer: 1-D; 2-C; 3-B; 4-A.

625. True or False? The Hawks have played in only two cities.
Answer: False. The Hawks have had franchises in four cities. They were
the Tri-Cities Blackhawks from 1949 to 1951; the Milwaukee Hawks
from 1951 to 1955; the St. Louis Hawks from 1955 through 1968; and the
Atlanta Hawks from 1968 to the present.

626. Match the teams with their original city.
1. Warriors   2. Rockets   3. Clippers   4. Grizzlies
A. Vancouver   B. San Diego   C. Philadelphia   D. Buffalo
Answer: 1-C; 2-B; 3-D; 4-A.

**627. Before they were the Sacramento Kings, what were their four
team names?**
Answer: Rochester Royals, Cincinnati Royals, Kansas City–Omaha Kings,
Kansas City Kings.

628. Match the following players with their New York places of birth.
1. Michael Jordan   2. Bob Cousy   3. Bernard King   4. Julius Erving
A. Roosevelt, New York   B. Brooklyn, New York   C. New York, New York
Answer: 1-B; 2-C; 3-B; 4-A.

HALL OF FAME

629. Which of the following Black pioneer players was the first to make the Hall of Fame?
A. Chuck Cooper   B. Nat Clifton   C. Earl Lloyd
Answer: C. Lloyd, the first to set foot on an NBA court when he played for the Washington Capitols on October 31, 1950, was elected in 2003. Cooper was the first player drafted and Clifton the first signed to an NBA contract.

630. The lone player to make the Hall of Fame from the draft class of 1975 was picked:
A. First   B. Second   C. Fourth   D. Fifth
Answer: A. David Thompson was selected first out of North Carolina State by the Atlanta Hawks, but chose to sign with the ABA's Denver Nuggets. The five-time All-Star had a nine-year professional career.

631. What Hall of Famer owns the immortal record for most points in a seven-game playoff series?
A. Elgin Baylor   B. Jerry West   C. Michael Jordan   D. Rick Barry
Answer: A. Baylor scored 284 points for the Lakers in the 1962 Finals (40.6 per game). He also averaged 17.9 rebounds, but the Celtics still prevailed in seven games.

632. Name the most recent player for the Bulls to be inducted into the Hall of Fame.
A. Dennis Rodman   B. Toni Kukoč   C. Scottie Pippen   D. Dwyane Wade
Answer: D. Wade, who played just one year with the Bulls, was inducted in 2023.

633. What Hall of Famer owns the record for most rebounds in a seven-game series?
A. Bill Russell   B. Wilt Chamberlain   C. Dennis Rodman
D. Charles Barkley
Answer: B. "The Stilt" grabbed 220 rebounds (31.4 per game) against the Celtics in a thrilling seven-game affair in the 1965 Eastern Division finals. He scored 30 points and grabbed 32 rebounds in Game 7, but the Celtics won the game 110–109.

634. The draft class of 1976 produced five Hall of Famers. Which of the following draftees did not make the Hall of Fame?
A. Adrian Dantley   B. Robert Parish   C. John Lucas   D. Alex English
E. Dennis Johnson
Answer: C. Ironically, Lucas was drafted first overall out of Maryland and played 14 NBA seasons.

635. Name the most recent Hall of Fame center to have played for the Hawks.
A. Walt Bellamy   B. Zelmo Beaty   C. Dikembe Mutombo
D. Moses Malone
Answer: C. The 7'3" shot-blocking machine, who swatted away 3,289 shots, played five of his 18 seasons with the Hawks.

636. Who was the last center to play for the Celtics to make the Hall of Fame?
Answer: Inducted into the Hall of Fame in 2016, Shaquille O'Neal played the last of his 19 years for the Celtics in 2011.

637. What Hall of Fame guard was voted to the NBA All-Defensive First Team every season from 1979 through 1983?
A. Dennis Johnson   B. Sidney Moncrief   C. Maurice Cheeks
D. Alvin Robertson
Answer: A. Johnson was a defensive stalwart who helped the Sonics to a title in 1979 and was named Finals MVP.

638. Which of the following Hall of Famers won Defensive Player of the Year in consecutive seasons?
A. Sidney Moncrief   B. Maurice Cheeks   C. Dennis Johnson
D. Joe Dumars
Answer: A. The Bucks guard won it in 1983 and 1984. "The Squid" was also on the NBA All-Defensive First Team from 1982 through 1985.

639. True or False? Jerry West was the leading scorer in the 1973 Finals.
Answer: False. Gail Goodrich averaged 21.8 points in the Lakers' five-game loss to the Knicks.

640. How many players drafted in the top 10 overall in 1962 made it to the Hall of Fame?
A. None   B. Two   C. Four   D. Six
Answer: C. Zelmo Beaty, who went on to play eight years and average 16 points and 10 rebounds, was picked third overall by the Hawks and was inducted to the Hall of Fame in 2016. Dave DeBusschere, inducted in 1983, was chosen fourth by the Pistons, posted 16 points and 11 rebounds per game, and played on the two Knicks championships in his 12-year career. The Royals chose Jerry Lucas sixth and he posted 17 points and 15.6 rebounds per game over 11 seasons and made the Hall of Fame in 1980. Drafted ninth by the Celtics, John Havlicek was the cream of the draft crop, playing 16 seasons, eight of them for NBA champions. He was the Finals MVP in 1974 and was inducted to the Hall in 1984.

641. True or False? Of the 39 NBA and ABA players who attended the University of Dayton, none made the Hall of Fame.
Answer: True.

642. Which of the following was the oldest to play in an NBA game to make the Hall of Fame?
A. Robert Parish   B. Bob Cousy   C. Kareem Abdul-Jabbar
D. Dikembe Mutombo
Answer: A. Parish played his last game on May 11, 1997, at the age of 43 years and 254 days.

643. Who was the youngest to play in an NBA game to make the Hall of Fame?

A. Tracy McGrady   B. Kobe Bryant   C. Magic Johnson   D. Karl Malone

Answer: B. Bryant was 18 years and 72 days old when he played his first game on November 3, 1996.

644. Name the first of these Lakers to be elected to the Hall of Fame.

A. Elgin Baylor   B. George Mikan   C. Jim Pollard   D. Vern Mikkelsen

Answer: B. The center who anchored their title teams was elected in 1959. He averaged 23.1 points and 13.4 rebounds.

645. Who was picked highest in the 1958 draft?

A. Wayne Embry   B. Guy Rodgers   C. Hal Greer   D. Elgin Baylor

Answer: D. Baylor was drafted first by the Minneapolis Lakers in the 1958 draft out of Seattle University. He went on to average 27.4 points and 13.5 rebounds a game in his Hall of Fame career.

646. Who were the two future Hall of Famers drafted in 1959?

A. Bob Ferry   B. Wilt Chamberlain   C. Dick Barnett   D. Bailey Howell

Answer: B and D. Chamberlain was inducted into the Hall of Fame in 1979. Howell, who was traded by the Bullets to the Celtics in 1966 for Mel Counts, helped the Celtics win titles in 1968 and 1969. He was inducted to the Hall of Fame in 1997.

647. True or False? No graduate of Temple made the Hall of Fame.

Answer: False. Point guard Guy Rodgers, who twice led the league in assists, made the Hall in 2014.

648. What two Hall of Famers coached in the 1957 All-Star Game?

A. Al Cervi   B. Red Auerbach   C. John Kundla   D. Bobby Wanzer

Answer: B and D. In the year his Celtics took their first title, Red led the East to a 109–97 win, as Bob Cousy (10 points, seven assists) took MVP honors in a controversial decision over teammate Neil Johnston (19 points, nine rebounds). Rochester coach Bobby Wanzer piloted the West.

649. What future Hall of Famer as a player and coach came off the bench in the 1971 All-Star Game to get 21 points to help the West win?
A. Lenny Wilkens   B. Chet Walker   C. Bob Love   D. Jeff Mullins
Answer: A. Playing just 20 minutes, the Sonics guard scored 21 as the West eked out a 108–107 win.

650. Who holds the record for most blocks in a game by a Hall of Famer?
A. Hakeem Olajuwon   B. Shaquille O'Neal   C. Ralph Sampson
D. Nate Thurmond
Answer: B. O'Neal's 15 blocks on November 20, 1993, are the most ever by a Hall of Fame player. Blocks have only been recorded as an official statistic since the 1973–74 season.

651. What coach who led his teams to three championships coached the 1958 All-Star Game?
A. Bobby Wanzer   B. Red Auerbach   C. Alex Hannum
D. George Senesky
Answer: C. Like Auerbach the year before, Hannum coached the All-Star Game and won his first title, leading the Hawks to a six-game victory over the Celtics. He also led the 76ers to a championship in 1967 and the Oakland Oaks of the ABA in 1969. His East troops lost 130–118, despite Bob Pettit's 28 points and 26 rebounds.

652. What two Hall of Famers were co-MVPs of the 1959 All-Star Game?
A. Cliff Hagan   B. Paul Arizin   C. Elgin Baylor   D. Bob Pettit
Answer: C and D. Baylor (24 points, 11 rebounds) and Pettit (25 points, 16 rebounds) led a 124–108 pasting of the East.

653. Which of the following teams were elected in the inaugural year of the Hall of Fame?
A. New York Renaissance   B. Buffalo Germans   C. Original Celtics
D. The First Team
Answer: C and D. Both teams were inducted in 1959. The Celtics, first formed in 1914, were composed of teenagers from Manhattan's West Side. The "First Team" were the 18 players, nine to a side, who participated in Dr. James Naismith's new invention, "basket ball," and competed in the first game in Springfield, Massachusetts, on December 21, 1891.

654. Name the Hall of Famer who scored 21 points in just 17 minutes to provide the East with a dominant victory in the 1968 All-Star Game.
A. Gus Johnson   B. Sam Jones   C. Hal Greer   D. John Havlicek
Answer: C. Playing before 18,422 fans at the new Madison Square Garden, Greer led his mates to a 144–124 win.

655. In which of these years did the number one draft pick make the Hall of Fame?
A. 1972   B. 1973   C. 1974   D. 1975
Answer: C and D. Bill Walton, the 6'11" center out of UCLA, won two titles in college and went on to win two in the pros with the Blazers and the Celtics. David Thompson, drafted by the Hawks, played most of his career with the Nuggets.

656. True or False? The most recent player who played with the Nets to make the Hall of Fame is Jason Kidd.
Answer: False. Kevin Garnett played two of his 21 seasons with the Nets in 2014 and 2015. The 15-time All-Star was inducted into the Hall of Fame in 2020.

657. Match the Hall of Famer with his nickname.
1. Kobe Bryant   2. Billy Cunningham   3. Wilt Chamberlain   4. Larry Bird
A. The Big Dipper   B. The Hick from French Lick   C. Kangaroo Kid
D. Black Mamba
Answer: 1-D; 2-C; 3-A; 4-B.

658. In which of these years did the number one draft pick make the Hall of Fame?
A. 1976   B. 1977   C. 1978   D. 1979
Answer: D. After leading Everett High in Lansing, Michigan, and leading Michigan State to an NCAA title, Magic Johnson was selected first in the 1979 draft and made his debut with the Lakers on October 12, 1979.

659. In which of these years did the number one draft pick make the Hall of Fame?
A. 1980   B. 1981   C. 1982   D. 1983
Answer: C and D. Drafted by the Lakers in 1982, James Worthy shone in a stellar 12-year career, helping the Lakers to win titles in 1985, 1987, and 1988. Drafted by the Rockets in 1983, Ralph Sampson played nine years in the NBA and was inducted into the Hall of Fame in 2012.

660. In which three of the following four years were centers drafted who made the Hall of Fame?
A. 1984   B. 1985   C. 1986   D. 1987
Answer: A, B, and D. Hakeem Olajuwon was picked first by the Rockets in 1984. The Knicks selected Patrick Ewing in 1985. The Spurs picked David Robinson first in 1987.

661. In which of these years did the number one draft pick make the Hall of Fame?
A. 1988   B. 1989   C. 1990   D. 1991
Answer: None. In the 1990 draft, Oregon State point guard and defensive maestro Gary Payton was picked second by the SuperSonics. He had a 17-year career and was inducted into the Hall of Fame in 2013.

662. True or False? No one who has ever won the annual Most Improved Player award is in the Hall of Fame.
Answer: False. Tracy McGrady, who made the Hall of Fame in 2017, won the award in 2001, when he raised his averages in assists, rebounds, and points, from 15.4 the previous year to 26.8.

663. In which of these years did the number one draft pick make the Hall of Fame?
A. 1992   B. 1993   C. 1994   D. 1995
Answer: A and B. Shaquille O'Neal was picked first in the 1992 draft. In 1993 Chris Webber was selected first.

664. In which of these years did the number one draft pick make the Hall of Fame?
A. 1996   B. 1997   C. 1998   D. 1999
Answer: A and B. The 76ers snatched Allen Iverson first in the 1996 draft. In 1997 the Spurs jumped on Wake Forest graduate Tim Duncan.

665. True or False? None of the top 20 picks in the draft of 1995 made it to the Hall of Fame.
Answer: False. In a draft that saw Maryland's Joe Smith picked first, none of the top 20 selections from college made the Hall of Fame. But Kevin Garnett, who leapt from high school to the pros, was chosen fifth by the Timberwolves, and enjoyed a 21-year NBA career. The 15-time All-Star, who was voted to the NBA's 75th Anniversary Team, was inducted in 2020.

666. True or False? The Mavericks have had just one coach who is in the Hall of Fame.

Answer: False. Their two are Don Nelson and Jason Kidd. Kidd began coaching for the Mavs in 2022. Nelson was at the helm from 1998 through 2005.

667. In which of these years did the number one draft pick make the Hall of Fame?

A. 2000   B. 2001   C. 2002   D. 2003

Answer: C. The Rockets picked Yao Ming first in the 2002 draft. It is very likely that LeBron James (drafted in 2003) will eventually be selected to the Hall of Fame.

668. In which of these years did the number one draft pick make the Hall of Fame?

A. 2004   B. 2005   C. 2006   D. 2007

Answer: None.

669. Which of the following Royals or Kings players are in the Hall of Fame?

A. Jerry Lucas   B. Bobby Wanzer   C. Oscar Robertson
D. Nate Archibald   E. Jack Twyman   F. All of them

Answer: F.

670. Name the first player to make the Hall of Fame who never played an NBA game.

A. Nikos Galis   B. Oscar Schmidt   C. Dražen Dalipagić
D. Krešimir Ćosić   E. Dino Meneghin   F. Sergei Belov

Answer: F. Known as "The Jerry West of Russia," Belov was a mainstay in the Summer Olympics from 1968 to 1980. He was inducted in 1992.

671. True or False? The first two players picked in the 1992 draft were centers.

Answer: True. Shaquille O'Neal was picked first and inducted to the Hall of Fame in 2016. Alonzo Mourning was picked second and was inducted in 2014.

672. True or False? Dirk Nowitzki is the only Dallas Mavericks player who made the Hall of Fame.

Answer: False. Nowitzki was just the latest. The six others are Adrian Dantley, Steve Nash, Dennis Rodman, Alex English, Tim Hardaway, and Jason Kidd

673. Of the 43 NBA and ABA players from the University of Nevada–Las Vegas, how many made the Hall of Fame?

A. None   B. Six   C. Seven   D. Nine

Answer: Improbably, no players from UNLV have ever made the Hall of Fame.

674. Name the Hall of Famer who was player-coach for the Pistons for three seasons in the 1960s.

A. Butch van Breda Kolff   B. Dave DeBusschere   C. Paul Seymour
D. Dick McGuire

Answer: B. DeBusschere began as a forward in 1962, playing while he was also a pitcher for the White Sox. In three seasons as the Pistons player-coach, he won 79 and lost 143. He played 12 seasons, was an All-Star eight times, and played for the championship Knicks in 1970 and 1973.

675. What player(s) drafted in the top 10 in 1955 made the Hall of Fame?

A. Ed Conlin   B. Jim Loscutoff   C. Tom Gola   D. Maurice Stokes
E. Jack Twyman

Answer: C, D, and E. C. Drafted first overall, "Mr. All-Around" was a five-time All-Star and played for the championship Warriors in 1956. He made the Hall of Fame in 1976. D. His career cut short after three seasons by post-traumatic encephalopathy, the 6'7" forward led the league in rebounds (16.3) his rookie season and was inducted to the Hall in 2004. E. A six-time All-Star, the small forward averaged 20 or more four times and made the Hall of Fame in 1983.

676. True or False? None of the top 20 picks in the 1986 draft made the Hall of Fame.

Answer: True. The 27th pick, Dennis Rodman, is a Hall of Famer.

677. Order the following players by when they made the Hall of Fame.

A. Allen Iverson   B. Ray Allen   C. Kobe Bryant   D. Steve Nash
Answer: 1-A, 2016; 2-B and D, 2018; 4-C, 2020.

678. True or False? No Fordham players have made the Hall of Fame.
Answer: True. Of the 11 NBA and ABA players who attended Fordham, none made the Hall of Fame.

679. True or False? Dave Bing was the only Hall of Famer from the 1966 draft.
Answer: False. Guard and small forward Lou Hudson, drafted fourth overall by the Hawks, averaged 20 points per game in seven of his 13 seasons and made the Hall in 2022.

680. What Hall of Famer made the most free throws in a season?
A. Tiny Archibald   B. Allen Iverson   C. Jerry West   D. Oscar Robertson
Answer: C. Jerry West made 840 of 977 free throws in 1966, both league-leading totals. West averaged 10.6 made per game out of 12.4 attempted. His averages were stellar: 31.3 points, 7.1 rebounds, and 6.1 assists per game.

681. Which Hall of Famer played for the most different teams?
A. Jason Kidd   B. Dennis Rodman   C. Shaquille O'Neal
D. LeBron James
Answer: C. O'Neal played with six teams, including the Magic, Lakers, Heat, Suns, Cavaliers, and Celtics.

682. Name the first Hall of Famer who coached either the Buffalo Braves, San Diego Clippers, or Los Angeles Clippers.
A. Dolph Schayes   B. Jack Ramsay   C. Paul Silas   D. Gene Shue
Answer: A. The center for the Syracuse Nationals coached the Braves in their inaugural 1970–71 season.

683. True or False? No Miami University (Ohio) player ever made the Hall of Fame.
Answer: False. The Oxford, Ohio, school produced one Hall of Famer. Wayne Embry, a 6'8" center and five-time All-Star known for his rebounding prowess, played eight of his 11 seasons with the Cincinnati Royals, and was inducted into the Hall of Fame in 1999.

684. True or False? No draftees from the first year of the new millennium made the Hall of Fame.
Answer: True. The 2000 draft hasn't produced a single Hall of Famer.

685. Rank the draft order of the following future Hall of Famers in the 1987 draft.

A. Scottie Pippen   B. David Robinson   C. Reggie Miller

Answer: 1-B, first pick; 2-A, fifth pick; 3-C, 11th pick.

686. What inventor of the 24-second clock made the Hall of Fame in 2000?

Answer: Danny Biasone, the owner of the Syracuse Nationals who won an NBA title in 1955, invented the clock in 1954.

687. Who was the first player from the Buffalo Braves to enter the Hall of Fame?

Answer: Bob McAdoo played for the Braves from 1973 through 1976, winning three straight scoring titles from 1974 through 1976. He was elected to the Hall of Fame in 2000.

688. What Hall of Famer delivered the most points for the West in the 1989 All-Star Game?

A. Alex English   B. Moses Malone   C. Dale Ellis   D. Clyde Drexler

Answer: B. The Mailman posted 28 points and nine rebounds to snatch MVP honors and lead the West to a 143–134 win.

689. Which players were elected to the Hall of Fame in 1982?

A. Hal Greer   B. Slater Martin   C. Frank Ramsey   D. Willis Reed
E. Thomas Barlow   F. All of the above

Answer: A, B, C, and D. A Trenton, New Jersey, native, Barlow played for the Philadelphia Sphas and Warriors in the ABA from 1926 to 1932. He was elected to the Hall of Fame in 1981.

690. Which Hall of Famer from the class of 1948 was drafted before the others?

A. Jack Coleman   B. Bobby Wanzer   C. Harry Gallatin
D. Dolph Schayes

Answer: D. The 6'8" forward and center from Syracuse was drafted fourth overall by the Knicks in the 1948 draft.

691. True or False? One player from McNeese State University made the Hall of Fame.

Answer: True. Of the six NBA and ABA players attending McNeese, Joe Dumars is the lone player inducted to the Springfield shrine. In his 18-year career he was a six-time All-Star, played on two Pistons title teams, and was the Finals MVP in 1989.

692. True or False? No players who played with the Hornets made the Hall of Fame.

Answer: False. Three players who played for the Hornets were inducted. Robert Parish played two of his 21 seasons with the Hornets and was inducted in 2003, Alonzo Mourning was inducted in 2014, and Vlade Divac made the Hall in 2019.

693. Name the Hall of Famer who played the most minutes in a seven-game series.

A. Kareem Abdul-Jabbar   B. Wilt Chamberlain   C. Jerry West
D. Stephen Curry

Answer: A. Playing for the Bucks, Jabbar played a staggering 345 minutes (49.3 minutes per game) in a seven-game Finals against the Celtics in 1974. Game 6 went to two overtimes, and Abdul-Jabbar played all 58 minutes and won the game on a 15-foot skyhook from the baseline. The Celtics won Game 7 on the road 102–87.

694. Name the first of the Knicks' starting five on their first title team to be elected to the Hall of Fame.

A. Bill Bradley   B. Walt Frazier   C. Dick Barnett
D. Dave DeBusschere   E. Willis Reed

Answer: E. "The Captain" was inducted in 1982.

695. What Hall of Famer got 20 assists in Wilt Chamberlain's 100-point game?

A. Al Attles   B. Guy Rodgers   C. Paul Arizin

Answer: B. The Hall of Fame point guard fed Wilt for the entire 48 minutes.

696. Which of the following players were picked in the top 10 of the 1963 draft and reached the Hall of Fame?

A. Nate Thurmond   B. Art Heyman   C. Rod Thorn   D. Eddie Miles

Answer: A. Drafted by the Warriors third overall, the 6'11" center averaged 15 points and 15 rebounds for his career. Oddly, Thorn was picked second, ahead of Thurmond, but played just eight seasons as a shooting and point guard, averaging 10.8 points per game and 2.6 assists. He was elected as a contributor.

697. Which of the following players drafted in 1964 made the Hall of Fame?

A. Wali Jones   B. Willis Reed   C. Jeff Mullins   D. Walt Hazzard
E. Luke Jackson

Answer: B. Selected for both the NBA's 50th and 75th Anniversary Teams, Reed's weak knees limited him to a 10-year career. But he was the Finals MVP in both of the Knicks' title seasons, 1970 and 1973. His career averages were 18.7 points and 12.9 rebounds per game.

698. Name the Hall of Fame forward who took MVP honors in the 1991 All-Star Game.

A. Bernard King   B. Dominique Wilkins   C. Charles Barkley
D. Kevin McHale

Answer: C. The "Round Mound" certainly did rebound, snatching 22 off the glass and scoring 17 points.

699. Match the Hall of Famers drafted first overall with the year of their debut.

1. David Robinson   2. Shaquille O'Neal   3. Allen Iverson   4. Tim Duncan
A. 1997   B. 1996   C. 1992   D. 1987
Answer: 1-D; 2-C; 3-B; 4-A.

700. True or False? There has been just one Hall of Famer from Wake Forest University.

Answer: True. Tim Duncan is the lone Wake Forest grad to be inducted into the Hall of Fame. He made the Hall in 2020.

701. How many Hall of Famers came from the 1961 draft?
A. None   B. One   C. Two   D. Three
Answer: B. Walt "Bells" Bellamy, who was drafted out of Indiana first overall and debuted on October 19, 1961, was inducted into the Hall of Fame in 1993.

702. Which Hall of Famer didn't play his entire career with one team?
A. Willis Reed   B. Elvin Hayes   C. Wes Unseld   D. Kobe Bryant
Answer: B. Hayes played 16 years, starting out as the league's leading scorer with the San Diego Rockets, who then moved to Houston in 1971. He played nine seasons with the Baltimore Bullets, Capital Bullets, and Washington Bullets. He finished his career with Houston and was elected to the Hall of Fame in 1990.

703. How many Hall of Famers recorded quadruple-doubles?
A. None   B. One   C. Two   D. Three
Answer: D. All three were Hall of Fame centers. The first was Nate Thurmond on October 18, 1974. Second was Hakeem Olajuwon on March 29, 1990, and the most recent was David Robinson on February 17, 1994.

704. Which of the following players won the Comeback Player of the Year Award and are also in the Hall of Fame?
A. Gus Williams   B. Paul Westphal   C. Bernard King
D. Tiny Archibald   E. Adrian Dantley
Answer: B, C, D, and E. B, Comeback Player of the Year 1983, Hall of Fame, 2019; C, CBY, 1981, HOF, 2013; D, CBY, 1980, HOF, 1991; E, CBY, 1984, HOF, 2008.

705. What Harlem Globetrotter was inducted into the Naismith Basketball Hall of Fame in 2003?
Answer: Meadowlark Lemon, the "Clown Prince of Basketball," played some 16,000 games from 1954 through 1978.

706. Rank the Hall of Fame players by points per game in a Finals.
A. Rick Barry   B. Elgin Baylor   C. Shaquille O'Neal   D. Michael Jordan
Answer: 1-D, 41 per game, six games, 1993; 2-A, 40.8, six games, 1967; 3-B, 40.6, seven games, 1962; 4-C, 38, 2000.

707. Name the most recent coach elected to the Hall of Fame who won 60 percent of his games.

A. George Karl   B. Pat Riley   C. Gregg Popovich   D. Bill Fitch

Answer: C. Elected in 2023, Popovich has won 1,366 and lost 761 and led the Spurs to five NBA titles through the 2022–23 season.

708. How many Hall of Fame players on the West team scored 20 or more points in the 1961 All-Star Game?

A. None   B. One   C. Two   D. Three

Answer: D. Bob Pettit (29), Clyde Lovellette (21), and game MVP Oscar Robertson (23) led the West to a 153–131 dusting of the East. Robertson nearly registered a triple-double with 14 assists and nine rebounds.

709. How many players drafted in the top 10 in the 1954 draft made the Hall of Fame?

A. None   B. One   C. Two   D. Three

Answer: C. Bob Pettit, drafted second overall by the St. Louis Hawks and one of the greatest power forwards of all time, was inducted in 1971. Baltimore Bullets point guard Slick Leonard was picked 10th overall. Leonard was inducted as a coach in 2014. He coached the ABA Indiana Pacers to titles in 1970, 1972, and 1973.

710. How many top 10 picks from the 1950 draft went to the Hall of Fame?

A. None   B. Three   C. Five   D. Six

Answer: B. Small forward Paul Arizin, picked third, made the Hall in 1978. Point guard Bob Cousy, selected fourth, was inducted in 1971. Small forward George Yardley, picked eighth, made the Hall in 1996.

711. How many Hall of Fame players were in the starting five for the West in the 1962 All-Star Game?

A. None   B. Two   C. Four   D. Five

Answer: D. Elgin Baylor (32 points), Oscar Robertson (26), Bob Pettit (25), Jerry West (18), and Walt Bellamy (23) combined for 124 points. For the second straight year the West topped the East by 20 with a 150–130 victory. Pettit drew MVP honors with 25 points and 27 rebounds, offsetting Wilt Chamberlain's 42 points and 24 rebounds for the East.

712. True or False? No player who attended DePaul was elected to the Hall of Fame.

Answer: False. George Mikan graduated DePaul. He played on five title teams for the Lakers and was voted to the Hall of Fame in 1959.

713. Which of the following Hall of Famers did not win Rookie of the Year?

A. Kareem Abdul-Jabbar   B. Walt Frazier   C. Earl Monroe
D. Jerry Lucas

Answer: B. Monroe won the award in Frazier's rookie season.

714. True or False? No player who attended LaSalle made it to the Hall of Fame.

Answer: False. Of the 24 pros who attended LaSalle, Tom Gola, drafted third overall by the Philadelphia Warriors in 1955, was the small forward and shooting guard who played on the championship Warriors of 1956 and later played with Wilt Chamberlain in the early 1960s.

715. True or False? Vince Carter is the only player drafted in the top 10 in 1998 in the Hall of Fame.

Answer: False. Having ended his career in 2020, Carter is not yet eligible for the Hall. Dirk Nowitzki, picked ninth overall, and Paul Pierce, picked 10th, are in the Hall of Fame.

716. Match the Hall of Famers from the 1960 draft with their colleges.

1. Oscar Robertson   2. Jerry West   3. Lenny Wilkens
4. Tom Sanders   5. Al Attles
A. West Virginia   B. New York University   C. Providence   D. North Carolina A&T   E. Cincinnati

Answer: 1-E; 2-A; 3-C; 4-B; 5-D.

717. Before Gregg Popovich, name the two NBA coaches who won championships who had been most recently elected to the Hall of Fame.

A. George Karl   B. Del Harris   C. Larry Costello   D. Rick Adelman
E. Bill Russell

Answer: C and E. Costello was the coach of the 1971 Bucks, the fastest expansion team to win an NBA title. Bill Russell, who was elected as a player in 1975, was inducted as a coach in 2021. As player-coach, "Bill the Hill" led the Celtics to championships in 1968 and 1969.

718. Among the following players, who was the most recent player inducted to the Springfield shrine?
A. Chris Bosh   B. Tim Duncan   C. Kobe Bryant   D. Kevin Garnett
Answer: A. The 6'11" center whose 13-year career included two titles with the Heat was inducted in 2021. The others were enshrined in 2020.

HISTORY

719. Which of the following players did not leap from high school to the pros?
A. Moses Malone   B. Julius Erving   C. Tracy McGrady   D. Kevin Garnett
Answer: B. Erving attended the University of Massachusetts.

720. What was the Lew Alcindor Rule?
Answer: The "Lew Alcindor Rule" banned dunking from college and high school basketball from 1967 through 1976. The ban was started to counter the dominance of Kareem Abdul-Jabbar (then known as Lew Alcindor), whose UCLA Bruins won three consecutive titles from 1967 to 1969. Abdul-Jabbar averaged 26 points, 15 rebounds, and shot an astounding .639 from the field. The Bruins won 88 and lost two in those three years.

721. True or False? More than one player has scored more than 25,000 points and 20,000 rebounds.
Answer: False. Wilt Chamberlain is the only one, having tallied 31,419 points and 23,924 rebounds in his inimitable career.

722. Rank the 1998 draftees in career NBA points.
A. Dirk Nowitzki   B. Vince Carter   C. Paul Pierce   D. Antawn Jamison
Answer: 1-A, 31,560 points; 2-C, 26,397 points; 3-B, 25,728 points; 4-D, 20,042 points.

723. Before the Nuggets took the Heat in five games in the 2023 Finals, name the last team to win a five-game Final.
A. Heat   B. Raptors   C. Cavaliers   D. Warriors
Answer: D. The Warriors topped the Cavs in five games in 2017.

724. True or False? The Lakers won a game by 63 points in 1972.
Answer: True. The Lakers beat the Warriors 162–99 on March 19, 1972. The 63-point differential was the largest margin of victory in league history at the time. The 1972 Lakers won 33 in a row and the championship that year.

725. Which two teams in the same division had .850 or better winning percentages after the first 20 games?
Answer: When the Warriors played the Suns on November 30, 2021, it was the first time in NBA history that two teams in the same division had .850 records after 20 games. The Warriors were 18-2 and the Suns 17-3. The Suns won the historic contest 104–96 to give both squads an 18-3 mark.

726. How many NBA teams have won 70 or more games in a season?
A. One   B. Two   C. Three   D. Four
Answer: B. The Bulls were 72-10 in 1996 and won the title. The Warriors were 73-9 in 2016, but lost in the Finals to the Cavaliers.

727. True or False? Wilt Chamberlain went straight from the University of Kansas to the NBA.
Answer: False. He signed to play with the Harlem Globetrotters in the summer of 1958 and his contract with them ran out in April 1959. He then joined the Warriors.

728. Name the team with the most 60-win seasons.
Answer: The Celtics have won 60 or more 13 times.

729. Match the last time the team won an NBA title with who was president then.
1. Wizards/Bullets   2. Knicks   3. 76ers   4. Hawks
A. Eisenhower   B. Reagan   C. Nixon   D. Carter
Answer: 1-D, 1978; 2-C, 1973; 3-B, 1983; 4-A, 1958.

730. Who invented the game of basketball?
A. Phog Allen   B. Red Auerbach   C. Alonzo Stagg
D. Dr. James Naismith
Answer: D. Dr. Naismith invented the game in Springfield, Massachusetts, in 1891.

731. When LeBron James became the ninth player in the 25,000 points/5,000 rebounds/5,000 assists club, what ABA player was not mentioned?

Answer: Julius Erving is omitted as a member of that club since his ABA statistics are not counted. Erving played five of his 16 years in the ABA, and he totaled 30,026 points, 10,525 rebounds, and 5,176 assists in 1,243 games played.

732. What is the record for the most overtimes ever played in an NBA game?

A. Four   B. Five   C. Six   D. Seven

Answer: C. The Indianapolis Olympians beat the Rochester Royals 75–73 in six overtimes on January 6, 1951. In the six extra periods the Olympians totaled just 10 points to the Royals' eight. The Royals' Arnie Risen led all scorers with 26 points.

733. Name the first Nuggets player to be an All-Star.

A. Spencer Haywood   B. Larry Jones   C. Wayne Hightower
D. Byron Beck

Answer: B. Selected in 1968, when the team was known as the Rockets, point guard Larry Jones was selected for the 1968 game, a season when Jones averaged 22.9 per game. He was also selected in 1969, a year he averaged 28.4 points.

734. True or False? Lakers center George Mikan was the first to reach 5,000 points.

Answer: False. While Mikan was first to cross the 10,000-point line, it was Jumpin' Joe Fulks, the Philadelphia Warriors' 6'5" power forward, who tallied 5,000 points first, reaching the mark during the 1950–51 campaign, his fifth year in the league. The two-time scoring champion was a star for the first team to win a championship, the 1947 Warriors.

735. No quintuple-double has been recorded in NBA history.

Answer: True. A quintuple-double would be achieving double digits in five categories, including points, rebounds, assists, blocks, and steals.

736. How many fewer games were required for Curry to break Ray Allen's all-time 3-point record?
A. 100 to 200   B. 200 to 300   C. 300 to 400   D. 400 to 500
E. 500 to 600
Answer: E. Curry took 511 fewer games than Allen played to break the mark. He broke Ray Allen's record of 2,973 3-pointers in 789 games. Allen played 1,300 games.

737. Name the team with the most wins all-time.
Answer: The Boston Celtics have 3,570 wins, ahead of the runner-up Lakers with 3,503.

738. Name the three players with 35,000 points.
A. Michael Jordan   B. LeBron James   C. Kareem Abdul-Jabbar
D. Kobe Bryant   E. Karl Malone
Answer: B, C, and E. James ranks first with 38,652 points. Abdul-Jabbar holds second place with 38,387 points. Malone ranks third with 36,928 points. Of course, James's total is higher because he did not play any college games and he began his NBA career at 18.

739. True or False? 73 points was the largest margin of victory in an NBA game.
Answer: True. On December 2, 2021, the Grizzlies beat the Thunder 152–79.

740. Before they were the Los Angeles Clippers in 1984, what other teams went by that name?
Answer: The franchise was in San Diego from the 1979 through 1984 seasons. Prior to those six years, they were the Buffalo Braves from 1971 through 1978.

741. Match the Hall of Fame players with the years they were born.
1. Wilt Chamberlain   2. Oscar Robertson   3. Bill Russell   4. Jerry West
A. 1938   B. 1934   C. 1935   D. 1936
Answer: 1-D; 2-A; 3-B; 4-A.

Wilt Chamberlain

742. How many times in NBA history has a team won three or more titles in a row?

A. One   B. Two   C. Three   D. Four   E. Five

Answer: E. The Minneapolis Lakers turned the trick first, winning titles from 1952 through 1954. The Celtics were next up and won eight times in a row from 1959 through 1966. The Bulls did it twice: from 1991 to 1993 and 1996 through 1998. The Lakers did it most recently, taking a trio of titles from 2000 through 2002.

743. Rank the following players in points per game in 1967.

A. Oscar Robertson   B. Jerry West   C. Wilt Chamberlain
D. Rick Barry   E. Elgin Baylor

Answer: Chamberlain had led the NBA in scoring over his first seven seasons, 1960–1966, and 1967 was the first time someone other than him did. He did average 24 points and 24 rebounds per game. 1-D, 35.6 points per game; 2-A, 30.5; 3-B, 28.7; 4-E, 26.6; 5-C, 24.

744. Of the following inactive franchises, which lasted the longest in the NBA?

A. Anderson Packers   B. Baltimore Bullets   C. Chicago Stags
D. Cleveland Rebels

Answer: B. The Bullets had the longest run by far. They played seven seasons, from 1947 to 1953, but compiled a poor won-lost mark of 158 wins and 292 losses.

745. Name the first NBA team to win five titles.

A. Warriors   B. Royals   C. Bullets   D. Lakers

Answer: D. The Minneapolis Lakers won five titles in six years from 1949 through 1954. Their best record was in 1950 when they won 51 and lost 17.

746. Which of the following players scored 25,000 points?

A. Jerry West   B. Dan Issel   C. Patrick Ewing   D. Ray Allen
E. Artis Gilmore

Answer: A and B. The Nuggets forward and center Dan Issel was well over the mark, with 27,482 points. Fellow Hall of Famer Jerry West posted 25,192 points.

747. Name the first season the Lakers beat the Celtics in the NBA Finals.

A. 1969   B. 1983   C. 1984   D. 1985

Answer: D. It was the first time in eight tries that the Lakers topped the Celtics. They won the sixth and final game at Boston Garden.

748. True or False? No team has won 90 percent of its games in the regular season.

Answer: True. The 2016 Warriors won 89 percent of their games with a record of 73-9.

749. Name the player who played with the Original Celtics in 1932 and played in two NBA games at the age of 46.

Answer: Matt Hickey. A native of Hoboken, New Jersey, born in 1902, the 5'11" guard made his debut on January 27, 1948, and played two games with the Providence Steamrollers of the Basketball Association of America (BAA) during the 1948–49 season. He missed three field goal attempts and made one free throw. Since the NBA counts the 1946–47 campaign as its first season, the Steamrollers were considered an NBA team.

750. Who was president of the United States in the first year of the NBA?

A. Harry Truman   B. Dwight Eisenhower   C. Franklin Roosevelt
D. Herbert Hoover

Answer: A. Harry Truman was president when the first NBA game was played on November 1, 1946.

751. What promotion was run the night of the first NBA game on November 1, 1946?

Answer: The Toronto Huskies' promotion, advertised with a newspaper ad, offered free admission to any fan taller than George Nostrand, the Huskies' 6'8" forward and center. Those 6'8" and under had to pay for tickets, which ranged from 75 cents to $2.50. The Knicks won 68–66 before a crowd of 7,090 fans at Maple Leaf Gardens.

752. Rank the following franchises by which has won the highest percentage of their Finals played in.

A. Spurs   B. Bulls   C. Celtics   D. Lakers   E. Warriors

Answer: 1-B, they won six of six Finals, 100 percent; 2-A, five of six, 83 percent; 3-C, 17 of 21, 81 percent; 4-E, six of 10, 60 percent; 5-D, 17 of 32, 53 percent.

IMMORTAL NUMBERS AND RECORDS

753. Who holds the record for games played in one regular season?
A. A. C. Green   B. Walt Bellamy   C. Len Wilkens   D. Wilt Chamberlain
Answer: B. Bellamy played 88 games in the 1968–69 season. The season
began when he played 35 for the Knicks. Then on December 19 he was
traded to the Pistons, who still had 55 games left on their schedule. The
record will likely remain unbroken. It was the fourth time that Bellamy
led the circuit in games played and sixth time he didn't miss a single
game in a season.

754. Who holds the record for 50-point games in a season?
A. Michael Jordan   B. Kobe Bryant   C. Wilt Chamberlain
D. Elgin Baylor
Answer: C. Incredibly, Wilt Chamberlain tallied 50 or more points 45
times during the 1961–62 season. He also scored 100 in one game that
season.

**755. Which player holds the record for most points per game by
a rookie?**
A. Bob Pettit   B. Julius Erving   C. Walt Bellamy   D. Wilt Chamberlain
Answer: D. "The Record Book" owns the record flat, averaging 37.8
points per game in his 1960 rookie campaign.

756. Who holds the record for most points in a game by a rookie?
A. Elgin Baylor   B. George Mikan   C. Wilt Chamberlain
D. Michael Jordan
Answer: C. "The Load" scored a record 58 points during his rookie campaign—and he did it twice. Chamberlain first led his Warriors to a 127–117 victory over the Pistons by logging 58 points and 42 rebounds. No misprint. The second contest was against the Knicks on February 21, 1960, when he scored 58 and grabbed 24 rebounds.

757. Which team has the record for most free throws made without a miss?
A. Heat   B. Warriors   C. Spurs   D. 76ers
Answer: A. On January 11, 2023, the Heat made all 40 of their free throws. Jimmy Butler, who made 23 of 23, made a free toss with 11 seconds left to give the Heat 40 straight and a 112–111 victory, breaking the Jazz's record of 39 straight in 1982. The Heat had trailed 111–106 with under a minute left.

758. True or False? Michael Jordan holds the Bulls' top 10 season records for points per game.
Answer: True. Excepting the two seasons he played baseball (1994–1995), Jordan owns the top 10 averages, ranging from 28.7 in 1998, to 37.1 in 1987, his personal high.

759. What player owns the mark for most rebounds in a game by a rookie?
A. Bill Russell   B. Wilt Chamberlain   C. Moses Malone
D. Nate Thurmond
Answer: B. Against the Syracuse Nationals on February 6, 1960, Chamberlain cleared the boards 45 times and scored 44 points. Five of his teammates scored in double figures, including Hall of Famers Paul Arizin and Guy Rodgers, each of whom tallied 16 in a 129–126 victory.

760. Which of the following teams won 40 home games in a season?
A. Celtics   B. Lakers   C. Spurs   D. Bulls
Answer: A and C. The 1986 Celtics did it first with a 40-1 mark at home during their championship season. Thirty years after the Celtics the 2016 Spurs were also 40-1. Despite a 67-15 mark, they lost in the Western Conference semifinals to the Thunder in six games.

761. Who was the only guard to be selected to the NBA All-Defensive First Team from 1969 through 1975?
A. Jerry West   B. Oscar Robertson   C. Jerry Sloan   D. Walt Frazier
Answer: D. Frazier was voted by head coaches to the defensive team for the first seven years the award was given.

762. Name the only forward voted to the NBA All-Defensive First Team for the first six years the award was given.
A. John Havlicek   B. Gus Johnson   C. Dave DeBusschere
Answer: C. From 1969 through 1974 the Knicks power forward was selected. The Knicks appeared in three Finals and won two in 1970 and 1973.

763. Rank the Nets' career leaders in points per game.
A. Rick Barry   B. Julius Erving   C. Kevin Durant   D. Kyrie Irving
Answer: 1-A, 30.6 points per game; 2-C, 29; 3-B, 28.2; 4-D, 27.1.

764. Name the all-time leader in offensive rebounds.
A. Robert Parish   B. Moses Malone   C. Buck Williams   D. Artis Gilmore
Answer: B. Since 1974 when the statistic was first kept, Moses Malone collected 7,382 offensive rebounds, leading the second-place finisher Gilmore by more than 2,000.

765. True or False? Only one player has accumulated 1,100 or more assists in a season.
Answer: False. John Stockton did it five times, including a record 1,164 assists in 1991. Isiah Thomas had 1,123 assists in 1985.

766. True or False? Only one player in NBA history has gathered 2,000 rebounds in a season.
Answer: True. In his second and third seasons, Wilt Chamberlain pulled down 2,149 and then 2,052 rebounds. He has the seven highest rebounding totals ever, established in a nine-year period from 1960 through 1968.

767. Who had the most steals in a single NBA playoff series?
A. Isiah Thomas   B. Alvin Robertson   C. Michael Jordan
D. Sidney Moncrief
Answer: A. Thomas had 20 steals in a series three different times: in a five-game series against the Bullets in 1988, in a seven-game finals against the Lakers in 1988, and in a seven-game series against the Bulls in 1990.

768. On January 2, 2023, Donovan Mitchell scored 71 points. It was the most points by any player in how many years?
A. 8   B. 16   C. 20
Answer: B. It was the most since Kobe Bryant scored 81 on January 22, 2006, against the Raptors. Mitchell had scored 58 in regulation leading the Cavs into an overtime after they were down 23 to the Bulls. He then scored 13 in overtime for a 145–134 win.

769. Name the most recent player with 30 rebounds in a game.
A. Dwight Howard   B. Enes Freedom   C. Andre Drummond
Answer: B. The Blazers' Enes Freedom snatched 30 boards in 37 minutes in a 118–103 win over Detroit on April 10, 2021. Of his 30 rebounds, 12 were on the offensive end and he scored 24 points.

770. Among players who competed in 10 or more Finals games, who had the highest points per game?
A. Michael Jordan   B. Karl Malone   C. Rick Barry   D. Kevin Durant
Answer: C. In 10 playoff games played against the 76ers in 1967 and the Bullets in 1975, the 6'7" forward from Elizabeth, New Jersey, scored 363 points for a finals average of 36.3.

771. True or False? Wilt Chamberlain has more 50-point games than the next four players combined.
Answer: True. Chamberlain had 118 50-point games. Michael Jordan had 31, Kobe Bryant 25, James Harden 23, and Elgin Baylor 27, for a total of 106.

772. True or False? Michael Jordan holds the record for most 40-point games in a season.
Answer: False. Wilt Chamberlain logged 63 games of 40 or more points during the 1961–62 season, when he averaged 50.4 points per game.

773. How many points did Wilt Chamberlain score in the second half of his 100-point game?
A. 43   B. 48   C. 51   D. 59
Answer: D. Chamberlain logged 41 points in the first half and 59 in the second half.

774. Which of the following players owns two of the top five single-season playoff scoring averages of all time?
A. Michael Jordan   B. Jerry West   C. Rick Barry   D. Elgin Baylor
Answer: D. Baylor scored 40.14 points per game in the 1962 playoffs and 38.62 in 1961. Those are the fourth and fifth highest season scoring averages in 76 seasons of NBA playoffs.

775. How many points did the Lakers' starting five average for the 1971–72 season?
Answer: 98.4 points per game. The Lakers won 69 games and topped their opponents by an average of 12.4 points per game.

776. Rank the following players in career playoff points per game.
A. Luka Dončić   B. Michael Jordan   C. Kevin Durant   D. Allen Iverson
Answer: 1-B, 33.45 points per game; 2-A, 32.54; 3-D, 29.73; 4-C, 29.39.

777. What player has the most rebounds in a game in the last 50 years?
A. Moses Malone   B. Kareem Abdul-Jabbar   C. Charles Oakley
D. Dennis Rodman
Answer: A. Since 1973 the highest total belongs to Moses Malone, who snagged 37 rebounds on February 9, 1979, against the Jazz. The Rockets won 106–99, as Malone added 33 points.

778. Who holds the mark for rebounds per game in a season?
A. Bill Russell   B. Wilt Chamberlain   C. Dennis Rodman   D. Bob Pettit
Answer: B. Chamberlain grabbed 27.2 rebounds per game over the 1960–61 season, his second year in the league.

779. True or False? Chamberlain had more 40-point games than the next two players combined.
Answer: False. But he's close. Chamberlain had 271 games with 40 or more points. Michael Jordan had 173 and Kobe Bryant had 122 for a total of 295.

780. True or False? Andre Drummond is the active player with the most 20-rebound games.

Answer: True. Drummond is first among active players with 88.

781. True or False? Wilt Chamberlain has more 60-point games than the next five players combined.

Answer: True. Chamberlain scored 60 or more 32 times, which is actually more than the next 14 players combined. Kobe Bryant (six), Damian Lillard (five), James Harden (four), Michael Jordan (four), and Elgin Baylor (three) have combined for 20 60-point games.

782. Rank the following players by how many times they led the league in rebounds.

A. Dennis Rodman   B. Bill Russell   C. Wilt Chamberlain
D. Moses Malone   E. Dwight Howard

Answer: 1-C, 11 times; 2-A, seven; 3-D, six; 4-B and E, five.

783. Who was the most recent player to record a quadruple-double in the NBA?

A. Nate Thurmond   B. Alvin Robertson   C. Hakeem Olajuwon
D. David Robinson

Answer: D. Robinson. In a 115–96 win over the Pistons on February 17, 1994, the Spurs center logged 43 points, 10 rebounds, 10 assists, and 10 blocks.

784. Who holds the record for most consecutive field goals made?

A. Wilt Chamberlain   B. Artis Gilmore   C. Jamal Crawford
D. Shaquille O'Neal

Answer: A. Unbelievably, Chamberlain hit 35 shots in a row over four games in 1967. On February 17 he began the streak hitting five of six attempts. On February 19 he hit 11 of 11 and on the 24th he hit 18 of 18. The streak ended on the 28th when he hit 11 of 14. He made 45 of 49 shots, and averaged 27 points, 10 assists, and 31 rebounds over the four games.

785. True or False? Michael Jordan had the most seasons with 2,000 or more points.

Answer: False. Karl Malone had 12 such seasons. Jordan is second with 11.

786. True or False? Wilt Chamberlain had the most seasons with 2,500 or more points.

Answer: True. Chamberlain did it seven times. Michael Jordan is second with six. No one else even has three.

787. True or False? No one ever grabbed 2,000 rebounds in a season.

Answer: False. Chamberlain did it twice. He peaked with 2,149 boards in 1961.

788. True or False? Only Wilt Chamberlain and Bill Russell have averaged 20 rebounds per game for a season in the NBA.

Answer: False. They are tied for first with 10 seasons each. Nate Thurmond and Jerry Lucas each did it twice and Bob Pettit did it once.

789. Who led the league in free throw percentage the most times?

A. Stephen Curry   B. Mark Price   C. Rick Barry   D. Bill Sharman

Answer: D. Sharman, the Hall of Fame Celtics guard and coach of the 1972 Lakers team that won a record 33 straight, led the league in free throw percentage a record seven times in nine seasons between 1953 and 1961. His best was 1959, when he shot .932 from the charity stripe.

790. What Eastern Conference player set the record for points in a Game 7?

A. Larry Bird   B. Jayson Tatum   C. Wilt Chamberlain   D. Rick Barry

Answer: B. Tatum tallied 51 on May 14, 2023, against the 76ers in a 112–88 blowout victory in Boston.

791. Which of the following players has the highest scoring average in a playoff series?

A. Wilt Chamberlain   B. Jerry West   C. Michael Jordan   D. Rick Barry

Answer: B. "Mr. Clutch" poured in 46.3 points per game in the Western Division finals against the Bullets in 1965. The Lakers star also averaged 5.8 rebounds and 6.8 assists to help defeat the Bullets in six games.

792. True or False? Magic Johnson holds the record for most assists in a Finals game.

Answer: True. He recorded 21 assists on June 3, 1984, against the Celtics.

793. Who played the most minutes in a game?
A. Dale Ellis   B. Kevin Johnson   C. Wilt Chamberlain   D. Paul Westphal
Answer: A. Playing for the Sonics, Ellis suited up for 69 minutes in a five-overtime contest against the Bucks on November 9, 1989.

794. Who holds the record for most field goals in a playoff game without a miss?
A. John Havlicek   B. Wilt Chamberlain   C. Michael Jordan
D. Chris Paul
Answer: D. The Suns guard connected on 14 without a miss against the Pelicans on April 28, 2022. His sharpshooting closed out the Pelicans in six, as he posted 31 points and eight assists in the 115–109 triumph.

795. Who holds the record for most points in a quarter?
A. Wilt Chamberlain   B. Stephen Curry   C. Bob Pettit
D. Klay Thompson
Answer: D. Thompson netted 37 points against the Kings on January 23, 2015.

796. Who posted the most field goals in a game without a miss?
A. Michael Jordan   B. Stephen Curry   C. Wilt Chamberlain
D. Oscar Robertson
Answer: C. "The Big Dipper" hit all 18 of his field goal attempts against the Bullets on February 24, 1967.

797. Name the player who averaged 20 or more points for the most seasons.
A. Kareem Abdul-Jabbar   B. Michael Jordan C. Dirk Nowitzki
D. LeBron James
Answer: D. James has averaged between 20.9 and 31.4 points in each of his 20 seasons.

798. True or False? More than one player has scored more than 20,000 points and 20,000 rebounds.
Answer: False. Only Chamberlain has accomplished the feat with 31,419 points and 23,924 rebounds.

799. Of the teams with the top 10 regular-season records, how many won championships that year?

A. Five   B. Six   C. Seven   D. Eight

Answer: C. The Warriors (73-9, 2016, lost in the Finals), Celtics (68-14, 1973, lost in the Eastern Conference finals), and the Mavericks (67-15, 2007, lost in the Western Conference first round) came up short despite achieving franchise regular-season records in those years.

800. What two teams tied for the third best regular-season record in NBA history?

A. Warriors   B. Lakers   C. 76ers   D. Bulls

Answer: B and D. The 1972 Lakers, who set the record with 33 straight wins, won 69 and lost 13 and beat the Knicks in five games in the Finals. The Bulls, following their 72-10 mark in 1996, finished 69-13 in 1997 and beat the Jazz in six in the Finals.

801. Name the two Lakers who averaged 38 points or more in one season in the playoffs.

A. Wilt Chamberlain   B. Jerry West   C. Elgin Baylor
D. Kareem Abdul-Jabbar

Answer: B and C. West averaged 40.64 over 11 games in the 1965 playoffs, second only to Jordan's 1986 season, when he averaged 43.67 (but in only three games). Baylor owns the fourth and fifth best scoring averages in the playoffs. He averaged 38.62 in 1962 and 38.08 in 1961.

802. Which squad turned the ball over the fewest times in a game?

A. Nuggets   B. Heat   C. Pacers   D. Spurs

Answer: A. The Nuggets committed just one turnover on February 23, 2021, against the Blazers. They won 111–106, led by Nikola Jokić, with 41 points and five assists.

803. True or False? Wilt Chamberlain owns the record for rebounds per game in the playoffs for a single season.

Answer: True. In 1966 Chamberlain averaged 30.2 rebounds per game in a four games to one loss to the Celtics. He also averaged 28 points per game in that series. Chamberlain and the Celtics' Bill Russell own 23 of the top 25 rebounding averages for the playoffs in a season. The other two marks belong to Wes Unseld and Nate Thurmond.

804. Who holds the mark for steals in a season?
A. John Stockton   B. Michael Ray Richardson   C. Don Buse
D. Alvin Robertson
Answer: C. Playing point guard for the Indiana Pacers in the ABA, Buse had 346 swipes during the 1976 season, an average of 4.1 per game. The two-time All-Star also led the league in assists that year. Steals records were kept in the ABA starting in 1973 and in the NBA since 1974.

805. Who holds the NBA mark for steals in a season?
A. Alvin Robertson   B. Don Buse   C. John Stockton
D. Michael Ray Richardson
Answer: A. Robertson, the Spurs' four-time All-Star guard, amassed 301 steals in 1986.

806. Rank the following players in career blocks per game in the playoffs.
A. Hakeem Olajuwon   B. Manute Bol   C. Mark Eaton   D. Elvin Hayes
Answer: Blocks have only been officially recorded since the 1973–74 season and thus stalwart defenders such as Wilt Chamberlain, Bill Russell, and Nate Thurmond are thereby excluded. 1-A, 3.26 blocks per game; 2-C, 2.84; 3-B, 2.66; 4-D, 2.61.

807. How many players scored 30,000 points and grabbed 20,000 rebounds?
A. None   B. One   C. Two   D. Three
Answer: B. Chamberlain scored 31,419 points and 23,924 rebounds in his career.

808. Rank the following players by career 3-point field goals.
A. Kyle Korver   B. Reggie Miller   C. Ray Allen   D. Stephen Curry
E. James Harden
Answer: 1-D, 3,390 3-pointers made; 2-C, 2,973; 3-E, 2,574; 4-B, 2,560; 5-A, 2,450.

809. Who holds the record for rebounds in an NBA game?
A. Bill Russell   B. Bob Pettit   C. Dennis Rodman   D. Wilt Chamberlain
Answer: D. Chamberlain grabbed 55 rebounds and scored 34 points in a losing effort to the Boston Celtics on November 24, 1960.

810. Who holds the record for points in a playoff game without overtime periods?
A. Elgin Baylor   B. Michael Jordan   C. Wilt Chamberlain   D. Rick Barry
Answer: A. Elgin Baylor scored 61 points and grabbed 22 rebounds on April 14, 1962. Jordan scored 63 on April 20, 1986, in a double-overtime loss to the Celtics, with 54 of those points scored during regulation time.

811. Who holds the record for most rebounds in an NBA playoff game?
A. Dennis Rodman   B. Bill Russell   C. Wilt Chamberlain
D. Nate Thurmond
Answer: C. Playing for the 76ers, Chamberlain swept the boards for 41 rebounds in Game 3 of the 1967 division finals against the Celtics on April 5, 1967. He also recorded 20 points and nine assists in the 76ers' 115–104 victory.

812. What player had the highest scoring average in a four-game playoff series?
A. Hakeem Olajuwon   B. Michael Jordan   C. Bob Pettit   D. Elgin Baylor
Answer: A. In the first round of the Western Conference playoffs against the Mavericks in 1988, Olajuwon averaged 37.5 points and 16.8 rebounds. He also blocked 2.8 shots per game. The Mavericks won three games to one.

813. Who holds the record for most assists in an NBA playoff game?
A. Scott Skiles   B. John Stockton   C. Bob Cousy   D. Magic Johnson
Answer: B and D. The Hall of Famers share the record with 24 assists. Stockton also scored 23 points in a 111–109 loss against the Lakers in the Western Conference semifinals on May 17, 1988. Johnson tallied his assists in a vital 118–102 victory against the Suns in the Western Conference finals on May 15, 1984.

814. What player had the most rebounds in a Game 7 of the Finals?
A. Nate Thurmond   B. Jerry Lucas   C. Wilt Chamberlain   D. Bill Russell
Answer: D. Russell snatched 40 rebounds in Game 7 of the Finals against the Lakers on April 18, 1962. The Celtics prevailed 110–107 in overtime. Russell also scored 30 points.

815. True or False? LeBron James holds the record for most career playoff points scored.
Answer: True. James has scored 8,023 in 282 playoff games.

816. What player scored the most points in the clinching game of a Finals series?
A. Jerry West   B. Rick Barry   C. Elgin Baylor
D. Giannis Antetokounmpo   E. Bob Pettit   F. Stephen Curry
Answer: D and E. Antetokounmpo scored 50 in Game 6 to eliminate the Suns in six games on July 20, 2021. He connected on 16 of 25 field goal attempts and grabbed 14 rebounds. Hawks forward Bob Pettit closed out the defending champion Celtics with 50 points and 19 rebounds in Game 6 of the 1958 Finals.

817. How many players have averaged 40 points in a season?
A. One   B. Two   C. Three   D. Four
Answer: A. Wilt Chamberlain did it twice, posting 50.36 points per game with the Philadelphia Warriors during the 1961–62 campaign and following up with 44.39 per game in 1962–63.

818. True or False? No one playing 80 or more games averaged 48 minutes per game over a season.
Answer: False. Wilt Chamberlain averaged 48.525 minutes per game in 1962, when he led the league in games played with 80.

819. Which of the following ABA players holds the record for most minutes in a season?
A. Rick Barry   B. Artis Gilmore   C. Gerald Govan   D. Spencer Haywood
Answer: D. In 1970, when he played in 84 games, Haywood amassed 3,808 minutes or 45.33 minutes per game.

820. Wilt Chamberlain's record for field goals in a season is how far ahead of the second-place player?
A. Less than 100   B. More than 200   C. More than 400
D. More than 500
Answer: C. Chamberlain made 1,597 field goals during the 1962 season, which averaged out to 20 per game over his 80-game season. The second-place finisher is Kareem Abdul-Jabbar, who scored 1,159 in 1972, which is 438 less than Chamberlain.

821. Who holds the mark for most assists in a season?
A. Bob Cousy   B. John Stockton   C. Magic Johnson   D. Jason Kidd
Answer: B. Stockton had 1,164 in 1991, an average of 14.2 per game.

822. Rank the following players for free throws made in a season.
A. Michael Jordan   B. Jerry West   C. Wilt Chamberlain
D. Adrian Dantley
Answer: 1-B, 840, 1966; 2-C, 835, 1962; 3-A, 833, 1987; 4-D, 813, 1984.

823. Rank the ABA players in games played all-time.
A. Louis Dampier   B. Byron Beck   C. Gerald Govan   D. Fred Lewis
Answer: 1-A, 728 games; 2-B, 694 games; 3-D, 686 games; 4-C, 681 games.

824. Name the first player with at least 200 points, 100 rebounds, and 50 assists in a single playoff series.
A. Wilt Chamberlain   B. Bob Pettit   C. Kareem Abdul-Jabbar
D. Giannis Antetokounmpo
Answer: D. The two-time MVP scored 237 points, grabbed 103 rebounds, and posted 50 assists in the 2022 conference semifinals against the Celtics. It wasn't enough, as Boston rolled in Game 7.

825. Who holds the record for assists in a half?
A. Magic Johnson   B. Bob Cousy   C. Dick McGuire   D. John Stockton
Answer: B. The "Houdini of the Hardwood" amassed 19 assists in a half against the Lakers on February 27, 1959.

826. Rank the following five in career blocks per game.
A. Elmore Smith   B. David Robinson   C. Hakeem Olajuwon
D. Manute Bol   E. Mark Eaton
Answer: 1-E, 3.50 per game; 2-D, 3.34; 3-C, 3.09; 4-B, 2.99; 5-A, 2.90

827. Name the four players who grabbed 40 rebounds in a game.
Answer: Wilt Chamberlain, 15 times; Bill Russell, 11 times; 3-Jerry Lucas, 4-Nate Thurmond.

828. True or False? Bill Russell holds the record for rebounds per game in a season.
Answer: False. Russell's 24.74 per game in 1964 is in fourth place. Chamberlain owns the three best season averages, with an all-time high of 27.2 in 1961.

829. Who holds the record for free throw attempts for a season?
A. Michael Jordan   B. Wilt Chamberlain   C. Jerry West
D. Shaquille O'Neal
Answer: B. "The Big Dipper" owns the top five season marks for free throws attempted. His personal best was 1,363 attempts in 1961–62, meaning he attempted just over 17 a game.

830. Rank the 1972–73 regular-season assist leaders.
A. Jerry West   B. Nate Archibald   C. Lenny Wilkens   D. Dave Bing
Answer: 1-B, 11.4 assists. He remains the only player ever to lead in points and assists in the same season. He averaged 34 points. 2-A, 8.8; 3-C, 8.4; 4-D, 7.8.

831. Who holds the NBA record for blocks in a season?
A. Elmore Smith   B. Manute Bol   C. Artis Gilmore   D. Mark Eaton
Answer: D. Eaton, the 7'4" center for the Utah Jazz, blocked 456 shots during the 1984–85 season. His feat remains the record since blocked shots became an official statistic in 1973–74.

832. Which of the following players holds the record for blocks in a game?
A. Mark Eaton   B. Elmore Smith   C Manute Bol   D Shaquille O'Neal
Answer: B. Blocks were first tracked in the 1973–74 season and Smith blocked 17 on October 28, 1973. He also logged 12 points and 16 rebounds to secure an unusual triple-double. The Lakers' 7-foot center led the league with 4.9 blocks per game during the 1973–74 season.

833. Which player blocked 10 or more shots in a game the most times?
A. Manute Bol   B. Hakeem Olajuwon   C. Mark Eaton   D. Andrew Bynum
Answer: C. The Jazz's 7'4" center blocked 10 or more an astounding 19 times. Bol ranked second, doing it 18 times.

834. What two players share the mark for steals in a game?
A. Walt Frazier   B. Larry Kenon   C. Kendall Gill   D. John Stockton
Answer: B and C. Both had 11 steals in a game. Playing for the Spurs, Kenon did it against the K.C. Kings on December 26, 1976. Competing for the Nets, Gill did it against the Heat on April 3, 1999.

835. Name the seven players who have played on four championship teams and won multiple regular-season MVPs.

Answer: 1. Bill Russell, 11 championships, five MVPs; 2. Kareem Abdul-Jabbar, six championships, six MVPs; 3. Michael Jordan, six championships, five MVPs; 4. Magic Johnson, five championships, three MVPs; 5. Tim Duncan, five championships, two MVPs; 6. LeBron James, four championships, four MVPs; 7. Stephen Curry, four championships, two MVPs.

836. Which of the following players averaged 30 points in a season five or more times.

A. Jerry West   B. Michael Jordan   C. Oscar Robertson

D. Adrian Dantley   E. Wilt Chamberlain

Answer: E, nine times; B, eight times; C, six times; A and D, four times.

MILESTONES

837. Which of the following players reached 30,000 points?
A. Wilt Chamberlain   B. Julius Erving   C. Moses Malone
D. Shaquille O'Neal
Answer: A and B. Chamberlain posted 31,419 points and Erving, with his NBA and ABA points combined, reached 30,026.

838. Rank the following players in games played.
A. John Stockton   B. Dirk Nowitzki   C. Robert Parish
D. Kareem Abdul-Jabbar   E. Vince Carter
Answer: 1-C, 1,611 games played; 2-D, 1,560; 3-E, 1,541; 4-B, 1,522; 5-A, 1,504.

839. How many players who played for the Lakers reached 30,000 points?
A. One   B. Two   C. Three   D. Four
Answer: C. LeBron James scored 38,652 points, Abdul-Jabbar scored 38,387, and Kobe Bryant tallied 33,643.

840. Name the two players who amassed 12,000+ assists.
A. Jason Kidd   B. Chris Paul   C. John Stockton   D. Steve Nash
Answer: A and C. Stockton compiled 15,806 assists. Kidd posted 12,091.

841. Name the first player to reach 15,000 points.
A. Dolph Schayes   B. George Mikan   C. Bob Pettit   D. Wilt Chamberlain
Answer: A. Having finished the 1959–60 season 13 points shy of 15,000, the Syracuse power forward surpassed the 15,000-point mark in his 11th season.

842. How many of the following players amassed 20,000 rebounds?
A. Kareem Abdul-Jabbar   B. Wilt Chamberlain   C. Moses Malone
D. Bill Russell
Answer: B and D. Chamberlain tallied 23,924 rebounds. Russell plucked 21,620 off the boards.

843. True or False? Dolph Schayes was the first NBA player to reach 1,000 games played.
Answer: False. Schayes played in 996 games. Hal Greer played his 1,000th game near the end of the 1970–71 season. The Hall of Fame guard finished his career in 1973 with 1,122 games played.

844. Name the first player to play in 1,000 consecutive games.
A. Dolph Schayes   B. Randy Smith   C. A. C. Green   D. Bob Cousy
Answer: C. From November 1986 until April of 2001, Green played in 1,192 consecutive games.

845. Rank the following players in career triple-doubles.
A. Jason Kidd   B. LeBron James   C. Magic Johnson
D. Oscar Robertson   E. Russell Westbrook
Answer: The NBA started tracking triple-doubles in 1979–80, when Magic Johnson popularized the achievement. But, since rebounds became an official statistic in 1950–51, we can compile a list. 1-E, 198 triple-doubles; 2-D, 181; 3-C, 138; 4-A and B, 107.

846. Rank the career leaders in blocks.
A. Hakeem Olajuwon   B. Mark Eaton   C. Kareem Abdul-Jabbar
D. Dikembe Mutombo   E. Artis Gilmore
Answer: Blocks have only been recorded since the 1973–74 season in the NBA and 1971–72 in the ABA. Otherwise, Abdul-Jabbar, who didn't have his blocks recorded until his fifth season, would likely rank ahead of Olajuwon and Mutombo. 1-A, 3,830; 2-D, 3,289; 3-C, 3,189; 4-E, 3,178; 5-B, 3064.

847. True or False? Until 1961 no player had posted double-digits in triple-doubles.
Answer: True. Oscar Robertson had 26 during the 1960–61 season, topping several players who reached nine.

848. Bob Cousy finished his career with 33 triple-doubles and was then the all-time leader. Who passed him to take the lead?

A. Sam Jones   B. Oscar Robertson   C. John Havlicek   D. Walt Frazier

Answer: B. Robertson passed Cousy during the 1961–62 season and finished with 181 triple-doubles.

849. Rank the career leaders in steals.

A. John Stockton   B. Chris Paul   C. Jason Kidd   D. Gary Payton
E. Michael Jordan

Answer: 1-A, 3,265; 2-C, 2,684; 3-B, 2,544; 4-E, 2,514; 5-D, 2,445. Steals became an official statistic in the NBA in 1973–74.

850. How many years had the Cleveland Cavaliers been without a title when they won in 2016?

A. 38 years   B. 43 years   C. 45 years   D. 51 years

Answer: C. Since Cleveland's inaugural season when they won 15 and lost 67 in 1971, no Cavaliers team had even made the Finals until 2015, when they lost to the Warriors in six games. In 2016 they trailed the Warriors three games to one before winning three straight, including two games on the road. They won Game 7 93–89.

851. Name the two players who played 63 minutes in the same game on February 2, 1969.

A. Nate Thurmond   B. Clyde Lee   C. Wilt Chamberlain
D. Rudy LaRusso

Answer: A and C. Once teammates with the Warriors, the two Hall of Famers each played every tick of the clock in a triple-overtime contest between the Warriors and Lakers. The Warriors won 122–117. Thurmond also scored 24 points and 34 rebounds. Chamberlain scored 23 points and 35 rebounds.

852. What happened in the third Final between the Lakers and Celtics?

Answer: It was Game 6 of the Finals in 1963 with the Lakers down three games to two and clawing back from an 11-point deficit at the half. They were playing at the Los Angeles Memorial Sports Arena. Their top scorers Elgin Baylor and Jerry West combined for 60 points as the Lakers got within three. But in what would become a familiar tale, the Lakers' two-pronged attack succumbed to the rounded attack of the Celtics, including Bill Russell (24 rebounds); Tommy Heinsohn, 22 points; Bob Cousy, 18 points; Tom Sanders, 18 points; and John Havlicek, 18 points. The Celtics won 112–109 to win their fifth consecutive Finals.

853. What happened at the end of regulation play in Game 7 of the 1957 Finals?

Answer: Bill Russell blocked Jack Coleman's layup that would have won the game for the Hawks in Game 7 of the 1957 Finals. Instead, the game went into one overtime and then a second. The Celtics won in double overtime 125–123 to win their first title. Of Russell's block, teammate Tommy Heinsohn said, "I've seen memorable plays in the NBA, but that has to be the most memorable play I've ever seen."

854. Who won the last ABA game?

A. Nuggets   B. Spurs   C. Nets   D. Squires

Answer: C. On May 13, 1976, the Nets trailed Denver by 22 points in the third quarter of Game 6 of the ABA Finals before 15,434 fans at the Nassau Veterans Memorial Coliseum in Uniondale, New York. But the Nets' starting five, led by Julius Erving with 31 points and 19 rebounds, tallied 100 points combined and stormed back to win 112–106. It was the Nets' second title in three seasons.

855. Name the player who posted 36 points, 19 assists, and seven rebounds in Game 7 of the 1970 Finals.

A. Jerry West   B. Elgin Baylor   C. Walt Frazier   D. Dick Barnett

Answer: C. It was Frazier having the game of his life to bring the Knicks a 113–99 victory and their first world championship.

856. What team scored the most points in a Finals game?

A. Celtics   B. Lakers   C. Spurs   D. Bulls

Answer: A. The Celtics beat the Lakers in Game 1 of the 1985 NBA Finals 148–114.

857. True or False? Stephen Curry was the youngest ever with a triple-double.

Answer: False. On January 3, 2022, Thunder guard Josh Giddey, then 19 years and 84 days old, recorded 17 points, 14 assists, and 13 rebounds in a 95–86 loss to the Mavericks.

858. True or False? Klay Thompson scored 50 points during the 2023 season.

Answer: True. Thompson scored 54 in a double-overtime win against the Hawks on January 2, 2023. It was his highest total in more than six years, dating to when he scored 60 against the Pacers in just three quarters on December 5, 2016.

859. Name the leading scorer in the 1985 Finals.
A. Kareem Abdul-Jabbar   B. Magic Johnson   C. Larry Bird
D. Kevin McHale
Answer: A. The oldest player on the floor at 38, Abdul-Jabbar, playing with six other Hall of Famers, was the leading scorer and the Finals Most Valuable Player. He averaged 25.7 points and shot .604 from the field, completely outplaying his opponent Robert Parish. After losing Game 1 148–114, with Abdul-Jabbar getting buried by the press, the Lakers won four of five to beat the Celtics in the Finals for the first time after eight failed attempts dating to 1959.

860. What was Shaquille O'Neal's highest block total in a game?
Answer: On November 20, 1993, Shaquille O'Neal had a personal best with 15 blocks. He also scored 24 points and grabbed 28 rebounds in an 87–85 victory over the Nets.

861. Name the last NBA player to score 70 points in a losing effort.
A. Damian Lillard   B. Donovan Mitchell   C. Devin Booker
D. David Thompson
Answer: C. Booker logged 70 points against the Celtics on March 24, 2017, but the Suns lost to the Celtics in Boston 130–120.

NICKNAMES

862. Match the players with their nicknames.
1. Vin Baker   2. Shaquille O'Neal   3. Chris Webber
4. Anfernee Hardaway
A. The Truth   B. Penny   C. Shake and Bake   D. The Big Aristotle
Answer: 1-C; 2-D; 3-A; 4-B.

863. Match the players with their nicknames.
1. Wayne Rollins   2. Donald Watts   3. Eddie Johnson   4. Ricky Pierce
A. Piggy   B. Slick   C. Tree   D. Big Paper Daddy
Answer: 1-C; 2-B; 3-A; 4-D.

864. Match the players with their nicknames.
1. Joel Embiid   2. Kevin Durant   3. Russell Westbrook   4. Chris Paul
A. The Skate Instructor   B. Mr. Triple Double   C. Do-a-180
D. Slim Reaper
Answer: 1-C; 2-D; 3-B; 4-A.

865. Match the players with their nicknames.
1. Elvin Hayes   2. John Havlicek   3. Bob Pettit   4. Walt Frazier
A. The Bombardier from Baton Rouge   B. The Big Enigma
C. Hondo   D. Clyde
Answer: 1-B; 2-C; 3-A; 4-D.

866. Match the players with their nicknames.
1. Gary Payton   2. Bobby Jones   3. Willis Reed   4. Jerry West
A. Mr. Clutch   B. The Secretary of Defense   C. Wolf   D. The Glove
Answer: 1-D; 2-B; 3-C; 4-A.

Jerry West

867. Match the players with their nicknames.
1. Julius Erving   2. Michael Jordan   3. Allen Iverson   4. Earvin Johnson
A. Air   B. The Answer   C. Dr. J   D. Magic
Answer: 1-C; 2-A; 3-B; 4-D.

868. Match the players with their nicknames.
1. Hakeem Olajuwon   2. Robert Horry   3. Kevin McHale   4. Kobe Bryant
A. Big Shot Bob   B. The Dream   C. Herman Munster
D. The Black Mamba
Answer: 1-B; 2-A; 3-C; 4-D.

869. Match the players with their nicknames.
1. Karl Malone   2. Dennis Rodman   3. LeBron James   4. David Robinson
A. The Chosen One   B. The Admiral   C. The Worm   D. The Mailman
Answer: 1-D; 2-C; 3-A; 4-B.

870. Match the players with their nicknames.
1. Phil Jackson   2. Wilt Chamberlain   3. Ray Allen   4. Jason Williams
A. The Load   B. Jesus Shuttlesworth   C. White Chocolate
D. The Zen Master
Answer: 1-D; 2-A; 3-B; 4-C.

871. Match the players with their nicknames.
1. Pete Maravich   2. Bryant Reeves   3. Darryl Dawkins
4. Gilbert Arenas
A. Agent Zero   B. Pistol   C. Big Country   D. Chocolate Thunder
Answer: 1-B; 2-C; 3-D; 4-A.

872. Match the players with their nicknames.
1. Gilbert Arenas   2. Stacey Augmon   3. Alfred Beard
4. Tyrone Bogues
A. Muggsy   B. The Hibachi   C. Plastic Man   D. Butch
Answer: 1-B; 2-C; 3-D; 4-A.

873. Match the players with their nicknames.
1. Vern Mikkelsen   2. Slater Martin   3. Bob Davies   4. Bobby Wanzer
A. Dugie   B. Li'l Abner   C. Hooks   D. The Great Dane
Answer: 1-D; 2-A; 3-B; 4-C.

874. Match the players with their nicknames.
1. Ray Allen   2. Kareem Abdul-Jabbar   3. Giannis Antetokounmpo
4. Carmelo Anthony
A. The Alphabet   B. Skinny Walt   C. The Captain   D. Captain America
Answer: 1-B; 2-C; 3-A; 4-D.

875. Match the players with their nicknames.
1. Tim Duncan   2. Vinnie Johnson   3. Kenny Smith   4. Shawn Kemp
A. The Microwave   B. The Big Fundamental   C. The Reign Man
D. The Jet
Answer: 1-B; 2-A; 3-D; 4-C.

876. Give the nicknames for the NBA's first champions, the 1946–47 Philadelphia Warriors.
1. Joe Fulks   2. George Senesky   3. Alexander Rosenberg
4. John Murphy
A. Handcuffs   B. Pete   C. The Kuttawa Clipper   D. Moe
Answer: 1-C; 2-A; 3-B; 4-D.

877. Give the nicknames for the NBA's second champion, the 1947–48 Baltimore Bullets.
1. Carl Meinhold   2. John Abramovic   3. Paul Hoffman   4. Herm Fuetsch
A. Brooms   B. Red   C. Dutch   D. Bear
Answer: 1-B; 2-A; 3-D; 4-C.

878. Give the nicknames for the NBA's third champion, the 1948–49 Baltimore Bullets.
1. Don Carlson   2. George Mikan   3. Earl Gardner   4. Ed Kachan
A. Swede   B. Red   C. The Monster   D. Whitey
Answer: 1-A; 2-C; 3-B; 4-D.

879. Give the nicknames for the NBA's fifth champion, the 1950–51 Rochester Royals.
1. William Holzman   2. Jack Coleman   3. Arnie Risen   4. Bobby Wanzer
A. Hooks   B. Stilts   C. Red   D. Old Ranche
Answer: 1-C; 2-D; 3-B; 4-A.

880. Give the nicknames for the NBA's ninth champion, the 1954–55 Syracuse Nationals.
1. Red Kerr   2. Earl Lloyd   3. Red Rocha   4. Dolph Schayes
A. The Thin Man   B. The Rainbow Kid   C. Iron Man   D. Big Cat
Answer: 1-C; 2-D; 3-A; 4-B.

881. Give the nicknames for the NBA's 10th champion, the 1955–56 Philadelphia Warriors.
1. Tom Gola   2. Neil Johnston   3. Ernie Beck   4. Walt Davis
A. Boom Boom   B. Ol' Hoss   C. Mr. All-Around   D. Buddy
Answer: 1-C; 2-B; 3-A; 4-D.

882. Give the nicknames for the NBA's 11th champion, the 1956–57 Boston Celtics.
1. Tommy Heinsohn   2. Bill Sharman   3. Andy Phillip   4. Frank Ramsey
A. Gunner   B. The Whizzer   C. Bullseye   D. The Kentucky Colonel
Answer: 1-A; 2-C; 3-B; 4-D.

883. Give the nicknames for the NBA's 12th champion, the 1957–58 St. Louis Hawks.
1. Bob Pettit   2. Cliff Hagan   3. Jack McMahon   4. Med Park
A. Irish   B. Bulldozer from Missouri   C. Big Blue   D. Li'l Abner
Answer: 1-C; 2-D; 3-A; 4-B.

884. Give the nicknames for the NBA's 17th champion, the 1962–63 Boston Celtics.
1. Sam Jones   2. Bill Russell   3. John Havlicek   4. Clyde Lovellette
A. Country Boy   B. Mr. Clutch   C. The Stuffer   D. The Whale
Answer: 1-B; 2-C; 3-A; 4-D.

885. Give the nicknames for the NBA's 23rd champion, the 1968–69 Boston Celtics.
1. Em Bryant   2. Larry Siegfried   3. Don Chaney   4. Tom Sanders
A. The Pest   B. Duck   C. Sieggy   D. Satch
Answer: 1-A; 2-C; 3-B; 4-D.

886. Match the players with the nicknames of the first ABA champions, the 1967-68 Pittsburgh Pipers.

1. Art Heyman   2. Connie Hawkins   3. Ira Harge   4. Tom Kerwin

A. The Man   B. The Pest   C. Large   D. Captain Hook

Answer: 1-B; 2-A; 3-C; 4-D.

887. Match the players with the nicknames of the 24th NBA champions, the 1969-70 New York Knicks.

1. Nate Bowman   2. Walt Frazier   3. Willis Reed   4. Dave Stallworth

A. Mr. Cool   B. The Captain   C. The Snake   D. The Rave

Answer: 1-C; 2-A; 3-B; 4-D.

888. Match the players with the nicknames of the second ABA champions, the 1968-69 Oakland Oaks.

1. Rick Barry   2. Warren Jabali   3. Jim Eakins   4. Larry Brown

A. Jumbo   B. Mad Dog   C. The Miami Greyhound   D. Little General

Answer: 1-C; 2-B; 3-A; 4-D.

889. Match the players with the nicknames of the third ABA champion, the 1969-70 Indiana Pacers.

1. John Barnhill   2. Roger Brown   3. Bill Keller   4. Fred Lewis

A. Rabbit   B. Fritz   C. The Rajah   D. Mickey Rooney

Answer: 1-A; 2-C; 3-D; 4-B.

890. Match the players with the nicknames of the fourth ABA champion, the 1970-71 Utah Stars.

1. Zelmo Beaty   2. Ron Boone   3. Merv Jackson   4. Wayne Hightower

A. Instant Offense   B. Magician   C. The Franchise   D. Spain

Answer: 1-C; 2-A; 3-B; 4-D.

891. Match the players with the nicknames of the fifth ABA champion, the 1971-72 Utah Stars.

1. Rick Mount   2. Darnell Hillman   3. Mel Daniels   4. George McGinnis

A. Baby Bull   B. Big D   C. The Rocket   D. Dr. Dunk

Answer: 1-C; 2-D; 3-B; 4-A.

892. Match the players with the nicknames of the sixth ABA champion, the 1972–73 Indiana Pacers.
1. Craig Raymond   2. Don Buse   3. Bill Newton   4. Gus Johnson
A. Boo   B. Stretch   C. Fig   D. Honeycomb
Answer: 1-B; 2-A; 3-C; 4-D.

893. Match the players with the nicknames of the seventh ABA champion, the 1973–74 New York Nets.
1. Julius Erving   2. Mike Gale   3. Larry Kenon   4. Willie Sojourner
A. Rainbow   B. Big Cat   C. Black Moses   D. Flipper
Answer: 1-C; 2-D; 3-B; 4-A.

894. Match the players with the nicknames of the eighth ABA champion, the 1974–75 Kentucky Colonels.
1. Artis Gilmore   2. Ted McClain   3. Ron Thomas   4. Dan Issel
A. The Plumber Duck   B. Horse   C. Hound Dog   D. Late Sleeper
Answer: 1-D; 2-C; 3-A; 4-B.

895. Match the players with the nicknames of the ninth ABA champion, the 1975–76 New York Nets.
1. Al Skinner   2. John Williamson   3. George Bucci   4. Rich Jones
A. Supe   B. Smoke   C. House   D. The King
Answer: 1-B; 2-A; 3-D; 4-C.

896. Match the players with the nicknames of the 25th NBA champion, the 1970–71 Milwaukee Bucks.
1. Kareem Abdul-Jabbar   2. Dick Cunningham   3. Bob Dandridge
4. Jon McGlocklin
A. The Tower of Power   B. The Original Buck   C. Pick   D. Cement Mixer
Answer: 1-A; 2-D; 3-C; 4-B.

897. Match the players with the nicknames of the 26th NBA champion, the 1971–72 Los Angeles Lakers.
1. Gail Goodrich   2. Jim McMillian   3. Wilt Chamberlain
4. Flynn Robinson
A. Big Musty   B. Electric Eye   C. Butterball   D. Stumpy
Answer: 1-D; 2-C; 3-A; 4-B.

898. Match the players with the nicknames of the 27th NBA champion, the 1972–73 New York Knicks.
1. Henry Bibby   2. Jerry Lucas   3. Dean Meminger   4. Phil Jackson
A. Mr. Memory   B. The Dream   C. Instant Offense   D. Action
Answer: 1-C; 2-A; 3-B; 4-D.

899. Match the players with the nicknames of the 28th NBA champion, the 1973–74 Boston Celtics.
1. Dave Cowens   2. Paul Silas   3. Don Chaney   4. Phil Hankinson
A. Papa Bear   B. Big Red   C. Duck   D. Spider
Answer: 1-B; 2-A; 3-C; 4-D.

900. Match the players with the nicknames of the 29th NBA champion, the 1974–75 Golden State Warriors.
1. Charles Johnson   2. Bill Bridges   3. Charles Dudley   4. Jeff Mullins
A. Grasshopper   B. The Train   C. Pork Chop   D. Jack
Answer: 1-D; 2-B; 3-A; 4-C.

901. Match the players with the nicknames of the 30th NBA champion, the 1975–76 Boston Celtics.
1. Steve Kuberski   2. Henry White   3. Dave Cowens   4. Charlie Scott
A. The Polish Powerhouse   B. Dave the Rave   C. Jo Jo   D. Great Scott
Answer: 1-A; 2-C; 3-B; 4-D.

902. Match the players with the nicknames of the 31st NBA champion, the 1976–77 Portland Trail Blazers.
1. Herm Gilliam   2. Maurice Lucas   3. Bill Walton   4 Dave Twardzik
A. Grateful Red   B. The Enforcer   C. The Trickster   D. Pinball
Answer: 1-C; 2-B; 3-A; 4-D.

903. Match the players with the nicknames of the 32nd NBA champion, the 1977–78 Washington Bullets.
1. Greg Ballard   2 .Elvin Hayes   3. Wes Unseld   4. Larry Wright
A. Bug-eyes   B. The Oak Tree   C. Billiards   D. The Bionic Man
Answer: 1-C; 2-D; 3-B; 4-A.

904. Match the players with the nicknames of the 33rd NBA champion, the 1978–79 Seattle SuperSonics.
1. Dennis Johnson   2. Gus Williams   3. Jack Sikma   4. Dick Snyder
A. The Wizard   B. The Duck   C. Banger   D. Airplane
Answer: 1-D; 2-A; 3-C; 4-B.

905. Match the players with the nicknames of the 34th NBA champion, the 1979–80 Los Angeles Lakers.
1. Jim Chones   2. Magic Johnson   3. Norm Nixon
4. Kareem Abdul-Jabbar
A. Cap   B. The Storm   C. Buck   D. Aircraft Carrier
Answer: 1-D; 2-C; 3-B; 4-A.

906. Match the players with the nicknames of the 35th NBA champion, the 1980–81 Boston Celtics.
1. Larry Bird   2. M. L. Carr   3. Cedric Maxwell   4. Kevin McHale
A. Lunchbox   B. Kodak   C. Black Hole   D. The Rubberband Man
Answer: 1-B; 2-A; 3-D; 4-C.

907. Match the players with the nicknames of the 36th NBA champion, the 1981–82 Los Angeles Lakers.
1. Kurt Rambis   2. Mike McGee   3. Jim Brewer   4. Eddie Jordan
5. Magic Johnson
A. Papa   B. Monty   C. Clark Kent   D. The Offensive Machine
E. The Deejay
Answer: 1-C; 2-D; 3-A; 4-B; 5-E.

908. Match the players with the nicknames of the 37th NBA champion, the 1982–83 Philadelphia 76ers.
1. Moses Malone   2. Andrew Toney   3. Julius Erving   4. Steve Mix
A. The Mayor   B. Chairman of the Boards   C. The Boston Strangler
D. Little Hawk
Answer: 1-B; 2-C; 3-D; 4-A.

909. Match the players with the nicknames of the 38th NBA champion, the 1983–84 Boston Celtics.
1. Robert Parish   2. Cedric Maxwell   3. Dennis Johnson   4. Larry Bird
A. Kodak   B. Airplane   C. Ced   D. Slim
Answer: 1-D; 2-C; 3-B; 4-A.

910. Match the players with the nicknames of the 39th NBA champion, the 1984–85 Los Angeles Lakers.
1. James Worthy   2. Kareem Abdul-Jabbar   3. Chuck Nevitt
4. Magic Johnson
A. Tragic   B. Human Victory Cigar   C. The Tower of Power   D. Ice Man
Answer: 1-D; 2-C; 3-B; 4-A.

911. Match the players with the nicknames of the 40th NBA champion, the 1985–86 Boston Celtics.
1. David Thirdkill   2. Robert Parish   3. Bill Walton   4. Rick Carlisle
A. Red Baron   B. The Chief   C. The Sheriff   D. Flipper
Answer: 1-C; 2-B; 3-A; 4-D.

912. Match the players with the nicknames of the 41st NBA champion, the 1986–87 Los Angeles Lakers.
1. Wes Matthews   2. Mike Smrek   3. A. C. Green
4. Mychal Thompson   5. Magic Johnson
A. Diesel   B. Wild Wild Wes   C. Iron Man   D. Sweet Bells   E. Junior
Answer: 1-B; 2-A; 3-C; 4-D; 5-E.

913. Match the players with the nicknames of the finalists in the 42nd NBA Finals between the 1987–88 championship Los Angeles Lakers and the Detroit Pistons.
1. Rick Mahorn   2. Adrian Dantley   3. Tony Campbell   4. Milt Wagner
A. Top Cat   B. Ice   C. The Teacher   D. McNasty
Answer: 1-D; 2-C; 3-A; 4-B.

914. Match the players with the nicknames of the finalists of the 43rd NBA Finals between the 1988–89 championship Detroit Pistons and the Los Angeles Lakers.
1. Bill Laimbeer   2. Isiah Thomas   3. Vinnie Johnson
4. Orlando Woolridge
A. Pocket Magic   B. The Prince of Darkness   C. 007   D. Tree
Answer: 1-B; 2-A; 3-C; 4-D.

915. Match the players with their nicknames.
1. Shaquille O'Neal   2. Paul Pierce   3. Shawn Marion   4. Shane Battier
A. Warrior   B. The Matrix   C. The Truth   D. Batman
Answer: 1-A; 2-C; 3-B; 4-D.

916. Match the players with their nicknames.
1. James Harden   2. Ray Allen   3. Fred Carter   4. George Mikan
A. Mr. Basketball   B. The Beard   C. Mad Dog   D. Skinny Walt
Answer: 1-B; 2-D; 3-C; 4-A.

917. Match the players with their nicknames.
1. Bill Russell   2. Oscar Robertson   3. Jerry West   4. Wilt Chamberlain
A. Zeke from Cabin Creek   B. Whiskers   C. The Big O   D. Whipper
Answer: 1-B; 2-C; 3-A; 4-D.

918. Match the players with their nicknames.
1. Nate Archibald   2. Elgin Baylor   3. Rudy LaRusso   4. Alex English
A. The Blade   B. The Skate   C. The Ivy Leaguer with Muscles
D. Tick Tock
Answer: 1-B; 2-D; 3-C; 4-A.

919. Match the players with their nicknames.
1. Damian Lillard   2. Bobby Smith   3. Russell Westbrook
4. Jerry Lucas
A. The Computer   B. Bingo   C. Sub Zero   D. The Brodie
Answer: 1-C; 2-B; 3-D; 4-A.

ODDITIES

920. True or False? No player has ever recorded a 20-20 and 5-5-5 (20 or more on any two stats and at least five of the remaining three stats).
Answer: False. Jusuf Nurkić of the Portland Trail Blazers, the 6'11" Bosnia native, posted an amazing line on New Year's Day in 2019. He scored 24 points, grabbed 23 rebounds, and got seven assists, five steals, and five blocks.

921. What player has the most 20-point games off the bench since 1983?
A. Jamaal Crawford   B. Ricky Pierce   C. Eddie Johnson
D. Lou Williams
Answer: D. Between 2008 and 2020, when his career ended, Williams scored 20 an amazing 208 times in games he didn't start.

922. Name the player whose point total in one half equaled the entire opposing team?
A. Stephen Curry   B. Jayson Tatum   C. Jrue Holiday   D. Luka Dončić
Answer: D. Dončić scored 27 in the first half of Game 6 of the conference semifinals against the Suns on May 16, 2022. The Mavericks led 57–27 at halftime.

923. Who won the MVP in the 1990 All-Star Game while playing on the losing team?
A. Hakeem Olajuwon   B. Magic Johnson   C. Michael Jordan
D. Kevin McHale
Answer: B. The West lost 130–113 but it was no fault of Johnson's. In 25 minutes he logged 22 points, six rebounds, and four assists to win the award at the Miami Arena.

924. Which team overcame the biggest deficit in a game to win?
A. 76ers   B. Bulls   C. Celtics   D. Jazz
Answer: D. With 20 seconds left in the second quarter, the Jazz trailed the Nuggets by 36 points. They overcame the 70–34 deficit by finishing the game on a 73–33 spurt to win 107–103 on November 27, 1996. Karl Malone led the way with 31 points and 17 rebounds.

925. Who won the first Finals MVP ever awarded?
A. Jerry West   B. John Havlicek   C. Bob Cousy   D. Willis Reed
Answer: A. West won it in 1969—for the losing team. The Lakers lost in seven to the Celtics. He averaged 37.9 points and 7.4 assists for the Finals series.

926. In the 40 years the Sixth Man of the Year award has been given, how many recipients have made the Hall of Fame?
A. One   B. Two   C. Five   D. Eight
Answer: C. Oddly, the first four recipients of the award made the Hall. They are Bobby Jones (1983), Kevin McHale (1984–1985) and Bill Walton (1986). Toni Kukoč (1996) and Manu Ginóbili (2008) later won it.

927. What two teams are tied for the most points in a regulation game?
A. Bulls   B. Pistons   C. Celtics   D. Suns
Answer: C and D. The Celtics starting five scored 128 and they topped the Lakers 173–139 on February 27, 1959. The Suns downed the Nuggets 173–143 on November 10, 1990. Cedric Ceballos led the way with 32, as five Suns surpassed 20 points.

928. Which player scored the most consecutive points in a game?
A. Carmelo Anthony   B. Michael Jordan   C. Jerry West   D. Karl Malone
Answer: A. Anthony tallied 26 consecutive points for the Nuggets against the Timberwolves on December 10, 2008. He scored 45 as the Nuggets won 116–105.

929. What is the largest point differential by one team over another in a quarter?
A. 21   B. 23   C. 35   D. 36
Answer: D. The Lakers outscored the Kings 40–4 in the first quarter on February 4, 1987, and went on to win 128–92.

930. What team had the fewest assists in a game in the last 50 years?
A. Wizards   B. Knicks   C. Celtics   D. 76ers
Answer: B. The Knicks had only three assists on March 28, 1976. Earl Monroe, John Gianelli, and Butch Beard each had one assist as the Celtics won 100–94.

931. What was unusual about the second recorded quadruple-double in NBA history?
Answer: On February 18, 1986, Spurs guard Alvin Robertson got double digits in steals instead of getting them in blocks. He recorded 20 points, 11 rebounds, 10 assists, and 10 steals.

932. What is the largest differential of scoring in a half?
A. 42 points   B. 47 points   C. 50 points   D. 61 points
Answer: C. The Mavericks held a 50-point lead over the Clippers, leading 77–27 after the first half at the Staples Center on December 27, 2020. They won by 51, 124–73.

933. What is the most rebounds a team grabbed in a game?
A. 77   B. 91   C. 99   D. 112
Answer: D. The Celtics secured 112 against the Pistons in a 150–106 victory at the Boston Garden on December 24, 1960.

934. What is the fewest rebounds by a team in one game?
A. 15   B. 17   C. 23   D. 27
Answer: B. The Nets got outrebounded by the Thunder 41–17 and lost 120–95 on January 31, 2014. Paul Pierce was the Nets' leading rebounder with five.

935. What is the fewest turnovers committed in a game?
A. None   B. One   C. Three   D. Five
Answer: B. The Nuggets turned it over just once against the Trail Blazers on February 23, 2021. Even with the nearly perfect handling of the ball, the Nuggets barely won, 111–106.

936. Name the most recent player to play for 12 different franchises.

A. Joe Smith   B. Tony Massenburg   C. Jim Jackson   D. Chucky Brown

Answer: A. All four have tied for the record of playing for 12 teams. Smith was the most recent. From 1998 to 2011 he played with the Warriors, 76ers, Timberwolves, Pistons, Bucks, Nuggets, Bulls, Cavaliers, Thunder, Hawks, Nets, and Lakers.

937. True or False? In each of the games Chamberlain scored 70 or more points, his team won.

Answer: False. Chamberlain scored 70 or more six times. His team lost three of them, including two to the Lakers and one to the Nationals.

PECKING ORDER

938. Rank the Mavericks' all-time leaders in assists.
A. Brad Davis   B. Derek Harper   C. Jason Kidd   D. Dirk Nowitzki
Answer: 1-B, 5,111 assists; 2-A, 4,524; 3-C, 4,211; 4-D, 3,651.

939. Rank the following players by adding their career points and rebounds per game.
A. Bob Pettit   B. Wilt Chamberlain   C. Elgin Baylor   D. Bill Russell
E. George Mikan
Answer: 1-B, 53 (30.1 points and 22.9 rebounds); 2-A, 42.6 (26.4 points and 16.2 rebounds); 3-C, 40.9 (27.4 points and 13.5 rebounds); 4-D, 37.6 (15.1 points and 22.5 rebounds); 5-E, 36.5 (23.1 points and 13.4 rebounds).

940. Rank the Pelicans' all-time leaders in points per game.
A. Jamal Mashburn   B. Brandon Ingram   C. Anthony Davis
D. Baron Davis
Answer: 1-C, 23.7 points per game; 2-B, 23.4; 3-A, 21.5; 4-D, 20.2.

941. Rank the following Trail Blazers in career rebounds per game.
A. Sidney Wicks   B. Marcus Camby   C. Jusuf Nurkić   D. Bill Walton
Answer: 1-D. Walton averaged 13.5 rebounds per game as a Blazer. His best season was 1977, their title season, when he posted 14.4 per game. 2-A, 10.3; 3-B, 10; 4-C, 9.8.

942. Rank the following Hall of Fame players by number of years played.
A. Kevin Garnett   B. Robert Parish   C. Kareem Abdul-Jabbar
D. Kobe Bryant
Answer: 1-A and B, 21 years; 3-C and D, 20 years.

943. Rank the following players by their number of 30-point games.
A. Wilt Chamberlain   B. LeBron James   C. Karl Malone
D. Michael Jordan   E. Kobe Bryant
Answer: 1-D, 562 30-point games; 2-B, 523; 3-A, 516; 4-C, 435; 5-E, 431.
Chamberlain averaged 42.3 in his games. Jordan was second with 37.5.

944. Rank the Pacers in total rebounds.
A. Rik Smits   B. Jeff Foster   C. Dale Davis   D. Mel Daniels
Answer: 1-D, 7,643 rebounds; 2-C, 6,006; 3-A, 5,277; 4-B, 5,248.

945. Rank the following teams by regular-season winning percentage.
A. 1996 Bulls   B. 2016 Warriors   C. 1967 76ers   D. 1972 Lakers
E. 1987 Bulls
Answer: 1-B, 73-9, .890; 2-A, 72-10, .878; 3-D and E, 69-13, .841; 5-C,
68-13, .840.

**946. Rank the following players by who has the most games with
10 assists since the 1982–83 season.**
A. Magic Johnson   B. Jason Kidd   C. Chris Paul   D. John Stockton
Answer: 1-D, 863 games; 2-C, 578; 3-B, 569; 4-A, 520.

947. Rank the players by most games with 20 field goals.
A. Michael Jordan   B. Kareem Abdul-Jabbar   C. Wilt Chamberlain
D. George Gervin   E. Rick Barry
Answer: 1-C, 141 games, more than all the other players here combined;
2-A, 28; 3-B, 14; 4-D and E, 13.

948. Rank the following Magic players by career rebounds per game.
A. Nikola Vučević   B. Rony Seikaly   C Horace Grant   D. Dwight
Howard   E. Shaquille O'Neal
Answer: 1-D, 13 rebounds per game; 2-E, 12.5; 3-A, 10.8; 4-B, 8.7; 5-C, 8.2.

**949. In the 75-year history of the Warriors, rank them by who has
scored the most points.**
A. Rick Barry   B. Paul Arizin   C. Stephen Curry   D. Chris Mullin
E. Wilt Chamberlain
Answer: 1-C, 21,712 points; 2-E, 17,783; 3-A, 16,447; 4-B, 16,266; 5-D,
16,235.

950. Rank the following franchises by most NBA titles.
A. Celtics   B. Lakers   C. Warriors   D. Bulls
Answer: 1-A and B, each has won 17 titles; 3-C and D, each has won six titles.

951. Rank the Suns by points per game in a season.
A. Devin Booker   B. Amar'e Stoudemire   C. Charles Barkley
D. Tom Chambers
Answer: 1-D, 27.2 points per game, 1990 (Chambers also owns the sixth best in 1989); 2-A, 26.8, 2022 (Booker also has the third and fourth best in 2019 and 2020); 5-B, 26, 2005; 7-C, 25.6, 1993.

952. Rank the Suns' players in assists per game in a season.
A. Chris Paul   B. Steve Nash   C. Kevin Johnson   D. Jason Kidd
Answer: 1-C, 12.2 assists per game, 1993 (Johnson also holds the fourth best season in 1990); 2-B, 11.6, 2007 (Nash holds the third, 2005; fifth, 2011; sixth, 2008; and seventh best 2010); 8-A, 10.8; 9-D, 10.8, 1999.

953. Rank the players in the order they were chosen in the 1984 draft.
A. Hakeem Olajuwon   B. Michael Jordan   C. Sam Perkins
D. Charles Barkley   E. Sam Bowie
Answer: 1-A; 2-E; 3-B; 4-C; 5-D.

954. Rank the following players by how many points they scored for the Bulls.
A. Jerry Sloan   B. Michael Jordan   C. Luol Deng   D. Bob Love
E. Scottie Pippen
Answer: 1-B, 29,277 points; 2-E, 15,123; 3-D, 12,623; 4-C, 10,286; 5-A, 10,233.

955. Rank the SuperSonics/Thunder all-time leaders in points per game.
A. Kevin Durant   B. Ray Allen   C. Spencer Haywood   D. Paul George
Answer: 1-A, 27.4 points per game; 2-D, 25.0; 3-C, 24.9; 4-B, 24.6.

956. Rank the following players by who won the highest percentage of the Finals he appeared in.
A. Sam Jones   B. Bill Russell   C. Michael Jordan
Answer: 1-C, 100 percent, Jordan played in six Finals and won all six; 2-B, 91.66 percent, Russell won 11 of the 12 Finals he played in (lost to the Hawks in 1958 Finals); 3-A, 90.9 percent, Jones won 10 of the 11 Finals he played in (also lost to the Hawks in 1958 Finals).

957. Rank the following top five in career free throw percentage (combined NBA and ABA).
A. Mark Price   B. Peja Stojaković   C. Stephen Curry   D. Steve Nash
E. Rick Barry
Answer: 1-C, .9087; 2-D, .9043; 3-A, .9039; 4-E, .8998; 5-B, .8948.

958. Rank the Pistons' all-time leaders in points per game.
A. Bob Lanier   B. Grant Hill   C. Dave Bing   D. Jerry Stackhouse
Answer: 1-A, 22.7; 2-C, 22.6; 3-D, 22.1; 4-B, 21.6.

959. Rank the 76ers' all-time leaders in field goal percentage.
A. Charles Barkley   B. Wilt Chamberlain   C. Darryl Dawkins
D. Ben Simmons
Answer: 1-B, .583; 2-A, .576; 3-D, .560; 4-C, .555.

960. Rank the following players in career points scored for the Bucks.
A. Sidney Moncrief   B. Kareem-Abdul-Jabbar
C. Giannis Antetokounmpo   D. Glenn Robinson   E. Michael Redd
Answer: 1-C, 16,280; 2-B, 14,211; 3-D, 12,010; 4-A, 11,594; 5-E, 11,554.

961. Rank the Suns' all-time leaders in points scored.
A. Alvan Adams   B. Walter Davis   C. Shawn Marion   D. Kevin Johnson
E. Devin Booker
Answer: 1-B, 15,666 points; 2-A, 13,910; 3-D, 12,747; 4-E, 12,688; 5-C, 12,134.

962. Rank the 76ers in points per game in a season.
A. Wilt Chamberlain   B. Joel Embiid   C. Charles Barkley   D. Allen Iverson
Answer: 1-A, 33.5, 1965–66; 2-B, 33.1, 2022–23 (Embiid also owns the seventh and eight best); 3-D, 33.0, 2005–6 (Iverson owns the fourth through sixth and ninth best); 10-C, 28.3, 1987–88.

963. Rank the 76ers players in rebounds per game in a season.
A. Moses Malone   B. Dolph Schayes   C. Red Kerr   D. Wilt Chamberlain
Answer: 1-D, 24.6 rebounds per game, 1965–66 (Chamberlain also holds the team record for second and third best seasons); 4-B, 16.4, 1951; 5-A, 1983; 6-C, 14.7, 1962.

Giannis Antetokounmpo

964. Rank the following top five in career assists per game.
A. Magic Johnson   B. Chris Paul   C. Isiah Thomas
D. Oscar Robertson   E. John Stockton
Answer: 1-A, 11.19 per game; 2-E, 10.51; 3-D, 9.51; 4-B, 9.47; 5-C, 9.26.

965. Rank the following players in career steals per game.
A. Mookie Blaylock   B. Michael Jordan   C. Michael Ray Richardson
D. Fatty Taylor   E. Alvin Robertson
Answer: Steals per game have only been kept since the 1973–74 season.
1-E, 2.71 steals per game; 2-C, 2.63; 3-D, 2.40; 4-B, 2.35; 5-A, 2.33.

966. True or False? There are more than 10 players with 25,000 points
and 14,000 rebounds.
Answer: False. There are seven: Wilt Chamberlain, Kareem Abdul-Jabbar,
Karl Malone, Moses Malone, Elvin Hayes, Tim Duncan, and Kevin Garnett.

967. Rank the top picks in the 1982 draft.
A. Terry Cummings   B. Dominique Wilkins   C. Bill Garnett
D. James Worthy
Answer: 1-D; 2-A; 3-B; 4-C.

968. Rank the following coaches by winning percentage.
A. Phil Jackson   B. Billy Cunningham   C. Steve Kerr   D. Larry Bird
Answer: 1-A, .704; 2-B, .698; 3-D, .687; 4-C, .665.

969. Rank the order of the following picks in the 1970 draft.
A. Dave Cowens   B. Rudy Tomjanovich   C. Bob Lanier
D. Pete Maravich
Answer: 1-C, center; 2-B, power forward; 3-D, guard; 4-A, center.

970. Rank the following players by their highest points per game in a
single season.
A. Rick Barry   B. Elgin Baylor   C. James Harden   D. Jerry West
Answer: 1-C, 36.13 in 2019; 2-A, 35.59, 1967; 3-B, 34.77, 1961; 4-D, 31.34,
1966.

971. Rank the Royals/Kings players for the season record in points per game.
A. Tiny Archibald   B. Oscar Robertson   C. Jack Twyman
Answer: 1-A, 34.0 points per game, 1973; 2-B, 31.4, 1964 (Robertson also holds the third best and fifth through 10th team records in points per game); 4-C, 31.2, 1960.

972. Rank the top five picks from the 1973 draft.
A. Ernie DiGregorio   B. Jim Brewer   C. Doug Collins   D. Mike Green
E. Kermit Washington
Answer: 1-C; 2-B; 3-A; 4-D; 5-E.

973. Rank the following players by career 3-point percentage.
A. Steve Kerr   B. Joe Harris   C. Seth Curry   D. Hubert Davis
Answer: 1-A, .454; 2-D, .441; 3-B, .437; 4-C, .435.

974. Rank the following players by free throw percentage in a season.
A. Calvin Murphy   B. Mahmoud Abdul-Rauf   C. Ray Allen
D. José Calderón
Answer: 1-D, .9805 in 2008–9; 2-A, .9581, 1980–81; 3-B, .9563, 1993–94; 4-C, .9518, 2008–9.

975. Rank the leaders in playoff points per game in 2022.
A. Luka Dončić   B. Nikola Jokić   C. Giannis Antetokounmpo
D. Jimmy Butler
Answer: 1-A and C, 31.7 points per game; 2-B, 31; 4-D, 27.4.

976. Rank the leaders in regular-season points per game in 2022.
A. Joel Embiid   B. Luka Dončić   C. Trae Young
D. Giannis Antetokounmpo
Answer: 1-A, 30.6 points per game; 2-D, 29.9; 3-B, 28.4; 4-C, 28.4.

977. Rank the leaders in steals in 2022.
A. Dejounte Murray   B. Matisse Thybulle   C. Chris Paul
D. Gary Trent Jr.
Answer: 1-A, 2.0 steals per game; 2-C, 1.99; 3-D and B, 1.7.

978. Rank the following guards in assists per game over a single season.
A. Kevin Porter   B. Magic Johnson   C. John Stockton   D. Isiah Thomas
Answer: 1-C, 14.54 assists per game, 1989–90 (Stockton also has the
second highest total with 14.20 over the 1990–91 campaign and owns
the fourth through sixth highest); 2-D, 13.86, 1984–85; 3-A, 13.40, 1978–
79; 4-B, 13.06, 1983–84.

979. Rank the order in which the following Hall of Famers were drafted in 1967.
A. Pat Riley   B. Earl Monroe   C. Mel Daniels   D. Walt Frazier
E. Phil Jackson
Answer: 1-B, second pick, Bullets; 2-D, fifth pick, Knicks; 3-A, seventh
pick, Rockets (inducted as a coach); 4-C, ninth pick, Royals; 5-E, 17th
pick, Knicks (inducted as a coach).

980. Rank the following ABA guards in assists per game over a single season.
A. Bill Melchionni   B. Al Smith   C. Mack Calvin   D. Don Buse
Answer: 1-A, 8.36, 1971–72, New York Nets (Melchionni also owns the
second highest total, 8.30 in 1970–71); 2-D, 8.20, 1975–76, Indiana Pacers;
3-B, 8.14, 1973–74, Denver Rockets; 4-C, 7.70, 1974–75, Denver Nuggets.

981. Rank the teams with the most NBA titles since 2000.
A. Warriors   B. Lakers   C. Spurs   D. Heat
Answer: 1-B, six; 2-C, four; 3-A and D, three each.

PLAYOFFS

982. True or False? Luca Dončić averaged more points in the 2022 conference semifinals versus Phoenix than he did in the conference finals versus Golden State.
Answer: True. His scoring average against Phoenix was 32.6 points per game and it was 32 against Golden State. A major difference, however, was that he hit 47.6 percent of his field goals against Phoenix but only 41.5 against Golden State.

983. Name the player with the most missed shots in an NBA playoff game.
A. Rick Barry   B. Elgin Baylor   C. Joe Fulks   D. Russell Westbrook
Answer: C. The Warriors power forward missed 38 shots in Game 4 of the 1948 semifinals against the St. Louis Bombers.

984. Who holds the dubious record for most turnovers in a playoff game?
A. James Harden   B. Luka Dončić   C. LeBron James
D. John Williamson
Answer: A. Playing for the Rockets, "The Beard" turned it over 12 times in Game 5 of the 2015 Western Conference finals against the Warriors. The Warriors won 104–90 to take the series in five games.

985. What team holds the record for most points in a playoff game?
A. Celtics   B. Lakers   C. Bulls   D. Suns
Answer: A. The Celtics beat the Knicks 157–128 on April 28, 1990, in Game 2 of the first round of the playoffs. The victory gave the Celtics a 2–0 series lead, but the Knicks won three straight to take the series.

986. What player(s) attempted the most field goals in a playoff game?
A. Wilt Chamberlain   B. Elgin Baylor   C. Joe Fulks   D. Rick Barry
Answer: A and D. Playing for the Warriors, Wilt took 48 shots and made 22 against Syracuse on March 22, 1962. He finished with 56 points and 35 rebounds. Against Wilt's 76ers in the 1967 Finals, Barry took 48 shots and made 22, logging 55 points. The 76ers won the series in six games.

987. Who holds the record for most points in a five-game playoff series?
A. Wilt Chamberlain   B. Kobe Bryant   C. Michael Jordan
D. Karl Malone
Answer: C. Jordan netted 226 points against the Cavaliers for a 45.2 average in the first round of the Eastern Conference playoffs in 1988. He scored 39 points and added six assists to help the Bulls to a victory in Game 5.

988. Who holds the Celtics' record for points scored in an elimination game?
A. Dave Cowens   B. Larry Bird   C. Sam Jones   D. Jayson Tatum
Answer: C. The Hall of Fame guard scored 47 against the Royals in Game 7 of the Eastern Division finals in 1963. The Celtics won 142–131 to advance to the Finals, where they beat the Lakers in six games.

989. Name the player who made the most 3-point goals in a playoff game.
A. Stephen Curry   B. Reggie Miller   C. Damian Lillard
D. Klay Thompson
Answer: C. Lillard connected for 12 of 17 3-pointers against the Nuggets on June 1, 2021, in a double-overtime 147–140 defeat. Lillard netted 55 points and had 10 assists. In the same series Lillard tied Vince Carter's record by making eight 3-pointers in a half.

990. True or False? The Grizzlies made it to a conference finals.
Answer: True. In 2013, under five-year coach Lionel Hollins, the Grizzlies finished a stellar 56-26. They beat the Clippers and Thunder in the first two rounds but were swept out of the playoffs by the Spurs in the conference finals.

991. Name the player who set a Celtics' record for points scored in a quarter during the 1974 playoff series with the Braves.

A. Jo Jo White   B. John Havlicek   C. Dave Cowens   D. Don Nelson

Answer: C. The Braves led by 12 after three quarters in Game 1, but Dave Cowens played like a man possessed, scoring 20 in the fourth period. The Celtics won the quarter 38–16 and took the contest 107–97. Each team won all its home games and the Celtics triumphed four games to two.

992. True or False? No teammates have had triple-doubles in the same playoff game.

Answer: False. It's happened twice. It took an overtime and triple-doubles by Stephen Curry (37 points, 13 rebounds, and 11 assists) and Draymond Green (18 points, 14 rebounds, and 11 assists) for the Warriors to win by two points, 119–117, and sweep the Blazers in the Western Conference finals on May 20, 2019. In Game 3 of the 2023 Finals, Jamal Murray and Nikola Jokić both had 30-point triple-doubles for the Nuggets against the Heat. Murray tallied 34 points, 10 rebounds, and 10 assists. Jokić posted 32 points, 21 rebounds, and 10 assists.

993. Name the player with the most steals in a playoff game.

A. Dennis Johnson   B. Allen Iverson   C. John Stockton
D. Darrell Walker

Answer: B. Playing for the 76ers, Iverson stole 10 against the Magic on May 13, 1999. Iverson's 33 points, five rebounds and assists, and 10 steals helped the Sixers to a 97–85 win.

994. Name the three players who are tied for the record with 10 blocks in a game.

A. Mark Eaton   B. Hakeem Olajuwon   C. Andrew Bynum   D. Manute Bol

Answer: A, B, and C. Jazz center Eaton was first, doing it in April 1985 against the Rockets. The Rockets' Olajuwon blocked 10 against the Lakers on April 29, 1990. Playing for the Lakers, Bynum did it against the Nuggets on April 29, 2012.

995. True or False? No NBA players had career playoff rebounding averages of 20 or more per game.

Answer: False. Centers Bill Russell and Wilt Chamberlain are the all-time leaders. Bill Russell owned a career average of 24.87 points per game. Wilt Chamberlain averaged 24.46.

996. True or False? Kevin Garnett's highest point per game average in the playoffs is higher than during that regular season.
Answer: True. Between 2002 and 2004 Garnett's playoff averages exceeded his regular-season averages. He averaged a career-high regular-season mark of 24.2 points per game in 2004 and averaged 25.8 in the playoffs that season.

997. Name the all-time leader in points per game in the ABA playoffs.
A. George Gervin   B. Dan Issel   C. Julius Erving   D. Rick Barry
Answer: D. Barry recorded an astounding 33.45 points per game in 31 ABA postseason games.

998. Which of the following teams has gone the longest without a championship?
A. 76ers   B. Knicks   C. Hawks   D. Wizards
Answer: C. The Hawks last won 65 years ago with Bob Pettit in St. Louis, when they bested the Celtics in a six-game Finals in 1958. The most recent team here to win was the Sixers, who took the title in 1983, led by Moses Malone and Julius Erving.

999. True or False? Bob Cousy holds the record for free throws made in a postseason game.
Answer: True. Cousy hit 30 of 32 free throws in a four-overtime game against the Syracuse Nationals in 1953.

QUOTES

1000. "I seek to leave the world a little better place than I found it."
—Dr. James Naismith, the physical education instructor from
McGill University in Quebec got his wish. He moved to Springfield,
Massachusetts, and invented the game. The first game of "Basket Ball"
was played in December 1891 in Springfield.

**1001. "The country was split. If you were white, you cheered for the
Celtics. If you were Black you cheered for the Lakers."**
—Magic Johnson, recalling the 1984 Celtics vs. Lakers Finals from the
2017 documentary *Celtics/Lakers: Best of Enemies*

**1002. "Julius Erving is the greatest forward ever to put on basketball
shoes." Who said it?**
A. Bill Walton   B. World B. Free   C. Lionel Hollins   D. George McGinnis
Answer: D. McGinnis, on teammate Erving. The two played on the 76ers
for two years, including the 1977 Finals against Portland.

**1003. "From the outside he could literally drill the ball in the basket.
George Gervin was a magnificent offensive player who could score
from anywhere. It was uncanny; he had such a soft touch, a beautiful
touch. He was an unstoppable offensive player."**
—Gene Shue, five-time All-Star guard and coach of the Baltimore Bullets

1004. "One thing I could do is finger roll." Who said it?
A. George Gervin   B. Wilt Chamberlain   C. Connie Hawkins
Answer: A. George Gervin, in a barbershop commercial with David Robinson and Tim Hardaway, who were laughing at Gervin and his 1970s fashions.

1005. "How could we stop Chamberlain without Willis? As always, I sat around the hotel, conserving energy for the game. I went over to the Garden early, trying to find out if anyone knew of Reed's condition. Nobody knew." Who said it?
A. Dave DeBusschere   B. Bill Bradley   C. Dick Barnett   D. Walt Frazier
Answer: D. Frazier, Hall of Game Knicks guard, recalling Game 7 of the 1970 Finals. Chamberlain had scored 45 points and grabbed 27 rebounds in Game 6, when the Knicks played without Reed.

1006. "I'd say that Game 7 against the Lakers. I always tried to hit the open man; this night I was the open man. I'd come off the pick, and the shot would be there."
—Walt Frazier, recalling the greatest game of his career, when he posted 36 points, 19 assists, seven rebounds, and four steals to lead New York to a 113–99 victory over the Lakers in Game 7 of the Finals on May 8, 1970

1007. "Guys today because they can jump out of the gym, often don't develop the skills they should have. We boxed out on the rebounds. Many players today don't. And guys who can drive often can't shoot from the perimeter."
—Hall of Fame guard and Knicks broadcaster Walt Frazier

1008. "He [Isiah Thomas] is second all-time to Jordan as having the greatest highlight film material." Who said it?
A. Pat Riley   B. Chuck Daly   C. Magic Johnson   D. Bob Ryan
Answer: D. Ryan, of the *Boston Globe*, recalling Thomas scoring 16 points in 90 seconds in the first round of the playoffs against the Knicks in 1984.

1009. "The highest compliment that you can pay a man is that he made other people around him better. Russell did that more than anyone, ever." Who said it?

A. Sam Jones   B. John Havlicek   C. Tommy Heinsohn
D. Satch Sanders

Answer: B. Havlicek, Celtic forward and Russell's teammate for seven years, 1963–1969.

1010. "We were the players we were because of Russell. We also rose higher because of him. A quick man like Havlicek could make four to six more lay-ups because of Russell. I'm not saying we were better because of him. Russell made people more effective. We all added to our games because of him." Who said it?

A. Bob Cousy   B. Sam Jones   C. Tom Sanders   D. K. C. Jones

Answer: C. "Satch" Sanders, 6'6" forward and teammate of Russell's from 1961 to 1969.

1011. "I remember Arnold [Red Auerbach] saying to me 'We're getting a player who is going to change things.'" Who said it?

A. Bob Cousy   B. Ed Macauley   C. Bill Sharman   D. Frank Ramsey

Answer: A. Cousy recalling Red Auerbach describing the acquisition of Bill Russell.

1012. "Basketball is like war in that offensive weapons are developed first, and it always takes a while for the defense to catch up." Who said it?

A. Pat Riley   B. John Kundla   C. Red Auerbach

Answer: C. Auerbach, who coached the Celtics to eight straight championships from 1959 through 1966.

1013. "Nobody did the stuff that Maravich was doing. If Maravich was playing today, he'd be a god. He did things in game situations that you practice on the sandlot. You couldn't pick one move as his best because he did 20 different things." Who said it?

A. Magic Johnson   B. Isiah Thomas   C. Michael Jordan

Answer: B. Thomas, appreciating the ball-handling and wizardry of Pete Maravich.

1014. "This is a team game, and one man doesn't win, and one man doesn't lose. In the end, the best team usually wins." Who said it?
A. Bill Russell   B. Wilt Chamberlain   C. Guy Rodgers   D. Bob Cousy
Answer: B. Chamberlain's teams lost in the playoffs 11 times. Eight of the losses came to Boston, a team which boasted many future Hall of Famers, including Bill Russell, Bob Cousy, Tommy Heinsohn, Sam Jones, John Havlicek, and Bailey Howell.

1015. "I like the [red, white, and blue] colors of the basketball."
—Artis Gilmore, explaining why he chose to sign with the Kentucky Colonels of the ABA rather than play with the Bulls who drafted him

1016. "It was a real quandary for the league. Here was the face of the league and he didn't want to talk to anyone." Who said it?
A. Michael Cooper   B. Kurt Rambis   C. Jamaal Wilkes
Answer: C. Wilkes, teammate of the quiet Kareem Abdul-Jabbar who wouldn't speak to the media.

1017. "I was in awe. I don't think there's any questions that if they kept blocked shots statistics that he'd have more in his time than anyone now. And if he wasn't blocking your shots, he caused a lot of 'hurries and worries' on the defense." Who said it?
A. Walt Frazier   B. Dick Barnett   C. Jerry West   D. Elgin Baylor
Answer: A. Frazier, recalling what it was like to penetrate on Bill Russell.

1018. "I don't get as many easy baskets as I used to." Who said it?
A. Cedric Maxwell   B. Kevin McHale   C. Robert Parish
Answer: Parish, Hall of Fame center, after Bird retired in 1992.

1019. "Elgin Baylor caught my eye and I watched him most of the evening. After seeing him, I was skeptical about making it to the pros." Who said it?
A. Oscar Robertson   B. Jerry Lucas   C. Jerry West
Answer: C. West, a junior at West Virginia, seeing Baylor play against the Knicks at Madison Square Garden in his first pro season.

1020. "Pro basketball has just thrown away the mold. He was one of a kind, unique. Not just the best of the best, but the only one who ever did what he did. He was a true warrior. I will never forget the Celtics-Lakers battles." Who said it?

A. Pat Riley   B. Chuck Daly   C. Magic Johnson

Answer: A. Riley describing Kareem Abdul-Jabbar, whose Lakers faced the Celtics in the 1984, 1985, and 1987 Finals.

1021. "I don't know much about Angola, but I know they're in trouble." Who said it?

A. Patrick Ewing   B. Clyde Drexler   C. Charles Barkley

Answer: C. Barkley, responding to a question about what he knew about Angola at the 1992 Olympics.

1022. "You can talk all you want about eras and all you want about how guys shot for a higher percentage today and how there are fewer missed shots. But the players of my time simply wanted to rebound more, and we rebounded better. I went into games expecting to get 20 rebounds. So did Wilt, Russell and Nate Thurmond. Now when a guy gets 20 rebounds, it's an event. Back then, it was just doing your job. There were many games where I got 35 to 40 rebounds, and that felt normal." Who said it?

A. Jerry Lucas   B. Nate Thurmond   C. Walt Bellamy

Answer: A. Lucas was right. Only four men ever got 40 rebounds in an NBA game. Wilt (14 times), Russell (eight times), Nate (once), and Lucas (once on February 29, 1964).

1023. "DeBusschere got better every day. He was such a dominant force—rebounding, blocking shots and scoring." Who said it?

A. Phil Chenier   B. Wes Unseld   C. Gus Johnson   D. Bill Bradley

Answer: A. Chenier, Bullets guard during the rivalry between the Knicks and the Bullets.

1024. "He [Bernard King] was the greatest offensive player in the history of the Knicks." Who said it?

A. Trent Tucker   B. Ernie Grunfeld   C. Marv Albert

Answer: C. Albert, ball boy and then broadcaster for the Knicks.

1025. "In 1965–66, his first year with New York, Walt led the Knickerbockers and placed fifth in the league in scoring (23.2 points per game) and fifth in rebounding (16.0). During the four years that Walt played in New York, he averaged 18.9 points and 13.4 rebounds. In each of those years, Bellamy finished in the top 10 in rebounding. His four-year scoring average is fourth best in Knickerbocker history behind Bob McAdoo, Richie Guerin and Walt Frazier." Who wrote it?
A. Willis Reed   B. Walt Frazier   C. Dick Barnett   D. Dave DeBusschere
Answer: D. DeBusschere wrote a letter to the Basketball Hall of Fame in 1983, penned on New York Knicks stationery, and signed: "Sincerely, Dave DeBusschere, Executive Vice President." DeBusschere, whose trade to the Knicks in 1968 helped make them two-time champions, was recognizing the value of the Hall of Famer he was traded for.

1026. "[Dan] Issel scored his 25,000th point in New Jersey. I was there for the milestone, and I remembered it because he scored it off me! I don't recall the shot, but he abused me somehow. For a guy his size he had incredible mobility. He could shoot the jumper facing up or off the drive."
—Mike Gminski, Nets forward and center, recalling an ABA and NBA star

1027. "Earl didn't know what his next move was going to be, so how could I know?" Who said it?
A. Dave Bing   B. Jo Jo White   C. Walt Frazier   D. Jerry West
Answer: C. Frazier, explaining his exasperation trying to guard the Bullets' Earl Monroe

1028. "He was a floor general, could run the floor and was one of the best ever at getting his own shot. And he seemed to get that shot more in clutch situations. He is one of the great big-game players of all-time."
—Matt Guokas, guard and small forward and a rookie on the famed 1967 Sixers, recalling Bob Cousy

1029. "John Stockton is the Bob Cousy of the eighties and nineties. He is the modern point guard reference for point guards."
—Bob Ryan, *Boston Globe*.

1030. "Dave Bing had quickness and uncanny leaping ability. He also had great range on his jumper." Who said it?

A. Phil Chenier   B. Archie Clark   C. Lucius Allen   D. Walt Frazier

Answer: D. Hall of Fame guard Walt Frazier on opposing Pistons guard Dave Bing.

1031. "I was the other guard on that team the year he did that. It was my job to stay away as far as I could. He was a strong competitor, and he would find you. But that year took a toll on his body. He often initiated contact on the drive, and he ended up on the floor a lot." Who said it?

A. Phil Ford   B. Johnny Green   C. John Block   D. Matt Guokas

Answer: D. Guokas, the "other guard" on the KC-Omaha Kings, in 1973 when Nate Archibald became the first and last player to lead the league in scoring and assists, with averages of 34 points and 11.4 assists.

1032. "Whether I start or come off the bench makes no difference to me. My game has always been to go as hard as I can for as long as I can." Who said it?

A. Frank Ramsey   B. Sam Jones   C. John Havlicek   D. Bailey Howell

Answer: C. A swingman who played small forward and shooting guard, Havlicek began as one of Boston's "sixth men," and ended up playing on eight championship squads. The first Celtic to score 25,000 points, "Hondo" was also an eight-time All-Defensive player.

1033. "He's playing only away games depending which city it is . . . can't play in New York . . . therefore we had different lineups, different matchups depending on the game schedule. It made it difficult for us coaches to figure out who's going to play instead of Kyrie. It was difficult for us to manage that so yeah, it was part of that."

—Amar'e Stoudamire, who left the Nets as a player development assistant because Kyrie Irving, who refused to receive a COVID vaccination, could not play games in Brooklyn.

1034. "I'm a lot better coach when I have really good players."

—Hall of Fame coach Chuck Daly, who coached the Pistons to consecutive championships in 1989 and 1990 before coaching the Olympic "Dream Team" in Barcelona in 1992. If not for Larry Bird stealing Isiah Thomas's inbound pass in the 1987 playoffs and a foul called on Bill Laimbeer in 1988, he might have coached them to four straight titles.

1035. "I'm 77 years old, and right now I can do more push-ups than you can. You wanna go to the mat, let's go."
—Pat Riley, Miami Heat team president, to a beat writer, when asked if he planned on retiring anytime soon

1036. Howard Cosell: "Red, how is it that the Lakers could do to you what they did two nights ago and you come back to do what you did tonight?"
  Red Holzman: "It's that old adage about it being a new game."
—Coach Red Holzman after the Knicks' 113–99 Game 7 victory over the Lakers after the Lakers had won Game 6 135–113 with Wilt Chamberlain gathering 45 points and 27 rebounds

1037. "They kept saying, 'You wait until Julius gets here. You wait for Julius.' And I said, 'Who's Julius, I'm in the NBA. What do I care about Julius?'"
—Tom Hoover Jr., a 6'9" center for the New York Knicks and other teams, 1963–1969, recalling the arrival of Julius Erving at Rucker Park in Harlem. Hoover and others soon found out the answer to his question, as Erving did leaps and dunks none had ever seen at the famous court. People sat on the roof and hung from trees in numbers never seen before. "It wasn't even standing room only," recalled Hall of Famer Tiny Archibald. "People could not see enough of him."

1038. "When I say I'm going home to play ball, that basically means by myself. I never like to scrimmage against people. Even when I was young, I liked to practice by myself or with no more than one other guy. I always felt I could get more work done by myself than with three or four other guys standing around. The way I see it, if I put two hours in by myself, then someone who is working out with someone else has to put in four hours in order to beat me. That's the way I've always gone about it. That summer [1983] I went home and put in more hours than I ever had before, I couldn't get that Milwaukee mess out of my mind."
—Larry Bird, explaining his training philosophy, after being swept by the Bucks in the 1983 playoffs

Larry Bird

1039. "Give it to Wilt, give it to Wilt."
—The chant from a crowd of just 4,124 fans in Hershey, Pennsylvania, as Chamberlain neared 100 points against the Knicks on March 2, 1962. He set records for field goals (36), free throws (28), points in a quarter (31), and points in a half (59).

1040. "Toward the end of his career, we learned a lot from playing against him. Everything we were, we became because of the Celtics. Just as everything Chicago became is because of us." Who said it?
A. Isiah Thomas   B. Joe Dumars   C. Dennis Rodman   D. Bill Laimbeer
Answer: A. Isiah Thomas, on facing Larry Bird and the Celtics.

1041. "I remember when he came here 13 years ago. He looked like a country bumpkin. But when you looked into his eyes you could see he was no dummy. He knew what he wanted in life and what he needed to get there."
—Red Auerbach, Celtics GM, in August 1992, speaking about Larry Bird

1042. "Bob Pettit was usually in the top three or four in rebounds. He could hit the 18-footer, play in the low box. He wasn't super quick, but he could shoot coming off a pick. He was the master of the half-inch. Bob Pettit was still the best forward I ever saw play the game." Who said it?
A. Bill Russell   B. Frank Ramsey   C. Jim Loscutoff   D. Tommy Heinsohn
Answer: D. Heinsohn, Hall of Fame Celtic power forward, describes the best scorer and rebounder on the St. Louis Hawks, the only team to beat the Celtics between 1957 and 1966.

1043. "It was a once in a lifetime thing. I wasn't sure what was happening. I was getting the ball, shooting it, and it was going in. The whole thing happened in a blur, and I don't remember the individual shots or plays. I just knew I wanted the ball because I didn't think they could do anything to stop me."
—Bob Pettit, recalling Game 6 of the 1958 Finals, when his 50 points clinched the series for the Hawks and he set a record for points in a regulation playoff game

1044. "[Julius] Erving was doing Jordan-like things before Jordan. Erving went into a higher orbit than Baylor did. Had there been cable TV when he was in his prime, we would have witnessed him more often. At that time, he looked like a soaring apparition with a big afro." Who said it?

A. Mel Daniels   B. Bobby Jones   C. Bill Melchionni   D. Mike Gminski

Answer: D. The 14-year forward for the Nets and other teams was recalling Erving's play above the rim.

1045. "He was a forerunner of the high-flying acts. I was in the sixth grade and my coach took us to the old Madison Square Garden to see the Christmas tournament. Baylor was playing for Seattle and had one of those 48-point afternoons. I went home and told my father, 'I just saw the greatest basketball player I've ever seen.'" Who said it?

A. Jerry West   B. Matt Guokas   C. Bob Pettit   D. Oscar Robertson

Answer: B. The 76ers guard, recalling seeing Elgin Baylor for the first time.

1046. Before a Game 7 in the Finals, which coach said, "Well Howard, we'd rather win with him than without him."

A. Red Holzman   B. Red Auerbach   C. Tom Heinsohn
D. Butch van Breda Kolff

Answer: A. On May 8, 1970, Knicks coach Red Holzman didn't know if Willis Reed would be able to play. ABC broadcaster Howard Cosell asked, "Could you win without him?" Reed played 27 minutes and held Wilt Chamberlain at bay, and the Knicks won 113–99, thanks to 36 points, 19 assists, and seven rebounds from guard Walt Frazier.

1047. "He also had 25 rebounds that game. [Owner] Bob Short gave every member of the team cufflinks with a '71.' We all wore them proudly."

—Hot Rod Hundley, Elgin Baylor's teammate, recalling November 15, 1960, the night Baylor scored 71 points against the Knicks

1048. "That guy is the greatest basketball player I have even seen. He makes the most difficult plays look routine."

—Bob Pettit, Hall of Fame forward for the St. Louis Hawks, describing Elgin Baylor

1049. "I am sure that no man can derive more pleasure from money or power than I do from seeing a pair of basketball goals in some out of the way place."
—James Naismith, inventor of the game, 1891

1050. "Ok, I'll put it like this: I doubt we will see another All-American basketball athlete who is a Rhodes Scholar." Who said it?
A. Dick Barnett B. Jerry Lucas C. Kareem Abdul-Jabbar
D. Willis Reed
Answer: C. Abdul-Jabbar, himself an author, describing Knicks forward Bill Bradley.

1051. "The invention of basketball was not an accident. It was developed to meet a need. Those boys simply would not play 'Drop the Handkerchief.'"
—Dr. James Naismith, inventor of the game in 1891, recalling a game in which whatever player from two teams picks up a handkerchief off the floor first has won for his team

1052. "I took two dribbles over the halfcourt line and let it fly as the buzzer went off, and the damn ball went in the hole. It was one of those once-in-a-lifetime deals." Who said it?
A. Jim Pollard B. Bob Harrison C. Slater Martin D. Vern Mikkelsen
Answer: B. Harrison, describing his game-winning shot to win Game 1 of the 1950 Finals to give the Minneapolis Lakers a 68–66 victory over the Syracuse Nationals. The Lakers won the series in six games.

1053. "God played today disguised as Michael Jordan."
—Larry Bird, after Jordan scored 63 points in a double-overtime game in the first round of the 1986 playoffs

1054. "With a two- or three-on-one against Jordan, you don't have a guaranteed score. He can block the shot, steal the pass or force you to take the jump shot."
—Hall of Fame coach Hubie Brown on the defensive prowess of Michael Jordan

1055. "[Magic] Johnson obviously had the court vision and total awareness. He was a consummate half-court and full-court guard. He was the greatest end-to-end guard ever, ran classic fast breaks and expanded and adapted his game to become an all-around scorer."
—Bob Ryan, *Boston Globe*

1056. "When you're young, you don't need that warmup to play. I looked at it the other way. The opponents would be tired, and I could get a few cheap baskets. And from another aspect I could see how the game was developing and whether we needed offense or defense at that moment."
—John Havlicek recalling his rookie season when he was a sixth man coming off the bench

1057. "He can run the floor and catch and finish. It has also helped him no end that he plays with John Stockton."
—Hall of Fame coach Jack Ramsay on Karl Malone

1058. "He has said that he is most proud of his rebounding. I get a kick out of it when they call some guy the greatest rebounder ever. If Charles wasn't as good a scorer as he is and was just a rebounder, he would get 17, 18, or 19 a game. If he just wanted to pass the ball, he would get seven, eight or nine assists. He's an all-around player."
—76ers guard Matt Guokas

1059. "Tonight Oscar Schmidt will be the 13th best player on the floor."
—Charles Barkley, playing for the Dream Team, prior to playing Brazil with their legend Schmidt

1060. "Jerry West was the captain of the all-clutch team. And it's there in print to see. He was consistent, glorious even in defeat."
—Dr. Jack Ramsay, Hall of Fame coach, recalling the Lakers guard in the playoffs

1061. "McHale was the surest two points in the history of basketball. He is the only 60-80 man in the history of basketball." Who said it?

A. Larry Bird   B. Robert Parish   C. Kurt Rambis   D. Bob Ryan

Answer: D. Ryan, writer for the *Boston Globe*, describing a 60-80 player as one who shot 60 percent from the field and 80 percent from the free throw line. McHale shot .604 from the field and .836 from the free throw line in 1987.

1062. "Our failure to win a championship can be traced to not getting Dolph Schayes. We've always missed because we never had a man who could average about 20 points over a season." Who said it?

A. Dick McGuire   B. Al McGuire   C. Sweetwater Clifton   D. Ned Irish

Answer: D. Ned Irish, owner of the Knicks, lamenting that Dolph Schayes went to Syracuse of the NBL for $7,500 a year as a rookie and that the Knicks, of the BAA, couldn't offer more than $5,000. The Knicks made the Finals from 1951 through 1953 but never won.

1063. "Losing the use of my right hand was the best break I ever got. I developed a left-handed shot that made me twice as effective."

—Dolph Schayes, on turning himself into an ambidextrous shooter after his right wrist was broken in 1952

1064. "The guy had legitimate 25- to 30-foot range. You could add five points to his career average if they had the 3-point shot back then."

—Alex Hannum, Syracuse coach, on Dolph Schayes's perimeter shooting

1065. "Schayes was something of a revolutionary, because he was the first big man to develop a great outside shot. Few people—and I wasn't one of them—believed that anyone taller than 6'6" had the coordination and the fine touch to be consistent beyond 20 feet. Until Schayes came along, all the good long shooters were little weasels who couldn't get close to the basket enough to score in any other way." Who said it?

A. Tom Gola   B. Carl Braun   C. Bob Cousy   D. Joe Lapchick

Answer: D. Lapchick, Knicks coach, on the long-range bombing of Dolph Schayes.

1066. "We didn't know if Moses would be able to adjust to our team because he came from Houston, a team that did not run. . . . We also had some apprehension about whether Doc and Moses could play together. After two days in training camp, we had our answer. Moses would make the adjustments. He did everything we asked of him. Each player changed his game. Doc concentrated more on defense and passing than scoring. Moses concentrated more on defensive rebounding and making the outlet pass rather than carrying the load with his offensive rebounding. This had happened with Wilt Chamberlain as well. Wilt had averaged 50 points a game one season and had achieved all the individual goals. But [in 1967] he showed he was a complete basketball player, making passes, blocking shots and rebounding."
—Billy Cunningham, as coach of the 1983 Sixers and as teammate of Chamberlain on the 1967 Sixers

1067. "The truth is that it [the shot] came by accident. I was playing in the Catholic Club League in Philadelphia and our games were on a slick dance floor. When I tried to hook, my feet would go out from under me. I jumped; the ceiling was low and I had to throw line drives; I just never changed." Who said it?
A. Neil Johnston   B. Paul Arizin   C. Joe Fulks   D. Andy Phillip
Answer: B. Arizin, Warriors Hall of Fame guard on perfecting his jump shot.

1068. "Someone would bring up Arizin's jump shot, and we'd try to figure out how to stop him. 'What makes him click?' someone would ask. 'A jump shot,' would be the answer. 'Let's stop it,' we'd say, but we knew we couldn't. His jump shot was perfect. There was no stopping it."
—Dolph Schayes, Nationals forward, recalling team meetings before facing the Warriors' Paul Arizin

1069. [Dave] DeBusschere and Gus [Johnson] had tremendous battles; you had to be there to see it. They were warriors; they didn't look to the referees for calls, never got mad at each other. They were so fierce that they were the epitome of professionalism." Who said it?
A. Bill Bradley   B. Phil Chenier   C. Wes Unseld   D. Jack Marin
Answer: B. Chenier, guard and three-time All-Star for the Bullets who played with Johnson and against DeBusschere.

1070. "People should not forget Dave DeBusschere. Today he would be a monster because he had three-point range. Each of the Knicks' forwards had more range than their guards, Frazier, Barnett, and Monroe. He was a rugged rebounder and personified the power forward of that time."
—Bob Ryan, *Boston Globe*

1071. "One of the best shooters ever in the history of basketball."
—Wilt Chamberlain on Jerry Lucas from his book, *A View from Above*

1072. "I feel like we can come back."
—Stephen Curry, when asked about the Warriors future after their six-game defeat to the Lakers in the 2023 Western Conference semifinals.

1073. "There was a time when the surest way to get two points was to throw the ball to Bernard King. There was a stretch when he was a devastating offensive course. First of all, he had an astonishingly quick release. He caught the ball and shot. It was like [Pittsburgh second baseman] Bill Mazeroski getting rid of the ball to complete the double play. I don't know how he did it. He had explosive quickness off the blocks and was a great fast-break finisher. He had that relentless, phenomenal truly high-level desire to score two points. Issel had it. Barry had it. It was an obsession in life at that moment to get the ball in the basket."
—Bob Ryan, *Boston Globe*

1074. "The bitch won't get 40 against us." Who said it?
A. M. L. Carr   B. Larry Bird   C. Kevin McHale   D. Cornbread Maxwell
Answer: D. Maxwell, referring to Bernard King, after King had scored 213 points in a five-game series against the Pistons in 1984, averaging 43 for the series. But King scored 46 in one game of the conference finals, won by the Celtics in seven games. King averaged 29 for the series.

1075. "The best thing about that Series was saying good-bye to Bernard King for the rest of the playoffs. During those playoffs, Bernard was automatic—the best scoring machine I have ever seen. His release was amazing. You'd always seem to come within a fraction of getting a piece of his shot, but he wouldn't allow it. He always had you off balance. And the Knicks seemed to go to him every time. We tried to get the ball out of his hands, but we always seemed to be late."
—Larry Bird, in *Drive*, recalling the seven-game conference finals in 1984 against the Knicks

1076. "I'm the first player to make the All-Star game without an ACL [anterior cruciate ligament]."
—Bernard King, playing in the 1991 All-Star Game after suffering a massive knee injury in March 1985

1077. "We sometimes need adversity to fathom our true depths."
—Pat Riley, from his book *The Winner Within: A Life Plan for Team Players*

1078. "Hayes was a real power player. He could post up and hit the jumper. He was an All-NBA First Team player three times, and second three times. He was also a 12-time All-Star."
—Former coach Hubie Brown on Hall of Fame power forward Elvin Hayes

1079. "He was just a phenomenal athlete, faster than people realize. He was a greyhound running the court and could score inside and out. I still remember one of his great feats, getting 35 rebounds against the Knicks at Madison Square Garden, an awesome display of toughness. He had one of the quickest jumpers."
—Guard Butch Beard on Elvin Hayes

1080. "Kevin McHale was the best back to the basket post man ever. Among all players not just forwards."
—Jack Ramsay, coach of the 1977 championship Trail Blazers

1081. [Oscar Robertson] was tough on defense too. He had great physical strength and was big and strong and would beat guys up."
Who said it?
A. Connie Hawkins   B. Walt Frazier   C. Dave Bing   D. Jerry West
Answer: A. Hawkins, Hall of Fame forward.

1082. "If there is one complete player, it's Oscar Robertson. He does everything flawlessly and is a perfectionist."
—Lenny Wilkens, Hall of Fame guard and coach

1083. "You can make a case for several guys being the greatest ever. There's Russell, Kareem, Bird, Erving, Magic, Oscar and Jordan."
—Red Auerbach, who coached the Celtics to eight straight titles from 1959 through 1966, whose list makes rival Wilt Chamberlain conspicuous by his absence

ROOKIES

1084. What two players tied for most assists in a game by a rookie?
A. Bob Cousy   B. Dick McGuire   C. Nate McMillan   D. Ernie DiGregorio
Answer: C and D. DiGregorio was playing for the Buffalo Braves when he recorded 25 assists (and 20 points and nine rebounds) on January 1, 1974, in a 120–119 win against the Blazers. McMillan posted his 25 playing for the Sonics against the Clippers in a 124–112 victory on February 23, 1987.

1085. True or False? Manute Bol holds the record for blocks in a game by a rookie.
Answer: True. The Bullets' 7'7" center from the Sudan got 15 blocks on January 25, 1986, against the Hawks.

1086. Who set records for points per game, total points, and total rebounds in his rookie season?
A. Kareem-Abdul Jabbar   B. Shaquille O'Neal   C. Tim Duncan   D. Wilt Chamberlain
Answer: D. Wilt averaged 37.6 points and tallied 2,707 points and 1,941 rebounds in his 1960 rookie season.

1087. True or False? Wilt Chamberlain holds the record for rebounds in a game by a rookie.
Answer: True. Chamberlain notched 45 rebounds for the Philadelphia Warriors against the Syracuse Nationals on February 6, 1960. He also scored 44 points as the Warriors won 129–126. Dolph Schayes logged 39 points and 24 rebounds and Red Kerr posted 35 points and 24 rebounds for the Nationals.

1088. Who won Player of the Week honors in his first week in the league?
A. David Robinson   B. Shaquille O'Neal   C. Tim Duncan
D. Magic Johnson
Answer: B. He also averaged 23.4 points, 13.9 rebounds (second in the league), and 3.53 blocks (second) in his first season as he rode his size and incredible quickness to immediate stardom.

1089. Whose team went from 21-61 before he arrived to 56-26 the year he arrived?
A. David Robinson   B. Patrick Ewing   C. David Cowens
D. Wilt Chamberlain
Answer: A. The plus 35 wins for the San Antonio Spurs in 1989–90 owed largely to Robinson's averages of 24.3 points, 12 rebounds, and 3.89 blocks per game. He also was selected to the All-Defensive Second Team and won Rookie of the Year honors.

1090. Who won Rookie of the Year and MVP in 1969?
A. Elvin Hayes   B. Willis Reed   C. Wes Unseld   D. Bob Rule
Answer: C. Like Chamberlain before him, Unseld took both honors. He finished second to Chamberlain with 18.2 rebounds. He beat out Elvin Hayes 53–25 in Rookie of the Year voting and beat Willis Reed 53–18 in first place votes for MVP honors.

1091. What rookie won the All-Star Game MVP in 1960?
A. Gene Shue   B. Wilt Chamberlain   C. Tom Gola   D. Jack Twyman
Answer: B. Playing in Convention Hall in Philadelphia in his rookie season, Wilt scored 23 points and had 25 rebounds to give the East a decisive 125–115 victory.

1092. Which of the following players led the league in scoring in their rookie season?
A. Elvin Hayes   B. Wilt Chamberlain   C. Oscar Robertson
D. George Mikan   E. Paul Arizin
Answer: A, B, and D. As a rookie with the San Diego Rockets in 1969, Hayes used his turnaround jumper to win the scoring title for the only time in his 15-year career with a 28.4 mark. Dominating the pivot with the Philadelphia Warriors, Chamberlain snatched his first of seven straight scoring crowns, posting 37.6 during the 1960 season. Mikan logged 28.3 points per game to earn his first of three straight titles for the Lakers in 1949.

1093. How many rookies in NBA history have averaged 30 points in a game?

A. None   B. One   C. Two   D. Three

Answer: D. Wilt Chamberlain (37.6, 1960), Walt Bellamy (31.6, 1960), and Oscar Robertson (30.5, 1961).

SEASONS

1094. In 2000, did any of the following players dish out 20 assists in a game?
A. Mookie Blaylock   B. Nick Van Exel   C. Sam Cassell   D. John Stockton
Answer: B. The man called "Nick at Nite" gave fans excitement for 12 years in the NBA. The 6'1" guard averaged a career best nine assists during the 1999–2000 campaign and got 20 for the Nuggets in a 115–100 victory against the Hawks on November 8, 1999.

1095. True or False? No player recorded 20 assists in a game during the 2021–22 75th anniversary season.
Answer: True. The highest total was 19, reached by Darius Garland and twice by Chris Paul.

1096. True or False? None of the following players got 30 rebounds in a game during the 50th anniversary of the NBA.
A. Patrick Ewing   B. Dennis Rodman   C. Ervin Johnson
D. Charles Barkley
Answer: False. Playing for the Rockets, Barkley led the pack with a 33-rebound game in a 110–95 victory against the Suns on November 2, 1996.

1097. Rank the leaders in regular-season rebounds in 2022.
A. Rudy Gobert   B. Nikola Jokić   C. Clint Capela   D. Domantas Sabonis
Answer: 1-A, 14.7 rebounds per game; 2-B, 13.8; 3-D, 12.1; 4-C, 11.9.

1098. True or False? Hakeem Olajuwon has the most seasons averaging four or more blocks per game.

Answer: False. Mark Eaton holds the record with four times. Olajuwon did it three times.

1099. What was the last year an NBA player averaged 25 rebounds per game for the season?

A. 1960   B. 1962   C. 1966   D. 1997

Answer: B. Wilt Chamberlain averaged 25.65 rebounds per game over 80 games of the 1961–62 season. That was the same year that he averaged 50.4 points per game.

1100. True or False? None of the six international players picked for the 75th Anniversary Team in 2021 were on the 50th Anniversary Team in 1996.

Answer: False. Patrick Ewing (Jamaica) and Hakeem Olajuwon (Nigeria) were on the 50th Anniversary Team.

SIZE

1101. Rank the following players by height.
A. Tacko Fall   B. Manute Bol   C. Mark Eaton   D. Gheorghe Muresan
Answer: 1-B and D, 7'7"; 2-A, 7'5"; 3-C, 7'4". Muresan is tied with Bol for the tallest player in NBA history.

1102. Who had nine blocks to help the Bullets to a one-point playoff win in the 1986 playoffs?
Answer: The 7'7" center Manute Bol did it against the 76ers in Game 1 of the first round of the Eastern Conference playoffs. The Sixers had four future Hall of Famers in the game: Julius Erving, Charles Barkley, Maurice Cheeks, and Bobby Jones.

1103. Match the players with their heights.
1. Bob Cousy   2. Allen Iverson   3. Isiah Thomas   4. Calvin Murphy
A. 6'1"   B. 6'0"   C. 5'9"
Answer: 1-A; 2-B; 3-A; 4-C.

1104. Stephen Curry, a 6'3" point guard, won the Finals MVP in 2022. Who was the only Finals MVP shorter than Curry?
Answer: The 6'1" Isiah Thomas won the 1990 Finals MVP, as the Pistons beat the Trail Blazers in five games. Thomas averaged 27 points, seven assists, and five rebounds for the series.

1105. Match the players with their heights.
1. Larry Bird   2. Dirk Nowitzki   3. Kevin McHale   4. Carmelo Anthony
A. 6'7"   B 7'0"   C 6'9"   D 6'10"
Answer: 1-C; 2-B; 3-D; 4-A.

STREAKS AND FEATS

1106. Name the only franchise that had two winning streaks of 19 or more consecutive games.

A. Warriors   B. Bucks   C. Lakers   D. Celtics

Answer: C. The 1972 Lakers won a record 33 straight games on the way to 69 wins, another record at the time, and grabbed an NBA championship. The 2000 Lakers, with the duo of Kobe Bryant and Shaquille O'Neal, won 19 in a row before losing to the Wizards 109–102 on March 16, 2000. The Lakers won 67 and lost 15 and captured their first of three consecutive titles.

1107. What players have the most consecutive 30-point games since 2000?

A. Tracy McGrady   B. Kobe Bryant   C. Kevin Durant
D. Shaquille O'Neal   E. James Harden

Answer: 1-E, 32 consecutive 30-point games, running from December 2018 through February 2019; 2-B, 16, between January and February 2002; 3-A, 14 consecutive from March to April 2003; 4-C, 12 games, January 2014; 5-D, 11 games, March–April 2001.

1108. Name the last team to win three consecutive Finals.

A. Celtics   B. Spurs   C. Bulls   D. Lakers

Answer: D. The Lakers, led by Shaquille O'Neal and Kobe Bryant, won three straight from 2000 to 2002.

1109. Who is the most recent player to win three consecutive scoring titles?

Answer: James Harden led from 2018 through 2020.

1110. True or False? Stephen Curry holds the record for most field goals made in a quarter.
Answer: False. His teammate Klay Thompson hit 9-of-9 in a quarter against the Kings on January 23, 2015. He also holds the record for most made in a quarter without a miss.

1111. Who is the most recent player to win three consecutive rebounding titles?
Answer: Andre Drummond led from 2018 through 2020.

1112. How many different NBA cities have won three consecutive NBA championships?
A. Two   B. Three   C. Four   D. Five
Answer: C. The Minneapolis Lakers won three straight titles from 1952 through 1954. The Celtics won eight in a row from 1959 through 1966. The Chicago Bulls won three in a row twice: from 1991 to 1993 and 1996 to 1998. The Los Angeles Lakers ran off three straight titles from 2000 through 2002.

1113. Who holds the record for most consecutive games with at least one 3-pointer?
Answer: On June 13, 2022, Stephen Curry broke a streak of 233 consecutive games with at least one 3-point field goal. He shot 0-for-9 in the Warriors' 104–94 win over the Celtics in Game 5 of the Finals.

1114. Name the team that won 20 straight in 1971 to tie an NBA record.
A. Celtics   B. Knicks   C. Bucks   D. Lakers
Answer: C. The Bucks' 20-game streak, following a 16-game win streak earlier in the season, began on February 6, 1971, with a 116–85 drubbing of the San Francisco Warriors. They lost to the Bulls 110–103 on March 9, 1971. The streak tied the Washington Capitols, who finished the 1947–48 season with five victories and then won 15 more to begin the 1948–49 season.

1115. Name the second team in NBA history to start a season 2-10 and still reach the conference finals.
A. Celtics   B. Timberwolves   C. Nuggets   D. Lakers
Answer: D. The 2023 Lakers, repeating the feat of the 1977–78 Seattle SuperSonics.

1116. Since 2000, how many different players have won back-to-back MVP awards?

A. One   B. Two   C. Three   D. Four   E. Six

Answer: E. Tim Duncan (2002–3), Steve Nash (2005–6), LeBron James (2009–10 and 2012–13), Stephen Curry (2015–16), Giannis Antetokounmpo (2019–20), and Nikola Jokić (2021–22).

1117. After the Celtics won eight straight titles from 1959 through 1966, what team was next to win consecutive championships?

A. Bucks   B. Lakers   C. 76ers   D. Knicks

Answer: B. It was more than 20 years before a repeat champion arose with the Lakers in 1987 and 1988.

1118. Name the player with the most consecutive points in a regular-season game.

A. Carmelo Anthony   B. Wilt Chamberlain   C. Bob Pettit
D. LeBron James

Answer: A. Anthony was hotter than a two-dollar pistol against the Timberwolves on December 10, 2008. He scored 26 consecutive points.

1119. Which of the following teams did not lose a game from November to January?

A. Warriors   B. Heat   C. Rockets   D. Lakers

Answer: D. The Lakers edged the Bullets 110–106 on November 5, 1971. They won 33 consecutive games before losing to the Bucks 120–104 on January 9, 1972. Fifty-one seasons later their record stands.

TEAM HISTORY

1120. Match the cities with their 1947 teams.
1. Washington   2. Toronto   3. Chicago   4. Pittsburgh
A. Huskies   B. Stags   C. Ironmen   D. Capitols
Answer: 1-D; 2-A; 3-B; 4-C.

1121. Match the cities with their team names from the 1949–50 season.
1. Syracuse   2. Anderson   3. Tri-Cities   4. Sheboygan
A. Packers   B. Blackhawks   C. Nationals   D. Red Skins
Answer: 1-C; 2-A; 3-B; 4-D.

1122. Name the player whose scoring average went down three consecutive years from 30 to 33 years old.
A. James Harden   B. Kevin Durant   C. Kyrie Irving   D. Stephen Curry
Answer: A. After averaging 34.3 in 2020, Harden fell to 24.6 the next year, then to 22 in 2022, and to 21 in 2023.

1123. Which of the following players holds the Trail Blazers' record for points per game in a season?
A. Damian Lillard   B. Clyde Drexler   C. Kiki Vandeweghe
Answer: A. Lillard averaged 32.2 points per game in 2023.

1124. What member of the Warriors was inducted into the Hall of Fame in 2014?
A. Chris Mullin   B. Mitch Richmond   C. Marques Johnson
D. Tim Hardaway
Answer: B. The 6'5" shooting guard was a six-time All-Star. He had a 14-year career, winning Rookie of the Year (1989) and averaging 21 points over his career.

1125. True or False? The Bulls' all-time leader in field goal percentage is Artis Gilmore.
Answer: True. Gilmore shot .587 with the Bulls from 1977 through 1982.

1126. Who played before his hometown fans to win the All-Star MVP in 1987?
A. James Worthy   B. Rolando Blackman   C. Moses Malone
D. Tom Chambers
Answer: D. Sonics forward Chambers scored 34 points to lead the West to a 154–149 overtime victory at the Kingdome in Seattle before 34,275 fans. Malone had 27 points and 18 rebounds.

1127. True or False? At least two of the following teams won championships: Rochester Royals, Cincinnati Royals, Kansas City–Omaha Kings, Kansas City Kings.
Answer: False. Playing in just the league's third Finals, the Rochester Royals won the franchise's only title in the 1950–51 season.

1128. Rank the Suns' all-time leaders in points scored.
A. Alvan Adams   B. Walter Davis   C. Devin Booker   D. Kevin Johnson
Answer: 1-B, 15,666 points; 2-A, 13,910; 3-D, 12,747; 4-C, 12,688.

1129. True or False? The Trail Blazers have won more games than they have lost.
Answer: True. Beginning play in 1970, the Blazers have won 2,238 games and lost 1,960 for an impressive winning percentage of .533.

1130. True or False? It took the Trail Blazers a decade before they played .500.
Answer: False. The Blazers were under .500 for six seasons. In their seventh they finished 49-33 (.598) and beat the 76ers in six games to win the championship.

1131. True or False? The Knicks have never lost 20 consecutive games.
Answer: False. When their leading scorer Bernard King went down with a knee injury in March of 1985 that sidelined him for two years, the Knicks hit the skids. They lost 20 straight from March 23, 1985. They didn't win again until they beat the Suns 103–92 on November 12 of the next season.

1132. Which of the following Mavericks, who played a minimum of five years with the team, is the all-time leader in rebounds per game?
A. Tyson Chandler   B. Popeye Jones   C. James Donaldson
D. Roy Tarpley
Answer: D. The 6'11" power forward from Michigan played all six of his seasons with the Mavericks and averaged 10 rebounds per game.

1133. Name the player who holds the Grizzlies record for assists per game in a season.
A. Mike Bibby   B. Ja Morant   C. Greg Anthony   D. Jason Williams
Answer: A. Bibby, the second pick overall for the Vancouver Grizzlies in the 1998 draft, posted 8.4 assists per game in 2001.

1134. Rank the following Lakers in blocks per game in a season.
A. Shaquille O'Neal   B. Elmore Smith   C. Kareem Abdul-Jabbar
Answer: 1-B, Smith blocked 4.9 per game in 1974, the first year that blocks statistics were kept (Smith also owns the eighth best season in Laker history); 2-C, 4.1 blocks in 1976 (Jabbar owns six of the top 10 Lakers' totals); 3-A. 3.0, 2000 (O'Neal owns the sixth and ninth best regular-season marks for the Lakers).

1135. True or False? The Hawks have a winning all-time record.
Answer: False. Since 1949 the Hawks have posted a 2,891-2,964 mark (.494).

1136. Name the Lakers' all-time leader in games, minutes, free throws, steals, and points.
A. Wilt Chamberlain   B. Jerry West   C. Magic Johnson
D. Kareem Abdul-Jabbar   E. Kobe Bryant
Answer: E. Bryant played 20 years with the Lakers and is the leader in those categories and more.

1137. Which team made the most 3-point shots in a game?
A. Pacers   B. Warriors   C. Bucks   D. Heat
Answer: C. The Bucks made 29 3-pointers against the Heat in a 144–97 victory on December 29, 2020. They made 29 of 51 and Jrue Holiday led the way by making six of 10 3-pointers.

1138. True or False? No Pelican has ever won Defensive Player of the Year.
Answer: True.

1139. True or False? No Pelican has ever won a scoring title.
Answer: True.

1140. What team had four All-Stars in the 2006 contest?
A. Lakers   B. Heat   C. Celtics   D. Pistons
Answer: D. Reserves Ben Wallace, Rasheed Wallace, Richard Hamilton, and Chauncey Billups, who had 15 points and seven assists, helped the East to a 122–120 victory.

1141. True or False? The Magic have played in one Finals.
Answer: False. They played in two. They were swept by the Rockets in the 1995 Finals and lost 4–1 to the Lakers in the 2009 Finals.

1142. True or False? Only one member of the Indiana Pacers scored 20,000 points.
Answer: True. Reggie Miller scored 25,279 points.

1143. True or False? The Magic have at least one 60-win season.
Answer: True. In 1996 they won 60 and lost 22 but were swept out of the conference finals by the Bulls.

1144. True or False? Reggie Miller is the Pacers' all-time leader in points per game.
Answer: False. Miller ranks ninth in Pacers' history with 18.2 points per game. Victor Oladipo is first with 20.6 and Miller's fellow Hall of Famers George McGinnis and Mel Daniels are ahead of him with 19.6 and 19.4 points, respectively.

1145. True or False? The Cavaliers have just one career 20-point scorer.
Answer: False. They have had four: LeBron James, 27.2 points per game; World B. Free, 23; Kyrie Irving, 21.6; Collin Sexton, 20.

1146. In how many games did the Pistons win their first 1980s Finals?
A. Four   B. Five   C. Six   D. Seven
Answer: A. They beat the Lakers in four in 1989.

1147. Name the team with the most players in the 2013 All-Star Game.
A. Lakers   B. Heat   C. Clippers   D. Knicks
Answer: B. The Heat trio of starters were LeBron James, Dwyane Wade, and Chris Bosh. They couldn't offset the West and MVP Chris Paul, who posted 20 points and 15 assists in a 143–138 win.

1148. Who played more games for the Hornets than any other player?
A. Kemba Walker   B. Muggsy Bogues   C. Dell Curry   D. Cody Zeller
Answer: C. Curry played 701 games for the franchise.

1149. Which of the following expansion teams has won more games than they lost in their history?
A. Pelicans   B. Timberwolves   C. Heat   D. Grizzlies
Answer: C. Through the 2023 season the Heat has won 1,475 and lost 1,328 for a percentage of .526.

1150. Which team had the most players in the All-Star Game in 1998?
A. Bulls   B. Lakers   C. Pacers   D. Magic
Answer: B. In Jordan's last year with the Bulls, Kobe Bryant, Shaquille O'Neal, Eddie Jones, and Nick Van Exel played for the Lakers. It wasn't enough as Jordan scored 23 and gathered eight assists, six rebounds, and three steals in a 135–114 romp by the East at Madison Square Garden.

1151. Who holds the Hawks' season record for points per game?
A. Trae Young   B. Bob Pettit   C. Dominique Wilkins
Answer: B. St. Louis Hawks forward Bob Pettit's 31.1 points per game in 1967 edged Wilkins's 30.7 points in 1988.

1152. Who holds the Hawks' record for rebounds per game?
A. Tree Rollins   B. Bill Bridges   C. Kevin Willis   D. Bob Pettit
Answer: Pettit holds the Hawks' top six marks in rebounds per season and eight of the top 10. His best was 20.1 rebounds per game in 1961.

1153. Who played more games for the Celtics than any other player?
A. Robert Parish   B. Paul Pierce   C. Kevin McHale   D. John Havlicek
Answer: D. "Hondo" played 1,270 games in his magnificent 16-year career, from 1963 to 1978.

1154. Against which team do the Hawks have a winning record all-time?
A. Celtics   B. Bucks   C. Lakers   D. Pistons   E. Knicks
Answer: E. The Hawks have won 200 and lost 188 against the Knicks, a .515 winning percentage.

1155. Rank the Celtics by who had the most triple-doubles.
A. Bob Cousy   B. Larry Bird   C. John Havlicek   D. Rajon Rondo
Answer: 1-B, 59; 2-A, 33; 3-C, 31; 4-D, 22.

1156. Who holds the Celtics record for minutes in a season?
A. Antoine Walker   B. Dave Cowens   C. Bill Russell   D. John Havlicek
Answer: D. Havlicek holds the top mark with 3,698 minutes in 1972, which averages to 45.1 minutes per game.

1157. Which Celtics have averaged 30 points a game for a season?
A. Jayson Tatum   B. Isaiah Thomas   C. Larry Bird   D. John Havlicek
Answer: A. Forward Jayson Tatum is the only Celtic to average 30 for a season, averaging 30.1 in 2023.

1158. True or False? Bill Russell owns the top 10 seasons in rebounds per game for the Celtics.
Answer: True. Amazingly, Russell has the best 10 seasons, with averages ranging from 21.7 (1967) to 24.7 (1964).

1159. Name the team with the longest losing streak.
A. Charlotte Bobcats   B. Cleveland Cavaliers   C. Philadelphia 76ers
D. Milwaukee Bucks
Answer: B and C. Two teams tied for this dubious honor. The Cavaliers lost 26 straight in 2010–11 and the 76ers in 2013–14.

1160. Name the team with the most turnovers in a season.
A. Knicks   B. Bobcats   C. Hawks   D. Nuggets
Answer: D. The 1976–77 Nuggets committed 2,011 turnovers, averaging 24.5 per game for the season. Still, they finished 50-32, making it to the second round of playoffs on the strength of the league's best defense.

1161. True or False? The Brooklyn Nets have gone by four names since their beginning.
Answer: True. They were the New Jersey Americans of the ABA in 1968, winning 36 and losing 42. They played eight more seasons as the New York Nets in the ABA, from 1969 through 1976, winning championships in 1975 and 1976. They were the New York Nets in 1977, their first year in the NBA. They played 35 years as the New Jersey Nets, from 1978 through 2012. They have been the Brooklyn Nets since 2013.

1162. True or False? None of the following teams have all-time records above .600.
A. Celtics   B. Spurs   C. Lakers   D. Bulls
Answer: False. Since 1976 the Spurs have won 2,283 games and lost 1,512 for a splendid percentage of .602. The Lakers (.592) and the Celtics (.590) barely fell short.

1163. What one-time Braves' All-Star came off the bench to lead the East to a come from behind victory in the 1978 All-Star Game?
A. Bob McAdoo   B. Randy Smith   C. Marvin Barnes   D. Jim McMillian
Answer: B. A 6'3" physical specimen from Bellport, New York, Smith played just 29 minutes but contributed 27 points, seven rebounds, and six assists to lead the East back. From 1972 to 1982 he played in a then record 906 consecutive games.

1164. What Denver Nuggets star won the MVP of the 1979 All-Star Game?
A. Bo Ellis   B. Dan Issel   C. George McGinnis   D. David Thompson
Answer: D. One of seven players for the West who scored in double-digits, Thompson logged a game-high 25 points, enough to offset 29 points from Julius Erving and 26 from George Gervin to help his squad to a 134–129 victory.

1165. Which team had the most road losses in a season?
A. Kings   B. 76ers   C. Pelicans   D. Bullets
Answer: A. The Kings won one and lost 40 on the road and were 24-17 at home during the 1990–91 season. Oddly, the Kings' 25-57 mark was an improvement over their 23-59 mark of the year before, despite the road mark.

1166. True or False? The Lakers had three players on the 2002 All-Star team.
Answer: False. Kobe Bryant was the only Laker on the West, but it was enough. He had 31 points to grab the MVP award and lead the West to a 135–120 win.

1167. Name the team with the most 50-win seasons.
A. Spurs   B. Lakers   C. Celtics   D. Suns
Answer: C. The Celtics edge the Lakers 35 to 33 in 50-win seasons. More impressive is that the Spurs, a newer team that began in 1977, has 27 50-win seasons.

1168. What two teams are tied for the fewest road losses in a season?
A. 1996 Bulls   B. 2016 Warriors   C. 1972 Lakers   D. 1997 Bulls
Answer: B and C. The Warriors posted a 34-7 mark in their 73-9 season in 2016. The historic 1972 Lakers, who ran off 33 straight wins, were 31-7 on the road and they were 2-1 in games played on a neutral court.

1169. True or False? No Nugget averaged 30 points per game in a season.
Answer: False. Spencer Haywood averaged 30 in 1970 for the ABA Nuggets, then known as the Rockets. The record holder for the NBA Nuggets is Alex English at 29.8.

1170. Which team had the fewest home wins in history?
A. Providence Steamrollers   B. Hornets   C. Kings
D. Fort Wayne Pistons
Answer: A. The Steamrollers didn't steam roll too many teams. They finished the 1948 season with a 6-42 mark (.125). Playing at the Rhode Island Auditorium, their home, they won two and lost 18. On the road they fared better with a 4-24 mark.

1171. True or False? One of the following franchises has an all-time record above .500.
A. Hawks   B. Nets   C. Hornets   D. Cavaliers
Answer: False. All of these teams lost more games than they have won.

1172. What team had the largest margin of victory in Game 7 of a Finals?
A. Hawks   B. Celtics   C. Lakers   D. Bulls
Answer: B. The Celtics topped the Hawks 122–103 for a record 19-point margin of victory in a Game 7 on April 9, 1960. The Celtics outscored the Hawks 41–23 in the second quarter to take control of the game.

1173. Who holds the Hawks' record for rebounds per game?
A. Tree Rollins   B. Bill Bridges   C. Kevin Willis   D. Bob Pettit
Answer: D. Pettit holds the Hawks' top six marks in rebounds per season and eight of the top 10. His best was 20.1 rebounds per game in 1961.

1174. When the Celtics were 40-1 at home in 1986, which was the only team to defeat them?
A. Trail Blazers   B. Lakers   C. Knicks   D. 76ers
Answer: A. The Blazers, who finished only 40-42, throttled the 67-15 Celtics 121–103 on December 6, 1985, handing them their only home loss.

1175. True or False? Prior to 2023, the Nuggets had beaten the Lakers in a playoff series at least once.
Answer: False. They met three times and the Lakers won all three.

1176. Match the Knicks with their post-career positions.
1. Bill Bradley   2. Dick Barnett   3. Dave DeBusschere   4. Walt Frazier
A. Sports management professor   B. ABA commissioner   C. US senator   D. Broadcaster
Answer: 1-C; 2-A; 3-B; 4-D.

1177. Who was the second straight Celtic to win the MVP in the 1982 All-Star Game?
A. Kevin McHale   B. Tiny Archibald   C. Robert Parish   D. Larry Bird
Answer: D. Bird flew high, registering 19 points, 12 rebounds, and five assists in a 120–118 victory over the West. Tiny Archibald won it in 1981.

1178. Name the team that had the All-Star Game MVP, league MVP, and won the title in 1983?
A. 76ers   B. Celtics   C. Lakers   D. Sonics
Answer: A. Julius Erving scored 25 in the East's 132–123 victory in the All-Star contest. Moses Malone averaged 24.5 points and 15.3 rebounds to take the league MVP and won the Finals MVP. The 76ers swept the Lakers in the Finals.

1179. Rank the Timberwolves by their career marks in assists per game.
A. Ricky Rubio   B. Terrell Brandon   C. Pooh Richardson
D. Stephon Marbury
Answer: 1-B and D, 8.3 assists per game; 3-A, 8.1; 4-C, 8.0.

1180. What Rockets' starter won the All-Star MVP in the 1985 contest?
A. Moses Malone   B. Hakeem Olajuwon   C. Ralph Sampson
D. Calvin Natt
Answer: C. The 7'4" center was most deserving, posting 24 points and 10 rebounds and leading the West to a 140–129 victory.

1181. Name the team(s) that have won more games than they lost all-time.
A. Knicks   B. Hawks   C. 76ers   D. Wizards
Answer: C. Since 1949 the 76ers have posted a record of 3,054 wins and 2,805 losses for an all-time percentage of .521.

1182. The only player who averaged 20 points, 20 rebounds, and shot 60 percent for a season played on what team?
A. Lakers   B. Celtics   C. 76ers   D. Warriors
Answer: C. Wilt Chamberlain averaged 24 points, 24 rebounds, seven assists, and shot 68 percent for the field in 1967.

1183. When the Lakers won the NBA title in 1972, how many years had it been since they won their last one?
A. 10 years   B. 13 years   C. 18 years   D. 21 years
Answer: C. The last time the Lakers had won was in 1954 when they beat the Syracuse Nationals in seven games.

Kareem Abdul-Jabbar

1184. The second player to make 500 career three-point shots in the playoffs plays for what team?
A. Lakers   B. 76ers   C. Warriors   D. Celtics
Answer: C. Klay Thompson connected for his 500th against the Lakers in the 2023 playoffs. Aside from the milestone, Thompson shot dreadfully, hitting just 34 percent of his shots for the series.

1185. True or False? The Knicks have had a Rookie of the Year since 2000.
Answer: False. The Knicks' most recent player to win the award was Mark Jackson in 1988.

1186. True or False? The Celtics haven't had a Rookie of the Year winner in this century.
Answer: True. Larry Bird was the last Celtic to take the award in 1980.

1187. True or False? Cleveland has two Rookies of the Year since 2000.
Answer: True. LeBron James won in 2004 and Kyrie Irving won in 2012.

1188. Rank the Clippers for the single-season bests in minutes per game.
A. Elmore Smith   B. Bob McAdoo   C. Bob Kauffman   D. Billy Knight
Answer: 1-B, 43.2 minutes per game, 1975 (McAdoo also owns second and third place for his 1974 and 1976 seasons); 4-C, 41.6, 1972; 5-A, 40.8; 6-D, 40.7, 1978.

1189. True or False? Shaquille O'Neal ranks among the top four Lakers in rebounds per game for a season.
Answer: False. Wilt Chamberlain holds the record with 21.1 rebounds per game during the 1969 season. (He also holds the third through fifth highest averages). Elgin Baylor ranks second with 19.8 boards per contest in 1961 (and holds the seventh, eighth, and 10th highest totals). Kareem Abdul-Jabbar ranks sixth with 16.9 in 1976. George Mikan posted the ninth best season with 14.1 in 1953.

1190. Which of the following numbers have been retired by the Hawks?
A. 9   B. 21   C. 23   D. 44   E. 55   F. All of the above
Answer: F. A, Bob Pettit; B, Dominique Wilkins; C, Lou Hudson; D, Pete Maravich; E, Dikembe Mutombo. Ted Turner has a retired jersey with no number, since he is honored as the owner.

1191. Before they were the Philadelphia 76ers, what was the name of the franchise?
Answer: The Syracuse Nationals. They were the Nationals from the 1949–50 season through the 1962–63 season. They started as the 76ers in the fall of 1963 and won 34 and lost 46 that season.

1192. True or False? Charlotte has never won 60 or more games in a season.
Answer: True. Their best season was a 54-28 mark in 1997. Coached by Hall of Fame center Dave Cowens, they lost in the first round of the playoffs to the Knicks.

1193. True or False? The Philadelphia 76ers, including their predecessor the Syracuse Nationals, won more Finals than they lost.
Answer: False. They have played in eight Finals, winning two and losing six.

1194. Who holds the Knicks record for points in a game?
A. Carl Braun   B. Richie Guerin   C. Bernard King   D. Carmelo Anthony
Answer: D. Anthony broke Bernard King's 60-point record when he logged 62 points against the Charlotte Bobcats at Madison Square Garden on January 24, 2014. The Knicks won 125–96. Anthony connected on 23 of 35 field goal attempts, including six for 11 from the 3-point line, and made all 10 of his free throws.

1195. What three Mavericks players share their top 10 season scoring averages?
Answer: Luka Dončić owns the highest mark with a 32.4 average in 2023 and four of the top 10 averages. Mark Aguirre and Dirk Nowitzki each own three of the top 10 marks.

1196. Which of the following Bulls were never selected for the NBA All-Defensive First Team?
A. Jerry Sloan   B. Michael Jordan   C. Scottie Pippen
D. Dennis Rodman   E. All were selected
Answer: E. Inducted to the Hall of Fame as a coach in 2009, Sloan was first, earning the distinction in 1969, 1972, 1974, and 1975.

1197. Which of the following Knicks were never selected for the NBA All-Defensive First Team?
A. Walt Frazier   B. Dave DeBusschere   C. Willis Reed   D. Michael Ray Richardson   E. Tyson Chandler   F. All were selected
Answer: F. The three-time steals leader and most recent honoree was Chandler, who was selected in 2013.

1198. Name the only team to make the playoffs in every season of the 1970s.
A. Knicks   B. Bullets   C. Lakers   D. Bucks   E. Celtics
Answer: B. From 1969, the Baltimore Bullets (who became the Washington Bullets in 1974) made the playoffs through 1980, which is 12 straight seasons. They won the Finals in 1978.

1199. Magic Johnson owns the top nine season averages in assists per game with the Lakers. Who holds the 10th spot?
A. Norm Nixon   B. Jerry West   C. LeBron James   D. Kobe Bryant
Answer: C. James had the 10th best total with 10.2 in 2020.

1200. Name the Clipper who set the league record for consecutive games played.
A. Randy Smith   B. Chris Paul   C. Norm Nixon   D. Ernie DiGregorio
Answer: A. Called the "Iron Man," Smith played an astounding 906 consecutive games from 1972 through 1982. The shooting guard from Bellport, New York, was known for his blazing speed from one end of the court to the other. He played his last game with the Clippers on March 13, 1983. He requested to be waived to play for a contender in 1983 and missed a game while waiting to clear waivers. A. C. Green broke his record in 1997 and finished with 1,192 straight games.

1201. How many teams have won 20 or more consecutive games?
A. One   B. Three   C. Five   D. Six
Answer: C. The Lakers won 33 straight in the course of the 1971 to 1972 season. The Heat threatened that record with a 27-game winning streak during the 2012–13 season. The 73-win Warriors won 24 in a row in the 2015–16 season. The Rockets ran off 22 in a row during the 2007–8 campaign. The Bucks won 20 straight during their 1970–71 championship season.

1202. True or False? At least one Bulls team made it to the Finals without Michael Jordan.

Answer: False. Since their first season in 1966–67, the Bulls made it to six Finals and won all of them. They reached the conference finals several times without Jordan, but never a Finals.

1203. True or False? The Mavericks have played in just one NBA Finals.

Answer: False. The 62-20 Mavericks lost in six to the Heat in 2006. But they avenged that lost by beating the Heat in six in 2011.

1204. What was the inaugural season of the Grizzlies?

A. 1994   B. 1995   C. 1997   D. 1998

Answer: B. The Vancouver Grizzlies had a most forgettable first season, finishing 15-67 (.183).

1205. Rank the Nuggets' all-time leaders in points per game.

A. Alex English   B. Allen Iverson   C. Larry Jones   D. Carmelo Anthony

Answer: 1-A, 25.9 points per game; 2-B, 25.6; 3-C, 25.4; 4-D, 24.8.

1206. True or False? The Knicks won more Finals than they lost.

Answer: False. They won two (1970, 1973) and lost six (1951, 1952, 1953, 1972, 1994, and 1999).

1207. In which season did the Knicks win their most games?

A. 1969   B. 1970   C. 1993   D. 1994

Answer: B and C. The Knicks were 60-22 in both seasons. The 1970 team finished the job, winning the Finals in seven games. In 1993 they lost in the conference finals to the Bulls, who went on to win the championship.

1208. Rank the Rockets by their highest points per game in a season.

A. Hakeem Olajuwon   B. Elvin Hayes   C. Moses Malone
D. James Harden

Answer: 1-D, 36.1 in 2019 (Harden also owns the second, fourth, fifth, and sixth marks for points per game); 3-C, 31.1, 1982; 7-B, 28.7, 1971 (Hayes also holds the record for eighth best); 9-A, 27.8, 1995.

1209. True or False? The Bucks were the fastest expansion team to win a championship.

Answer: True. The Bucks finished 66-16 in 1971 and swept the Baltimore Bullets in the Finals; it was just their third season. They were 27-55 in 1969, then leapt to 56-26 in 1970, Kareem Abdul-Jabbar/Lew Alcindor's first year.

1210. True or False? The Thunder, who began in 2008 after being the Seattle SuperSonics, have lost more Finals than they have won.

Answer: True. The SuperSonics/Thunder have played in four Finals total: the Sonics in 1978, 1979, and 1996 and the Thunder in 2011. The Sonics beat the Washington Bullets in 1979 but the two teams lost the other three.

1211. True or False? The Hawks never won 60 games in a season.

Answer: False. They turned the trick once in 2015, winning 60 and losing 22. That team made it to the Eastern Conference finals before losing four straight games to the Cavaliers.

1212. True or False? The Bucks have won more NBA Finals than they've lost.

Answer: True. The Bucks swept the Bullets in the Finals in 1971. They lost to the Celtics in seven games in 1974. In 2021 they topped the Suns in six games.

1213. True or False? Minnesota reached the .500 mark at least once in its first five years in the league.

Answer: False. They didn't reach .500 until their ninth season in 1998.

1214. True or False? Minnesota did reach a conference finals in the playoffs.

Answer: True. In 2004 they played against the Lakers in a conference finals. They lost in six games.

1215. What Bucks player owns the season record for points per game?

Answer: Kareem Abdul-Jabbar averaged 34.8 points during the 1972 season. He holds the Bucks' top four scoring averages and six of the top 10.

1216. Rank the Rockets by all-time free throw percentage.
A. Calvin Murphy   B. Kevin Martin   C. Chris Paul   D. Rick Barry
Answer: 1-D, .941; 2-B, .895; 3-A and C, .892.

1217. How many cities have the Pistons played in?
A. One   B. Two   C. Three   D. Four
Answer: B. The Pistons played in Fort Wayne from 1948 through 1957
and moved to Detroit for the 1957–58 season.

**1218. True or False? The Pistons have won three championships in
their history.**
Answer: True. The Fort Wayne Pistons lost back-to-back Finals in 1955
and 1956. They made up for those defeats by winning consecutive titles
in 1989 and 1990. They won again in 2004.

1219. Rank the Pistons for points per game in a season.
A. George Yardley   B. Dave Bing   C. Jerry Stackhouse
D. Kelly Tripucka
Answer: 1-C, the shooting guard averaged a career best 29.8 points per
game in the 2000–1 season; 2-A, 27.8, 1958; 3-B, 27.1, 1968 (and 27 in
1971); 4-D, 26.5, 1983.

**1220. With the 1969 All-Star Game played at the Baltimore Civic Center,
what Bullets trio scored in double figures?**
A. Kevin Loughery   B. Earl Monroe   C. Wes Unseld   D. Gus Johnson
Answer: B, C, and D. The virtuoso guard Monroe started and led with 21
points. Reserves Gus Johnson and Wes Unseld registered 13 and 11 points.
The East won 123–112 behind game MVP Oscar Robertson's 24 points.

1221. Name the Thunder's leading scorer in the 2012 Finals.
A. Russell Westbrook   B. James Harden   C. Kendrick Perkins
D. Kevin Durant
Answer: D. Durant not only led all Thunder scorers, but also surpassed
all Heat scorers, including LeBron James and Dwyane Wade. Durant
connected on 54.8 percent of his shots and averaged 30.6 points, six
rebounds, and two assists in a five-game loss to the Heat.

1222. Rank the Pistons by who logged the most games played.
A. Vinnie Johnson   B. Isiah Thomas   C. Joe Dumars   D. Bill Laimbeer
Answer: 1-C, 1,018 games; 2-B, 979; 3-D, 937; 4-A, 798.

Kevin Durant

1223. True or False? The Houston Rockets lost more NBA Finals than they won.
Answer: False. The Rockets lost Finals to the Celtics in 1981 and 1986. They won two in the next decade, beating the Knicks in 1994 and the Magic in 1995.

1224. True or False? The Warriors have won more Finals than they have lost.
Answer: True. The Warriors have been in 11 Finals and have won six and lost five. They won the first final ever played, beating the Chicago Stags in 1947. They lost the second one, losing to the Baltimore Bullets in 1948.

1225. Name the player who has the Warriors' career record for points per game.
Answer: Wilt Chamberlain is far and away the team leader, averaging 41.5 points per game in his six seasons as a Warrior.

1226. Rank the following players by how many times they led the league in points per game with the Warriors.
A. Joe Fulks   B. Paul Arizin   C. Wilt Chamberlain   D. Neil Johnston
Answer: 1-C, six times, 1960–1965; 2-D, three times, 1953–1955; 3-A and B, twice, Fulks, 1947, 1948, Arizin, 1952, 1957.

1227. Rank the Mavericks all-time leaders in points per game.
A. Mark Aguirre   B. Kristaps Porziņģis   C. Luka Dončić
D. Dirk Nowitzki
Answer: 1-C, 27.6 points per game; 2-A, 24.6; 3-D, 20.7; 4-B, 20.0.

1228. Rank the following Bulls for the team record in rebounds per game in a season.
A Tom Boerwinkle   B. Charles Oakley   C. Artis Gilmore
D. Dennis Rodman
Answer: 1-D, 16.1, 1997 (he also holds the second and third best seasons); 2-A, 13.8, 1971; 3-B and C, 13.1, Oakley, 1987, Gilmore, 1978.

1229. Rank the Bulls' "iron men" for minutes per game in a season.
A. Ron Mercer   B. Jalen Rose   C. Michael Jordan   D. Bob Love
Answer: 1-D, 43 minutes per game, 1971; 2-A, 41.6, 2001; 3-B, 40.9, 2003; 4-C, 40.4, 1988.

1230. Name the three Celtics and future Hall of Famers drafted in the 1956 draft.

A. Sam Jones   B. Tom Heinsohn   C. Bill Russell   D. K. C. Jones

Answer: B, C, and D. Russell was drafted second overall, Heinsohn sixth, and Jones 14th. Russell was inducted into the Hall of Fame as a player in 1975 and as coach in 2021. Heinsohn made the Hall as a player in 1986 and a coach in 2014. Jones was inducted in 1989.

1231. How many times did the Heat team with LeBron James and Dwyane Wade go to the Finals?

A. Two   B. Three   C. Four   D. Five

Answer: C. The Heat went to four consecutive Finals from 2011 through 2014. They lost to the Mavericks in 2011, and then beat the Thunder in 2012 and the Spurs in 2013. They lost to the Spurs in 2014.

1232. Rank the Bulls in all-time points per game.

A. Zach LaVine   B. Jalen Rose   C. Bob Love   D. Michael Jordan
E. DeMar DeRozan

Answer: 1-D, 31.5; 2-E, 26.2; 3-A, 24.4; 4-B, 21.4; 5-C, 21.3.

1233. Name the Bulls player who made the All-Star team four times in five years from 1970 to 1974.

A. Guy Rodgers   B. Jerry Sloan   C. Bob Love   D. Bob Boozer
E. Chet Walker

Answer: E. Small forward Chet "The Jet" averaged 22 points over those years and was a workhorse, missing just 11 contests in 410 games. They went to the conference finals in 1974, losing to the Bucks in four straight, and in 1975, losing in seven to the Warriors.

1234. Rank the all-time assist leaders for the Cavaliers.

A. LeBron James   B. Foots Walker   C. Mark Price
D. Terrell Brandon   E. John Bagley

Answer: 1-A, 6,228 assists; 2-C, 4,206; 3-E, 2,311; 4-D, 2,235; 5-B, 2,115.

1235. True or False? No Cavalier has ever averaged 10 assists per game in a season.

Answer: False. Andre Miller averaged 10.9 assists per game in 2002.

1236. True or False? No Cavalier besides LeBron James has ever won an MVP.
Answer: True. James won consecutive MVPs with the Cavs in 2009 and 2010.

1237. Name the first Cavalier to compete in an All-Star Game.
A. Bingo Smith   B. Lenny Wilkens   C. John Johnson   D. Butch Beard
Answer: C. Playing in the Cavs' inaugural season, Johnson, a 6'7" forward who led the team with 16.1 points per game, was the team's first All-Star in 1971. He played just two minutes in the game, didn't attempt a shot, and was credited with an assist.

1238. Name the first Cavaliers player to be inducted into the Hall of Fame.
Answer: Lenny Wilkens. He played two of his 15 seasons with Cleveland in 1973 and 1974 and was inducted into the Hall of Fame as a player in 1989.

1239. True or False? The Hornets have never won 50 games in a season.
Answer: False. The Hornets won 50 three times in four years. They were 50-32 with coach Allan Bristow in 1994–95. Then Dave Cowens led them to 54 wins in 1997 and 51 in 1998, riding the scoring of Glen Rice and scoring and rebounding of Anthony Mason to back-to-back playoff seasons.

1240. Name the Hornets' record holder for assists per game in a season.
A. Brevin Knight   B. Baron Davis   C. Muggsy Bogues   D. Kemba Walker
Answer: C. The 5'3" Bogues averaged 10.7 assists in 1990. He owns the second and third best team marks in assists per game and seven of the top 10 marks.

1241. Name the Hornets' record holder for points per game in a season.
A. Kemba Walker   B. Kelly Tripucka   C. Larry Johnson   D. Glen Rice
Answer: D. Rice poured in 26.8 points per game in 1997.

1242. Rank the Hornets' all-time leaders in rebounds.
A. Gerald Wallace   B. Larry Johnson   C. Cody Zeller   D. Emeka Okafor
Answer: 1-D, 3,516 rebounds; 2-B, 3,479; 3-A, 3,398; 4-C, 2,824.

1243. True or False? The Bulls clinched all three of their 1991–1993 titles on the road.
Answer: False. They won the 1991 and 1993 titles on the road, but they beat the Trail Blazers at home to win the 1992 championship.

1244. True or False? Only two players have eight or more assists per game for their Nets careers.
Answer: True. Jason Kidd averaged 9.1 assists per game and Stephon Marbury averaged 8.1.

1245. Which of the following Hawks is not in the Hall of Fame?
A. Cliff Hagan   B. Lou Hudson   C. Bob Pettit   D. Dominique Wilkins
E. Bill Bridges
Answer: E. Bridges averaged double digits in points and rebounds for 12 consecutive seasons. The forward from Hobbs, New Mexico, was also a three-time All-Star. But he was not inducted to the Hall of Fame.

1246. How many locations have the Hawks played in?
A. Two   B. Three   C. Four   D. Five
Answer: C. For the 1949–50 and 1950–51 seasons, they were the Tri-Cities Blackhawks, a location along the Mississippi River, next to Moline and Rock Island, Illinois, and Davenport, Iowa. They played in Milwaukee from the 1951–52 season through the 1954–55 season. They won their only title in 1958 while playing in St. Louis from 1955–56 through 1967–68. They have played in Atlanta since the 1968–69 season.

1247. True or False? No Hawks player ever averaged 20 rebounds per game in a season.
Answer: False, Bob Pettit averaged 20.3 in 1960–61.

1248. Rank the following Hawks in assists per game in a season.
A. Mookie Blaylock   B. Doc Rivers   C. Trae Young
Answer: 1-B, 10.0, 1986–87; 2-A, 9.7, 1993–94; 3-C, 9.7, 2021–22; and 9.4, 2020–21.

1249. Rank the following Hawks in all-time points scored.
A. Dominique Wilkins   B. Lou Hudson   C. Cliff Hagan   D. Bob Pettit
Answer: 1-A, 23,292 points; 2-D, 20,880; 3-B, 16,049; 4-C, 13,447.

1250. Who coached the Hawks to their only world championship?
A. Harry Gallatin   B. Ed Macauley   C. Andy Phillip   D. Alex Hannum
Answer: D. In his second season as an NBA coach, Hannum coached the
St. Louis Hawks to their only title in 1957–58. They beat the Celtics in six
games. The year before he led them to a seven-game Finals against the
Celtics, who prevailed in double overtime.

**1251. Name the Celtic who holds the record for assists per game for
a season.**
A. Bob Cousy   B. Tiny Archibald   C. Rajon Rondo   D. Sherman Douglas
Answer: C. Amazingly, Rondo holds the team's four highest marks, all
set between 2010 and 2012. He peaked during the 2010–11 season with
11.7 assists per game.

1252. Rank the Celtics' all-time leaders in points.
A. Paul Pierce   B. Larry Bird   C. Robert Parish   D. John Havlicek
E. Kevin McHale
Answer: 1-D, 26,395 points; 2-A, 24,021; 3-B, 21,791; 4-C, 18,245; 5-E, 17,335.

1253. Rank the Celtics by total rebounds.
A. Dave Cowens   B. Larry Bird   C. Bill Russell   D. John Havlicek
E. Robert Parish
Answer: 1-C, 21,620 rebounds; 2-E, 11,051; 3-A, 10,170; 4-B, 8,974; 5-D,
8,007.

1254. Rank the Celtics by total assists.
A. Paul Pierce   B. Bob Cousy   C. Larry Bird   D. Rajon Rondo
E. John Havlicek
Answer: 1-B, 6,935 assists; 2-E, 6,114; 3-C, 5,695; 4-D, 4,474; 5-A, 4,305.

**1255. Name the former NBA player who coached the Nets to two ABA
championships.**
A. Lou Carnesecca   B. Kevin Loughery   C. York Larese
D. Max Zaslovsky
Answer: B. A shooting guard out of Cardinal Hayes High in Brooklyn,
Loughery played most of his 11 NBA seasons with the Baltimore Bullets.
At the height of the Bullets-Knicks rivalry, he posted scoring averages
of 22.6 and 21.9 points per game in 1969 and 1970. He coached the Nets
to three consecutive seasons of 55 or more wins and ABA titles in 1974
and 1976.

1256. Name the Nets' record holder in assists per game over a season.
A. Kevin Porter   B. Jason Kidd   C. Kenny Anderson
D. Stephon Marbury   E. Deron Williams
Answer: A. The 6-foot Chicago native known as "The Conductor" led the league in assists per game four times, topping out with 13.4 for Detroit in 1979. In 1978 he averaged 10.8 for the New Jersey Nets, which remains a franchise record.

1257. What one-time winner of Comeback Player of the Year honors holds the Nets' record for steals in a season?
A. Brian Taylor   B. Micheal Ray Richardson   C. Eddie Jordan
D. Kendall Gill
Answer: B. "Sugar Ray" averaged three steals in 1985 to set the team mark. That was the same year that the 20-year-old guard won the Comeback award with 20.1 points and 8.2 rebounds a game.

1258. Rank the Nets' career leaders in assists.
A. Bill Melchionni   B. Kenny Anderson   C. Jason Kidd
D. Deron Williams
Answer: 1-C, 4,620 assists; 2-A, 3,044; 3-B, 2,363; 4-D, 2,078.

1259. Rank the SuperSonics/Thunder in career assists per game.
A. Gary Payton   B. Lenny Wilkens   C. Russell Westbrook
D. Slick Watts
Answer: 1-B, 9 assists per game; 2-C, 8.4; 3-A, 7.4; 4-D, 6.7.

1260. Rank the Nets' career leaders in points per game.
A. Julius Erving   B. Vince Carter   C. Kyrie Irving   D. Rick Barry
E. Kevin Durant
Answer: 1-D, 30.6; 2-E, 29; 3-A, 28.2; 4-C, 27.1; 5-B, 23.6.

1261. Name the player who leads the Nets in career points.
A. Vince Carter   B. Buck Williams   C. Brook Lopez
D. Richard Jefferson
Answer: C. Lopez scored 10,444 points, beating Williams by just four points. The 7-foot center from North Hollywood known as "Splash Mountain" split nine seasons with the Nets between New Jersey and Brooklyn and averaged 20+ points per game four times.

1262. Name the player who owns the Nets' record for points in a game.
A. Vince Carter   B. Bernard King   C. Julius Erving   D. Kyrie Irving
Answer: D. Irving tallied 60 points in a 150–108 victory over the Magic on
March 15, 2022.

**1263. Which was the only 1990s team to fall behind three games to two
but still win the Finals?**
A. Spurs   B. Bulls   C. Rockets   D. Pistons
Answer: C. In 1994 the Rockets fell behind three to two but won Games
6 and 7 at home against the Knicks.

**1264. Name the team which holds the record for most consecutive
playoff wins.**
A. Warriors   B. Celtics   C. Bulls   D. Spurs
Answer: A. The Warriors won 15 straight playoff contests in the spring of
2017. They won their first 121–109 against the Trail Blazers on April 16 and
didn't lose until June 9, when the Cavaliers topped them 137–116.

1265. Which of the following Knicks is not in the Hall of Fame?
A. Dick Barnett   B. Willis Reed   C. Bernard King   D. Bill Bradley
E. Dave DeBusschere
Answer: A. As a guard for the Nationals, Lakers, and Knicks, Barnett
averaged 20 or more points six times in his 15-year career and played on
two championship teams with the Knicks in 1970 and 1973.

1266. Which of the following Celtics is not in the Hall of Fame?
A. Tommy Heinsohn   B. Ed Macauley   C. Satch Sanders
D. K. C. Jones   E. Chris Ford
Answer: E. The Celtics coach and guard known for making the first
3-point shot in October 1979 is not in the Hall of Fame.

1267. Name the player who leads the Nets in most 40-point games.
A. Rick Barry   B. Julius Erving   C. Kevin Durant   D. Kyrie Irving
Answer: B. Erving posted an amazing 21 regular-season 40-point games
for the Nets from 1974 to 1976. He also scored 45 and 48 back-to-back
to begin the 1976 ABA Finals, which the Nets won in six games over the
Nuggets. Those were the last games played in the ABA.

Julius Erving

1268. How many points did the Lakers' starting five average for the 1971–72 season?

Answer: 98.4 points per game. The Lakers won 69 games and topped their opponents by an average of 12.4 points per game.

1269. What team has never won three road games in a single series in franchise history?

A. 76ers   B. Knicks   C. Celtics   D. Lakers

Answer: A. The most recent occurrence was in the 2023 Eastern Conference semifinals, when the 76ers didn't win a third road game and were blown out in Game 7 in Boston, 112–88.

1270. Name the most recent 76er to win MVP and be named to the first All-NBA team in the same season.
A. Wilt Chamberlain   B. Hal Greer   C. Billy Cunningham   D. Joel Embiid
Answer: D. Embiid did it in 2023. The center averaged 33 points and 10 rebounds.

1271. Besides Bob McAdoo, what Braves player averaged over 20 per game in the 1976 Eastern Conference semifinals?
A. Ernie DiGregorio   B. Randy Smith   C. Jim McMillian
D. John Shumate
Answer: B. The "Iron Man" with blazing speed, Smith posted a superb 23 points, 7.7 assists, and 6.6 rebounds. It was the misfortune of the exciting Braves to be knocked out of the 1974 and 1976 playoffs by the championship Celtics, both times in six games. Smith and McAdoo (26.8 points for the series) met their match in Dave Cowens (24.5 points, 17.8 rebounds) and Jo Jo White (23.8 points), as Boston won all four of its home games.

1272. Name the Magic player who holds the team record for points in a season.
A. Shaquille O'Neal   B. Tracy McGrady   C. Dwight Howard
D. Anfernee Hardaway
Answer: 1-B, 2,407 points, 2003. All told, McGrady owns four of the top 10 points totals. O'Neal posted three, Howard two, and Hardaway one.

1273. Which of the following is the newest team in the NBA?
A. Hornets   B. Pelicans   C. Grizzlies   D. Clippers
Answer: B. The New Orleans Pelicans played their inaugural season as the New Orleans Hornets in 2002–3.

1274. Rank the Raptors' all-time leaders in points.
A. Kyle Lowry   B. Chris Bosh   C. DeMar DeRozan   D. Vince Carter
Answer: 1-C, 13,296 points; 2-A, 10,540; 3-B, 10,275; 4-D, 9,420.

TRADES

1275. Name the year that Anthony Davis was traded to the Lakers.
A. 2018   B. 2019   C. 2020   D. 2021
Answer: B. In exchange for Davis the Pelicans received Lonzo Ball, DeAndre Hunter, Brandon Ingram, Josh Hart, and draft picks.

1276. Name the year that Wilt Chamberlain was traded to the Lakers.
A. 1966   B. 1967   C. 1968   D. 1969
Answer: C. On July 9, 1969, Chamberlain was traded from the 76ers to the Lakers for Darrall Imhoff, Jerry Chambers, and Archie Clark.

1277. In what season was Oscar Robertson traded to the Bucks?
A. 1969   B. 1970   C. 1971   D. 1972
Answer: B. Robertson was traded to the Bucks on April 21, 1970, for Charlie Paulk and Flynn Robinson. The trade helped the Bucks to win a title in 1971.

1278. What year was Kareem Abdul-Jabbar traded to the Lakers?
A. 1975   B. 1976   C. 1977   D. 1978
Answer: A. Abdul-Jabbar said, "It's just that socially and culturally I don't fit in Milwaukee." The comment was made in March 1975 and three months later he was traded with Walt Wesley to the Lakers for Elmore Smith, Brian Winters, and rookies Dave Meyers and Junior Bridgeman.

1279. What year was Dennis Rodman traded to the Chicago Bulls?

A. 1994 B. 1995 C. 1996 D. 1997

Answer: B. On October 2, 1995, he was traded to the Bulls for center Will Perdue. Rodman won three consecutive rebounding titles as the Bulls won three consecutive championships.

1280. In what year did the Hornets trade Kobe Bryant?

A. 1996 B. 1997 C. 1998 D. 1999

Answer: A. On July 11, 1996, the Hornets dealt their draft pick to the Lakers for center Vlade Divac. Bryant teamed with Shaquille O'Neal and went on to win five titles and an MVP with the Lakers.

1281. In what year was LeBron James traded to Miami?

A. 2009 B. 2010 C. 2011 D. 2012

Answer: B. The Cavaliers got five future draft picks when James took "his talents to South Beach" in July of 2010.

1282. In what year was Russell Westbrook traded to Houston?

A. 2019 B. 2020 C. 2021 D. 2022

Answer: A. Talk about a blockbuster. Having averaged three triple-doubles in a row from 2016 to 2018, Westbrook headed to Houston in exchange for Chris Paul, two future first-round picks, and two other pick swaps.

1283. In what year was Charles Barkley traded to the Suns?

A. 1991 B. 1992 C. 1993 D. 1994

Answer: B. On June 17, 1992, the Sixers traded Barkley to the Suns in exchange for Jeff Hornacek, Andrew Lang, and Tim Perry. In his first season with the Suns, Barkley averaged 25.6 points, 12.2 rebounds, and a personal best 5.1 assists. He earned the Most Valuable Player award and carried the Suns to the Finals, where they lost to the Bulls in six games.

1284. Who did the SuperSonics get in a trade for Scottie Pippen?

A. Gerald Henderson B. Mark Jackson C. Olden Polynice
D. Jeff Sanders

Answer: C. On June 22, 1987, they swapped Pippen along with a 1989 first-round pick (later Jeff Sanders) for Polynice, a 1988 second-round pick, and a 1989 first-round pick (B. J. Armstrong was later selected).

1285. In what year was Clyde Drexler traded to the Rockets?
A. 1993   B. 1994   C. 1995   D. 1996
Answer: C. On February 14, 1995, Drexler was traded with Tracy Murray to the Rockets and the Blazers received Otis Thorpe in return. With Drexler and Olajuwon teammates as they had been in Houston during their college days, the Rockets won a second straight title.

1286. In what year was Dave DeBusschere traded to the Knicks?
A. 1968   B. 1969   C. 1970   D. 1971
Answer: A. A Piston player-coach, DeBusschere was the power forward the Knicks sought. On December 19, 1968, they moved Walt Bellamy, a future Hall of Fame center, and guard Howard Komives. Now Willis Reed would be the center and Walt Frazier the guard who ran the Knicks. The future Hall of Famers and DeBusschere led the Knicks to titles in 1970 and 1973.

1287. In what year was Kevin Love traded to Cleveland?
A. 2013   B. 2014   C. 2015   D. 2016
Answer: B. It's a tough question since Love helped the Cavaliers to win their first title in 2016. But he was traded to them from Minnesota in 2014 in exchange for Anthony Bennett, Andrew Wiggins, and Thaddeus Young.

1288. In what year did the Knicks acquire Carmelo Anthony?
A. 2009   B. 2010   C. 2011   D. 2012
Answer: C. Anthony came with some of his mates, including Chauncey Billups, Anthony Carter, Sheldon Williams, and Corey Brewer. Denver received a haul in exchange, including Wilson Chandler, Raymond Felton, Danilo Gallinari, Timofey Mozgov, three future New York picks, and a pick swap with the Timberwolves in 2016.

1289. In what year was James Harden traded to the 76ers from the Nets?
A. 2019   B. 2020   C. 2021   D. 2022
Answer: D. Less than 13 months after he was traded to the Nets from the Rockets, Harden was out the door with Paul Millsap, in exchange for Seth Curry, Andre Drummond, Ben Simmons, and two future first-round picks.

1290. In what season was Earl Monroe traded from the Bullets to the Knicks?

A. 1970   B. 1971   C. 1972   D. 1973

Answer: B. Months after the Bullets were swept by the Bucks in the Finals, "The Pearl" was traded to the Knicks for Mike Riordan, Dave Stallworth, and cash on November 10, 1971.

1291. When was Elvin Hayes traded to the Bullets?

A. 1969   B. 1970   C. 1971   D. 1972

Answer: D. He had won a scoring title in his rookie season with the San Diego Rockets, won a rebounding title in his second season, and would go on to be a 12-time All-Star. After the 1972 season, his fourth, he said "I was expected to make a winner out of a team which didn't have the ability." He was dealt to the Bullets for Jack Marin. Bullets coach Gene Shue was optimistic. "With a change in location, we hope Elvin will have a change in attitude."

1292. In what year was Kevin Garnett traded to the Celtics?

A. 2006   B. 2007   C. 2008   D. 2009

Answer: B. After winning rebounding titles and perennial All-Star placements with the Timberwolves, Garnett was traded on July 31, 2007. The power forward brought to the Wolves Ryan Gomes, Gerald Green, Al Jefferson, Theo Ratliff, Sebastian Telfair, and two 2009 first-round draft picks. In his first season in Boston, the team finished 66-16 and beat the Lakers in six games in the 2008 Finals.

TWO-SPORT STARS

1293. Name the players who were drafted in at least two sports.
A. John Havlicek   B. Gene Conley   C. Dave Winfield   D. Brian Jordan
Answer: All of them. A, basketball and football; B, baseball and
basketball; C, basketball and baseball; D, baseball and football.

1294. What Minneapolis Lakers draft pick in 1958 played two pro sports?
A. Gene Conley   B. Steve Hamilton   C. Frank Howard
D. Chuck Connors
Answer: B. The 6'6" small forward was the ninth pick overall and
would play a total of 82 games over the 1959 and 1960 seasons. With
teammate Elgin Baylor he played in the 1959 Finals, but the Lakers were
swept by the Celtics. He played seven of his 12 baseball seasons with the
Yankees, where he became famous for his "folly floater" bloop pitch out
of the bullpen.

**1295. Which of the following players won titles in basketball and
baseball?**
A. Dave DeBusschere   B. Gene Conley   C. Chuck Connors
D. Danny Ainge
Answer: B. "Long Gene," the 6'8" forward, and pitcher, won titles
with the Celtics in 1959, 1960, and 1961, having already won with the
Milwaukee Braves in 1957.

1296. How many players with the following names played baseball and basketball?
A. Reggie Jackson   B. Jackie Robinson   C. Manny Ramírez
D. Rafael Palmeiro
Answer: A and B. Drafted by the Thunder in 2011, Jackson has played 11 NBA seasons. Baseball's Reggie Jackson hit 563 homers. Drafted in 1978 by the Rockets, Robinson played three NBA seasons, including with the championship 1979 Sonics.

1297. Name the player who didn't play in the NBA.
A. Gene Conley   B. Dave DeBusschere   C. Danny Ainge
D. Bob Gibson   E. Chuck Connors
Answer: D. A Hall of Fame pitcher for the Cardinals, Gibson played for the Globetrotters but not in the NBA.

UNIFORM NUMBERS

1298. Who wore the lowest uniform number retired by the Celtics?
A. Dennis Johnson   B. Kevin Garnett   C. Bill Russell   D. Robert Parish
Answer: Parish wore #00.

1299. How many players' numbers have the Bulls retired?
A. One   B. Two   C. Three   D. Four
Answer: D. They have retired Jerry Sloan (#4), Bob Love (#10), Michael Jordan (#23), and Scottie Pippen (#33). They also have jerseys retired for JK (Jerry Krause) and PJ (Phil Jackson).

1300. True or False? In their 33 seasons the Hornets haven't retired any numbers.
Answer: False. They retired #13 worn by guard Bobby Phills. Phills played the last three years (1998–2000) of his career with the Hornets. He was killed in a car accident in January of 2000.

1301. Whose number have the Mavericks not retired?
A. Jason Kidd   B. Rolando Blackman   C. Brad Davis
D. Dirk Nowitzki   E. Derek Harper
Answer: A. It is surprising, since Kidd was a key part of the 2011 title team, leading the Mavericks with 38 assists in the Finals.

1302. Which of the following players wore #7 and are in the Hall of Fame?
A. Tiny Archibald   B. Jermaine O'Neal   C. Lamar Odom
D. Pete Maravich
Answer: A and D.

1303. Which of the following players wore #2 and are in the Hall of Fame?
A. Alex English   B. Mitch Richmond   C. Joe Johnson   D. Moses Malone
Answer: A, B, and D.

1304. True or False? The Nets have retired no jersey numbers below 10.
Answer: False. Of the Nets six retired jerseys, two are below 10. They retired Dražen Petrović's #3 and Jason Kidd's #5. Their other retired numbers are 23 (John Williamson), 25 (Bill Melchionni), 32 (Julius Erving), and 52 (Buck Williams).

1305. Which player wore the lowest number retired by the Nuggets?
A. Fat Lever   B. Alex English   C. David Thompson   D. Dan Issel
Answer: B. English wore #2, their lowest number retired.

1306. Which of the following players wore #1 and are in the Hall of Fame?
A. Tracy McGrady   B. Tim Hardaway   C. Amar'e Stoudemire
D. Chauncey Billups
Answer: A and B.

1307. Which of the following players wore #3 and are in the Hall of Fame?
A. Allen Iverson   B. Ben Wallace   C. Dwyane Wade
D. Dennis Johnson   E. All of them
Answer: E.

1308. Which of the following numbers is not retired by the Knicks?
A. 10   B. 19   C. 24   D. 32
Answer: D. No one with #32 is retired.

1309. Match the players with their uniform numbers.
1. Michael Jordan   2. Bill Russell   3. Kareem Abdul-Jabbar
4. Wilt Chamberlain
A. 6   B. 33   C. 13   D. 23
Answer: 1-D; 2-A; 3-B; 4-C.

1310. Match the players with their uniform numbers.
1. Jerry West   2. Oscar Robertson   3. Elgin Baylor   4. Kobe Bryant
A. 22   B. 14   C. 44   D. 24
Answer: 1-C; 2-B; 3-A; 4-D.

1311. True or False? Wilt Chamberlain has his number retired by three teams.
Answer: True. Chamberlain's 13 is retired by the Warriors, 76ers, and Lakers.

1312. Match the players with their uniform numbers.
1. Bob Cousy   2. Elgin Baylor   3. George Mikan   4. Jerry West
A. 44   B. 99   C. 22   D. 14
Answer: 1-D; 2-C; 3-B; 4-A.

1313. Match the players with their uniform numbers.
1. Tim Duncan   2. Larry Bird   3. Magic Johnson   4. Julius Erving
A. 32   B. 6   C. 33   D. 21
Answer: 1-D; 2-C; 3-A; 4-B.

WHICH ONE?

1314. Which Duke player played for seven NBA and ABA teams and won a title with one?
A. Larry Cannon   B. Jack Marin   C. Art Heyman   D. Stephen Vacendak
Answer: C. "The Pest" was a 6'5" shooting guard who started with the Knicks in 1963, went to the Royals, the 76ers, the New Jersey Americans, and won a title with the Pittsburgh Pipers in 1968, the ABA's first season. Then Heyman played for the Minnesota Pipers in 1969, back to Pittsburgh in 1970, and finished with the Miami Floridians in 1970.

1315. Who scored 52 points in the 2017 All-Star Game?
A. Russell Westbrook   B. Anthony Davis   C. Kobe Bryant
D. LeBron James
Answer: B. The Pelicans power forward posted 52 points and 10 rebounds and grabbed MVP honors in the highest scoring game in All-Star history, a 192–182 win for the West.

1316. Which player received the most votes and got the MVP in the 2018 All-Star Game?
A. Russell Westbrook   B. Kevin Durant   C. LeBron James
D. Kyrie Irving
Answer: C. He nearly posted a triple-double with 29 points, 10 rebounds, and eight assists as Team LeBron beat Team Stephen.

1317. Who led eight double-digit scorers in points for the West in the 1995 All-Star Game?

A. Charles Barkley   B. Hakeem Olajuwon   C. Karl Malone

D. Mitch Richmond

Answer: D. Playing just 22 minutes as a reserve, Richmond, then a shooting guard for the Kings, connected on 10 of 13 shots to lead his team with 23 points. He took MVP honors as the West won going away, 139–112.

1318. Name the two players who recorded 20-20-20s in their career (meaning 20 or more in any three statistical categories).

A. Oscar Robertson   B. Russell Westbrook   C. LeBron James

D. Wilt Chamberlain

Answer: B and D. As with so many distinctions, Chamberlain was first. Wilt played 48 minutes and logged 22 points, 25 rebounds, and 21 assists for the 76ers to help beat the Pistons 131–121 on February 2, 1968. Westbrook led the Thunder over the Lakers 119–103 in April 2019 when he posted 20 points, 20 rebounds, and 21 assists.

1319. Which of the following coaches won 1,000 games?

A. Rick Adelman   B. Al Attles   C. Red Auerbach   D. Bernie Bickerstaff

Answer: A. In 23 years Adelman won 1,042 games, most with the Blazers. He peaked with 63 wins in 1991. He led his teams to two Western Conference championships, but never an NBA title.

1320. Name the guard who led a furious comeback to give the East a victory in the 2001 All-Star Game.

A. Vince Carter   B. Ray Allen   C. Stephon Marbury   D. Allen Iverson

Answer: D. With 25 points, five assists, and four steals, Iverson helped the East to overcome a 19-point deficit at the start of the fourth quarter to win 111–110.

1321. Which player who once grabbed 40 rebounds in a game was MVP of the 1965 All-Star Game?

A. Bill Russell   B. Nate Thurmond   C. Wilt Chamberlain   D. Jerry Lucas

Answer: D. The East survived a furious fourth quarter rush in which they were outscored 32–17 and won 124–123. Royals forward Lucas scored 25 points and had 10 rebounds.

1322. Which player drafted in the top 10 in 1993 made it to the Hall of Fame?
A. Anfernee Hardaway   B. Sam Cassell   C. Chris Webber
D. Allan Houston
Answer: C. Picked first overall, Webber, a career 15-point scorer in his 15-year career, was inducted into the Hall in 2021.

1323. Which of the following players did not win three consecutive scoring titles?
A. George Mikan   B. Kareem Abdul-Jabbar   C. Neil Johnston
D. Wilt Chamberlain
Answer: B. Abdul-Jabbar won scoring titles in 1971 and 1972 only.

1324. Name the player who fell short of the 30,000-point club by less than 500 points?
A. Moses Malone   B. Julius Erving   C. Elvin Hayes   D. Shaquille O'Neal
Answer: A. Malone posted a total of 29,580 points in the ABA and NBA.

1325. Name the player who fell short of the 20,000-point club by less than 500 points.
A. Bob Pettit   B. Mitch Richmond   C. John Stockton   D. Tom Chambers
Answer: C. The all-time assist leader had 19,711 points.

1326. Who holds the record for assists in an NBA game?
A. Kevin Porter   B. John Stockton   C. Scott Skiles   D. Oscar Robertson
Answer: C. Skiles amassed 30 assists for the Magic in a 155–116 victory against the Nuggets at the Orlando Arena on December 30, 1990.

1327. Which player holds the record for most offensive rebounds in a playoff game?
A. Dennis Rodman   B. Dave Cowens   C. Moses Malone   D. Jerry Lucas
Answer: C. Malone grabbed 15 off the offensive glass against the Bullets in Game 2 of the Eastern Conference semifinals on April 21, 1977. Moses finished with 31 points and 26 rebounds in a 124–118 victory.

1328. Which of the following players didn't make the NBA's top 50 players but made the top 75 team?
A. Dan Issel   B. Bernard King   C. Artis Gilmore   D. Dominique Wilkins
Answer: D. The Hall of Fame forward was picked for the top 75 team in October 2021.

John Stockton

1329. Which of the following players made the NBA's top 50 players and the top 75 team?
A. Jason Kidd   B. Damian Lillard   C. Shaquille O'Neal   D. Ray Allen
E. All of the above
Answer: C. Having played only three complete seasons, O'Neal was a controversial selection when the first team was chosen on October 29, 1996. At 24 years old he was the youngest player picked.

1330. Who holds the record for most free throws in a game without a miss?
A. Dirk Nowitzki   B. Rick Barry   C. Mark Price   D. Stephen Curry
Answer: A. Tallying 48 for Game 1 of the Western finals against the Thunder on May 17, 2011, Dirk scored 24 of them on free throws. He averaged 32 for the series as the Mavericks rolled in five games.

1331. Which of the following players did not win three consecutive scoring titles?
A. Bob McAdoo   B. George Gervin   C. Allen Iverson   D. LeBron James
Answer: C and D. Iverson won four scoring titles in 1999, 2001, 2002, and 2005, but never won three straight. James won a scoring title in 2008.

1332. Which of the following players did not win three consecutive scoring titles?
A. James Harden   B. Russell Westbrook   C. Kevin Durant
D. Stephen Curry
Answer: B and D. Westbrook won in 2015 and 2017. Curry won in 2016 and 2021.

1333. Which player does not have 20,000 points and 10,000 rebounds?
A. Walt Bellamy   B. Wilt Chamberlain   C. Bob Pettit   D. John Havlicek
Answer: D. A guard and small forward, "Hondo" tallied 26,395 points but just 8,007 rebounds.

1334. Name the Magic player who holds their record for blocks per game in a season.
A. Dwight Howard   B. Shaquille O'Neal   C. Bo Outlaw
Answer: B. O'Neal averaged 3.5 blocks per game in his rookie season in 1993. He posted four of the top 10 averages in team history. Howard posted five and Outlaw one.

WHO AM I?

1335. I got clear for a last second shot from the top of the key and hit it to lead my team to victory in the 1972 All-Star Game.
A. John Havlicek   B. Walt Frazier   C. Jerry West   D. Billy Cunningham
Answer: C. West tallied only 13 points in the game but hit the last-second shot that won the game 112–110 and was awarded the MVP.

1336. I was the leading scorer in the 2013 Finals.
A. LeBron James   B. Dwyane Wade   C. Kawhi Leonard   D. Tim Duncan
Answer: A. James was the only scorer above 20 with 25 and took home MVP honors.

1337. I had the highest scoring game in the 2012 Finals.
A. Kevin Durant   B. Dwyane Wade   C. Russell Westbrook
D. LeBron James
Answer: C. Westbrook netted 43 in Game 4 for the series high. It wasn't enough. The Thunder won the opener before losing four straight games to the Heat.

1338. I played at St. John's, was drafted 13th overall by the Pistons in 1962, and played 11 years, most of them with the Bullets. I then coached for 20 years and led two teams to ABA titles.
A. Leroy Ellis   B. Kevin Loughery   C. Jim Lynam   D. Terry Dischinger
Answer: B. The ABA championship teams that Loughery coached were the 1974 and 1976 Nets.

1339. I missed 58 percent of my shots in the 2011 Finals, but I still helped the winning team.
A. Shawn Marion   B. Dirk Nowitzki   C. Jason Kidd   D. Jason Terry
Answer: B. He shot only .416 from the field, but he averaged 26 points and 9.7 rebounds and was awarded the MVP as the Mavericks topped the Heat in six games.

1340. I was the only player picked in the top 10 in the 1974 draft who made the Hall of Fame.
Answer: Bill Walton was picked first overall by Portland. In just his third season the 6'11" center led the Trail Blazers to their first and only title in 1977.

1341. I was the leading scorer in the 2010 Finals despite missing 60 percent of my shots.
A. Kendrick Perkins   B. Paul Pierce   C. Kobe Bryant   D. Kevin Garnett
Answer: C. Bryant made just 40.5 percent of his shots for the series. He was awarded the MVP despite hitting just 6 of 24 attempts in Game 7.

1342. I scored 63 points on February 10, 1949, and that broke the NBA record of 48 points set 12 days before. I was also glad we won the game against the Indianapolis Jets 108–87.
Answer: "Jumpin'" Joe Fulks, the Philadelphia Warriors forward, eclipsed George Mikan's record by plenty. One of the first jump shooters, Fulks attempted 56 field goals and made 27 of them. He was also nine of 14 at the free throw line.

1343. I helped the West win an All-Star Game in 1967 after the East had won five in a row.
A. Rick Barry   B. Dave DeBusschere   C. Elgin Baylor   D. Jerry West
Answer: A. Barry led all scorers with 38 points to lead the West to a 135–120 win in front of his home fans at the Cow Palace in San Francisco.

1344. I became the first player in NBA history to reach 20,000 points and 10,000 assists.
A. Magic Johnson   B. Kobe Bryant   C. Chris Paul   D. Dwyane Wade
Answer: C. Paul turned the trick for the Suns on October 23, 2021, when he tallied 23 points and 14 assists in a 115–105 defeat of the Lakers.

1345. As a rookie during the 1961–62 season, I was runner-up in points per game. No one paid much attention to me though.
A. Bob Pettit   B. Jerry Lucas   C. Walt Bellamy   D. Willis Reed
Answer: C. "Bells" averaged 31.58 points per game, good enough for second place, but well behind Wilt Chamberlain's 50.4 points per game. Bellamy was also third behind Chamberlain and Bill Russell in rebounds per game with 18.99.

1346. I was the first player in NBA history to win three consecutive scoring titles.
A. George Mikan   B. Neil Johnston   C. Paul Arizin   D. Joe Fulks
Answer: A. The Lakers pivotman led the circuit from 1949 through 1951, the first to do so.

1347. I broke Wilt's streak of seven consecutive scoring titles from 1960 through 1966. Then I met him in the Finals.
A. Rick Barry   B. Jerry West   C. Elgin Baylor   D. Oscar Robertson
Answer: A. Playing for the San Francisco Warriors, Barry poured in points at a 35.6 clip in 1967. Then he met Wilt's 76ers in the Finals. He got better in the Finals, posting 40.8 points per game. But the 76ers won in six games.

1348. I was one of two Hall of Fame players drafted in the top 10 of the 1977 NBA Draft. I was drafted seventh and he was selected eighth.
A. Bernard King   B. Jack Sikma   C. Otis Birdsong   D. Walter Davis
Answer: A. King was selected seventh overall and Sikma eighth.

1349. There were three future Hall of Famers picked before me in the 1984 draft. I was chosen 16th overall but made the Hall of Fame too.
Answer: John Stockton, out of Gonzaga University, played 19 seasons and is the all-time assists leader.

1350. I was chosen first overall in the 1997 draft and played for a championship team in just my second year in the league.
Answer: Tim Duncan. Duncan played 19 seasons and did it all. He was Rookie of the Year, a five-time champ with the Spurs, two-time MVP, three-time Finals MVP, and voted to the NBA 75th anniversary squad.

1351. I played for the Bulls before they won any championships. I'm proud to be the only one of 21 players who attended Bradley to make the Basketball Hall of Fame.

Answer: Chet Walker. A 6'6" small forward, Chet "The Jet" was drafted by the Syracuse Nationals 14th overall in 1962. In 13 seasons he was an All-Star seven times. He played his last six seasons with the Bulls but won his only title as a member of the 1967 76ers.

1352. I am the first player to attend Syracuse University to make it to the NBA, and make the Hall of Fame.

Answer: Dave Bing, picked fifth overall in the 1966 draft, played 12 NBA seasons, averaging 20 points and six assists, and remains the only Syracuse grad to make the Hall of Fame.

1353. When you think of the 1978 draft, it's Larry Bird that comes to mind first. He was drafted sixth and made the Hall. I was drafted 35th, but I still made it.

Answer: Maurice Cheeks. One of the great small guards, Cheeks was a four-time All-Star, five-time All-Defensive Team choice, and the point guard for the 1983 champion Sixers.

1354. I'm the most recent guy to win back-to-back Finals MVPs.

Answer: Kevin Durant, who won the Finals MVP with the Warriors in 2017 and 2018. In 2017 he averaged 35 points, eight rebounds, and five assists in a five-game defeat of the Cavaliers.

1355. I hold the record for points in a quarter and points in a half of an NBA playoff game.

A. Michael Jordan   B. Eric Floyd   C. Rick Barry   D. Klay Thompson

Answer: B. His nickname was "Sleepy," but the Warriors point guard wasn't drowsy against the Lakers on May 10, 1987. Trailing the Lakers 3–0 in the Western Conference semifinal series, Floyd posted a game for the ages. He scored 51 points, including 29 points in the third quarter and 39 in the second half, to bring the Warriors back from a 65–57 halftime deficit to win 129–121.

1356. I broke a record by scoring 17 points in the overtime period of an NBA game.

A. Stephen Curry   B. Ray Allen   C. Reggie Miller   D. Gilbert Arenas

Answer: A. Curry turned the trick on May 9, 2016, when he led the Warriors to a 132–125 victory against the Trail Blazers in Game 4 of the Western Conference semifinals.

1357. Defenders were prone to foul me a lot, so I set a record for free throws attempted in a playoff game.

A. Wilt Chamberlain   B. DeAndre Jordan   C. Shaquille O'Neal

Answer: C. O'Neal had his most prolific Hack-a-Shaq game against the Pacers on June 9, 2000, when he shot 39 free throws and made just 18. The strategy didn't work, as the Lakers prevailed 111–104 behind O'Neal's 40 points and 24 rebounds. It didn't work for the series either, as "The Big Aristotle" averaged 38 points and 17 rebounds in the six-game tilt and was named MVP. The Lakers won their first of three consecutive Finals.

1358. Since they started giving out the Finals MVP award in 1969, I was the first to average 40 points in the Finals.

A. Rick Barry   B. Michael Jordan   C. Kareem Abdul-Jabbar
D. Jerry West

Answer: B. Jordan averaged 41 points, eight rebounds, and six assists in a six-game defeat of the Suns in 1993.

1359. I grabbed more than 20 rebounds per game in the Finals, which is more than the points I scored, and they awarded me the Finals MVP.

A. Wilt Chamberlain   B. Bill Russell   C. Hakeem Olajuwon
D. Moses Malone

Answer: A. In 1972 the Lakers ran off 33 straight wins and beat the Knicks in five in the Finals. Chamberlain posted 19.4 points per game, grabbed 23.2 rebounds—and played 47.2 minutes per game—to earn MVP honors.

1360. I won six MVP awards. They tell me that's more than anyone else won.

A. Michael Jordan   B. Bill Russell   C. Wilt Chamberlain
D. Kareem Abdul-Jabbar

Answer: D. The great center won them in 1971, 1972, 1974, 1976, 1977, and 1980. The first three were with the Bucks and the last three with the Lakers.

1361. I was the most recent player to win two All-Star Game MVP awards.

A. Kyrie Irving   B. Kevin Durant   C. Russell Westbrook   D. Kobe Bryant

Answer: B. Durant won his second MVP in 2019 when, as a Warrior, he scored 31 points in a 178–164 victory for the West. He had won his first with the Thunder in 2012, when he scored 36 in the West's 152–149 victory.

1362. Some people thought I should have won a Finals MVP in 1970 or 1973. I didn't win either. I did win the All-Star MVP in 1975 though.

A. Jerry West   B. Walt Frazier   C. Tiny Archibald   D. Rick Barry

Answer: B. Frazier posted 30 points on 10 field goals and 10 charity tosses. His teammate Willis Reed won both of those Finals honors. The East won 108–102.

1363. I was drafted third overall in 1963 and played center—as a teammate of Wilt Chamberlain.

Answer: Nate Thurmond played two seasons with Wilt for the Warriors and then watched his teammate get traded to the 76ers.

1364. I led the 1958 Finals against the Celtics in scoring, just enough to get us past Boston's balanced attack.

A. Cliff Hagan   B. Slater Martin   C. Bob Pettit   D. Jack Coleman

Answer: C. Pettit had a stellar series in the Hawks' six-game win, averaging 29.3 points and 17 rebounds.

1365. You think it was easy breaking the Celtics' streak of eight straight titles? But we did it in 1967, winning the Finals in six. I was the leading scorer on the winning team.

A. Hal Greer   B. Wali Jones   C. Chet Walker   D. Wilt Chamberlain
E. Rick Barry

Answer: A. The Sixers point guard and future Hall of Famer Hal Greer posted 26 points, eight rebounds, and six assists for the Finals in their victory over the Warriors.

1366. I led all scorers in the 1976 Finals. It was a tense series that the Celtics won in six.

A. Paul Westphal   B. Jo Jo White   C. Alvan Adams   D. John Havlicek

Answer: C. The 6'9" center averaged 23 points for the Suns, but it wasn't enough to top the Celtics.

1367. We lost some big series to the Knicks and Bucks in the early 1970s, but we finally triumphed in 1978. I helped with double digits in rebounds.

A. Bob Dandridge   B. Greg Ballard   C. Wes Unseld   D. Kevin Grevey

Answer: C. Unseld tallied nine points and 11.7 rebounds per game as the Bullets topped the Sonics in seven games.

1368. We avenged the Bullets big time in 1979, topping them in just five games. I led my team in scoring in four of those five.

A. Jack Sikma   B. Gus Williams   C. Dennis Johnson   D. Fred Brown

Answer: B. Williams was a scoring beast, scoring 30 or more three times.

1369. I didn't lead my team in scoring in the 2022 Finals. Curry took that prize. But I did lead us in rebounding and scored a bit too.

A. Klay Thompson   B. Andrew Wiggins   C. Draymond Green
D. Jordan Poole

Answer: B. Wiggins was second in scoring against the Celts with 18.3 points per game and also tallied the most rebounds (8.8) and blocks (1.5).

1370. I had a bust-out Finals in 2021, leading my team in scoring with 28.2 and even scored 42 and 40 in back-to-back games, but we lost both.

A. Deandre Ayton   B. Devin Booker   C. Mikal Bridges   D. Chris Paul

Answer: B. Booker's scoring exploits fell short as the league MVP was a bit better. Giannis Antetokounmpo shot an astounding 62 percent, and averaged 35 points, 13 rebounds, five assists, and 1.8 blocks. In Game 6 the "Greek Freak" posted a clinching game for the ages: 50 points, 14 rebounds, and five blocks.

1371. I gave it my all in the 2020 Finals, but the Lakers had LeBron James and Anthony Davis. I scored 40 and grabbed 11 rebounds to get us back in the series in Game 3.
A. Tyler Herro   B. Jae Crowder   C. Duncan Robinson   D. Jimmy Butler
Answer: D. Butler was stellar in the Finals, shooting 55 percent, scoring 26.2 a game, and bagging 9.8 rebounds. The Lakers won in six.

1372. I scored a lot in the 2019 Finals, got my share of rebounds, and led my squad in assists.
A. Pascal Siakam   B. Kyle Lowry   C. Fred VanVleet   D. Kawhi Leonard
Answer: B. Guard Lowry was solid across the board with seven assists and 16 points per game. His play, with that of MVP Leonard, helped the Raptors take the Warriors in six.

1373. I helped my team to a four-game sweep in which we outscored our opponents by 60 points in 2018. I led in four statistical categories.
A. Kevin Durant   B. Stephen Curry   C. Klay Thompson
D. Draymond Green
Answer: A. Durant led the Warriors in points (28.8), rebounds (10.8), assists (7.5), and blocks per game (2.3). They swept the Cavaliers.

1374. I was the MVP of the 2017 Finals.
A. LeBron James   B. Stephen Curry   C. Kyrie Irving   D. Kevin Durant
Answer: D. Durant led the Warriors to a five-game win over the Cavs. He posted 35.2 points, 8.2 rebounds, and 5.4 assists. He also shot 55.6 percent from the field.

1375. LeBron won the MVP of the 2016 Finals. I was the only other guy who averaged 20 in the series.
A. J. R. Smith   B. Tristan Thompson   C. Kevin Love   D. Kyrie Irving
Answer: D. Aside from draining the game-winner over the outstretched hand of Stephen Curry in Game 7, Irving averaged 27 for the Finals, just two less than James.

1376. I was the leading scorer in the 2015 Finals. Was I also the MVP?
Answer: No. Stephen Curry was the only Warrior with a 20-point average in the 2015 Finals. But Andre Iguodala averaged 16 a game on 52 percent shooting to cop MVP honors. He logged 25 points in the 105–97 clinching win at Cleveland in Game 6.

1377. I averaged 15 points, 15 rebounds, and four blocks in the 2009 Finals.

A. Pau Gasol   B. Lamar Odom   C. Dwight Howard   D. Rashard Lewis

Answer: C. Howard's stat line didn't help the outcome as the Lakers beat the Magic in five games, behind Kobe Bryant's MVP performance of 32 points, 5.6 rebounds, and seven assists per contest.

1378. I wasn't the highest scorer in the 2008 Finals, and I connected on an unimpressive 43 percent of my shots, but I was awarded the Finals MVP award.

A. Ray Allen   B. Paul Pierce   C. Kevin Garnett   D. Kobe Bryant

Answer: B. The Celtics beat the Lakers in six games as the small forward averaged 21.8.

1379. I led my team in points and assists for the 2007 Finals. But it wasn't enough to keep us from being swept. Who won the MVP of the 2007 Finals?

A. Tony Parker   B. Manu Ginóbili   C. LeBron James   D. Tim Duncan

Answer: C. James's 22 points, seven rebounds, and seven assists (but also an awful 36 percent field goal percentage) couldn't rescue the Cavaliers from a four-game sweep at the hands of the Spurs. Tony Parker led the way for the Spurs with 24 points, five rebounds, and three assists per game.

1380. I would win a Finals MVP later, but in 2006 I missed 61 percent of my shots in the Finals.

A. Jason Terry   B. Dirk Nowitzki   C. Dwyane Wade   D. Shaquille O'Neal

Answer: B. Nowitzki did average 22 points and 11 rebounds on 39 percent shooting for the Mavericks. The Heat won in six games and Nowitzki would get his MVP in the 2011 Finals, avenging the earlier loss to the Heat.

1381. In a seven-game Finals in 2005, only one team broke 100 points. We lost that one by 31 points, but won two of the next three and prevailed in seven games. I was Finals MVP.

A. Tony Parker   B. Tim Duncan   C. Chauncey Billups   D. Ben Wallace

Answer: B. He missed 58 percent of his field goal attempts, but still averaged 21 points, 14 rebounds, and two blocks per game.

1382. Not just Celtics were winning MVPs in the 1950s and 1960s. I was the first MVP winner and the first to get two.
A. George Mikan   B. Paul Arizin   C. Oscar Robertson   D. Bob Pettit
Answer: D. In 1959 he averaged 29 points and 16 rebounds to take his second award. He won his first in 1956.

1383. I was drafted a little low in the 1964 draft, 10th overall. My team went on to win two titles in the early 1970s and I was the Finals MVP in both.
Answer: Willis Reed. The Grambling State University center played only 10 seasons due to knee injuries, but he also won Rookie of the Year and was the MVP in 1970.

1384. I got picked 10th overall in the 1965 draft and played on two championship teams at UCLA before Lew Alcindor and Bill Walton got there. In the NBA I played on the Lakers' team that won a record 33 straight and we captured a championship.
Answer: Gail Goodrich. The point guard scored a record 42 points for the Bruins in the 1965 title game against favored Michigan.

1385. I was that other Celtic who played at the University of San Francisco with Bill Russell.
A. Sam Jones   B. K. C. Jones   C. Satch Sanders   D. Tom Heinsohn
Answer: B. The University of San Francisco won consecutive titles with Russell and reeled off a then record 60 straight wins.

1386. I led St. Bonaventure to the Final Four in 1970, but a knee injury kept me from playing in the semifinals against Jacksonville and we lost.
Answer: Bob Lanier.

1387. I still hold the record for career points in college and points per game.
Answer: Pete Maravich. "The Pistol" averaged 44.2 points per game over his three seasons at Louisiana State.

1388. I played center for Jacksonville in the 1970 NCAA Finals against UCLA. I got 19 points and 16 rebounds but we lost 80–69.
Answer: Artis Gilmore.

1389. I played on the University of Houston team dubbed "Phi Slamma Jamma," and I later joined an old teammate there to win my first NBA title.

Answer: Clyde Drexler was traded to the Rockets where he won a title with Hakeem Olajuwon in 1995.

1390. Out of Temple in 1958, I was chosen number one ahead of Elgin Baylor in the draft.

Answer: Guy Rodgers. The 6'1" point guard was tossing the ball to Chamberlain with the Warriors in their first seasons in the league. He was elected to the Hall of Fame in 2014.

1391. I was only chosen ninth in the NBA Draft, but I went on to score 26,395 points, more than the first eight picked, and played on eight championship teams.

Answer: John Havlicek.

1392. I played mostly right field in my Hall of Fame baseball career. But I was also drafted by the Hawks.

Answer: Dave Winfield was selected in the fifth round by Atlanta in 1973.

1393. I earned 65 percent of the first-place votes to win the MVP in 2022.

Answer: Nikola Jokić. The versatile center averaged 27.1 points, 13.8 rebounds, and 7.9 assists to earn the award.

1394. I surprised even my biggest supporters when I got 91 percent of the first-place vote to grab MVP honors in 2021.

Answer: Nikola Jokić. The Nuggets center won his first of consecutive MVPs with a line of 26.4 points, 10.8 rebounds, and 8.3 assists.

1395. You probably couldn't spell my name, but I won my second straight MVP award in 2020.

Answer: Giannis Antetokounmpo walked off with 85 percent of the first-place votes in 2020 after posting 29.5 points and 13.6 rebounds a game.

1396. I won Rookie of the Year in 2019. I got 21 points and seven rebounds a game, but I wanted our team to do better than 33 wins and 49 losses.

Answer: Luka Dončić drew 98 percent of the first-place votes.

Nikola Jokić

1397. I just barely beat out Bob Pettit for the Most Valuable Player in 1957.
Answer: Bob Cousy. The Celtics guard averaged 20.6 points and seven assists while shooting just .378 from the field. Pettit averaged 24.7 points and 14.6 rebounds while shooting 41.5 percent. But Cousy got 23 percent of the first-place votes to Pettit's 21 percent.

1398. My squad didn't win the title in 1958, but I did win the league MVP. I would rather have had that second straight title though.
Answer: Bill Russell. The Boston pivotman averaged 22.7 rebounds and 16.6 points, but the Celtics lost to the Hawks in a six-game Finals.

1399. You know, I like scoring and rebounding the ball, but I like winning a title more. I would trade my 1959 MVP award for a second title instead.
Answer: Bob Pettit. The St. Louis forward got 317 first-place points in the voting to Celtic Bill Russell's 144. But the Celtics took back the title they had lost the year before.

1400. I scored 47 points on my 38th birthday. We even won, something we hadn't been doing much of.
A. LeBron James   B. Wilt Chamberlain   C. Kareem Abdul-Jabbar
D. Julius Erving
Answer: A. James netted 47 on December 30, 2022. He also grabbed 10 rebounds and nine assists in a 130–121 road victory against the Hawks. The Lakers' record was just 15-21.

1401. I had my third 50-point game of the season to finish 2022 with a 126–125 victory over the Spurs.
Answer: Luka Dončić did this in his 37th game. By comparison, Chamberlain had 21 50-point games after playing the 37th game of the 1961–62 season on December 30, 1961. Wilt scored only 41 that night, ending a streak of seven consecutive 50-point efforts and 12 in 13 games. His high marks during that streak were 78 points and 60 points.

1402. I could board. Man, a lot of guys in the mid-1970s could go get it off the boards. So I was happy to lead in offensive rebounds in 1974, the first year they kept that stat.
A. Elvin Hayes   B. Paul Silas   C. Dave DeBusschere   D. Happy Hairston
Answer: A. The "Big E," the Capital Bullets power forward, led the NBA with 354 offensive rebounds in 1974.

1403. I knew I could board. But who knew I was first to get 500 offensive rebounds in a year?
A. Dennis Rodman   B. Moses Malone   C. Wes Unseld
D. Wilt Chamberlain
Answer: B. Malone got a record 587 offensive boards in the 1978–79 season to set a record that still holds. He also got 573 and 558 in seasons after and owns the top three marks of all time.

1404. I was in that other league, the ABA. I hold the record for offensive rebounds in a season there.
A. Spencer Haywood   B. Moses Malone   C. Mel Daniels
D. Artis Gilmore
Answer: A. Haywood got 533 in 1970, an ABA record.

1405. I couldn't believe it when they told me in 2015 that I tied the record of some great players with 18 offensive rebounds in a single game.
A. Zaza Pachulia   B. Rudy Gobert   C. Steven Adams
D. Andre Drummond
Answer: A. The Bucks center did it on March 20, 2015, tying the marks of Dennis Rodman and Charles Oakley.

1406. You may not have heard, but I was the first guy to reach 1,000 career assists way back in 1951.
A. Andy Phillip   B. Bob Cousy   C. Dick McGuire   D. Bob Davies
Answer: A. Phillip was the Warriors point guard, leading the league in assists per game for the second of three straight years that season.

1407. I was the first guy to get 10,000 assists.
A. Bob Cousy   B. Oscar Robertson   C. John Stockton
D. Magic Johnson
Answer: C. When he reached 10,000 in the 1995 season, he was not only the active and career leader in assists but also the record holder for assists in a season with 1,164, which he set in 1991. He is still the single-season and career assist leader with 15,806.

1408. I was the first to break the mark for 42 triple-doubles in a season.
A. Magic Johnson   B. Wilt Chamberlain   C. Lenny Wilkens
D. Russell Westbrook
Answer: D. Westbrook broke Oscar Robertson's mark that stood for 55 years when he got 45 triple-doubles in 2017.

1409. I still own the single-game record for points in a Finals game. I had 61 in a game in 1962.
A. Jerry West   B. Wilt Chamberlain   C. Elgin Baylor   D. Sam Jones
Answer: C. He not only got 61 but 22 rebounds to go with those points on April 14, 1962. Jordan is a distant second with 55 in the 1993 Finals.

1410. I have the record for points in a Finals game among active players with 51.
A. Stephen Curry   B. LeBron James   C. Russell Westbrook
D. Kevin Durant
Answer: B. James unloaded for those 51 in Game 1 of the 2018 Finals. The problem was the Warriors had three guys scoring between 24 and 29 points, and they won 124–114.

1411. All right, I don't have the record for points in a Finals game, but I'm tied for field goals in one game with 22, which I did in 1967.
Answer: Rick Barry. He hit 22 of 48 shots, got 55, and also had 12 boards.

1412. I know I don't want my name attached to how many field goals I missed in a single Finals game, but there it is. I missed 28 shots in a game.
A. Elgin Baylor   B. Rick Barry   C. Michael Jordan   D. LeBron James
Answer: B. The Warriors forward hit 15 of 43 and scored 37 in a Game 1 loss to the 76ers in the 1967 Finals.

1413. It's nice to have the record for most free throws in a Finals game. They may have called some light fouls, but 21 free throws is still impressive.

A. Bob Pettit   B. Jerry West   C. Cliff Hagan   D. Dwyane Wade

Answer: D. Wade equaled the entire Mavericks team when he hit 21 against them to give the Heat a 101–100 victory in Game 5.

1414. I was traded by the Celtics along with Ed Macauley in 1956 to the Hawks for Bill Russell. Russell and the Celtics won the next years. But in 1958 I helped my team win.

A. Slater Martin   B. Jack Coleman   C. Bob Pettit   D. Cliff Hagan

Answer: D. A guard, Hagan averaged 25.2 points and 9.7 rebounds in the Hawks' six-game victory over the Celtics in the 1958 Finals.

1415. I know I'm not Wilt or Russell or anyone of that caliber. But I'm proud of owning the record for blocks in a Finals game.

A. Dwight Howard   B. Bill Walton   C. Andrew Bynum   D. Patrick Ewing

Answer: A. The Magic center got nine blocks, 21 rebounds, and 16 points against the Lakers in the 2009 Finals. They lost to the Lakers 99–91 and dropped the series in five.

1416. I own the record for assists in a Finals game, but it brings up a bad memory for me.

A. Magic Johnson   B. Jerry West   C. Kevin Johnson
D. Dennis Johnson

Answer: A. Johnson got 21 assists and a triple-double for a victory in Game 3 of the 1984 Finals. Due to a stolen pass, poor clock management, and missed free throws, however, the Celtics won in seven games.

1417. Bill Walton said I didn't have the bulk for the inside game. I would give up 50 and 60 pounds to everybody inside. True enough. I was a running center.

A. Dave Cowens   B. Bob Rule   C. Bob Lanier   D. Bob McAdoo

Answer: D. Just 6'9" and 210 pounds, McAdoo still won three straight scoring titles for the Braves from 1974 to 1976.

1418. Phil Chenier said he wouldn't put me on his list of great centers, since I stuck out my knees when I set picks. But I still averaged 30 points in my rookie year, second only to Wilt.

A. Nate Thurmond   B. Rudy LaRusso   C. Walt Bellamy

Answer: C. Bellamy averaged 31 points and 19 rebounds in his rookie year and led in field goal percentage. He's in the Hall of Fame.

1419. A teammate of mine said "I had to be regarded as the top center in pro basketball" after the 1973 conference finals when I held Abdul-Jabbar to 43 percent shooting and only 22 points per game.

A. Walt Bellamy   B. Nate Thurmond   C. Bob Lanier

Answer: B. The quote is from Jeff Mullins after the Warriors beat the Bucks in six games. Abdul-Jabbar said that Thurmond defended him better than anyone else.

1420. Against Thurmond I scored my fewest points. When the ball went away from most guys, you were open. When the ball went away from Nate, he went with you.

A. Kareem Abdul-Jabbar   B. Willis Reed   C. Dave Cowens
D. Bob Lanier

Answer: Willis Reed, explaining why the 16-footer that he could get off against most centers he couldn't get off against the great defender Thurmond.

1421. You know, Bill Walton gave me high praise. He said I was a terrific player and worked hard but didn't have enough good teammates to get me a title.

A. Patrick Ewing   B. Bob Lanier   C. Jack Sikma   D. Bob McAdoo

Answer: A. Ewing is in the 20,000-10,000 club with 24,815 points and 11,607 rebounds.

1422. I scored more earlier in my career, but later I had some problems with mobility. I was proud of my rebounding, especially for a small center.

A. Dave Cowens   B. Wes Unseld   C. Willis Reed   D. Bob Lanier

Answer: B. At 6'7" he was called the greatest outlet passer of the centers. His rivalry with the Knicks was classic; in a Game 3 127–113 win in the Eastern semifinals against the Knicks in 1970, he had 34 rebounds and 23 points, perhaps his best postseason game ever. He averaged 10 points and 23 rebounds for the series.

1423. You better be rugged to play against Wilt, Kareem, and Thurmond. I was shorter than them, but I averaged 14 rebounds for my career.
A. Willis Reed   B. Bob McAdoo   C. Dave Cowens
Answer: C. Cowens also won an MVP and played on two champions with the Celtics in 1974 and 1976.

1424. I thought this is a helluva predicament to be in. Everybody in Madison Square Garden is saying everything's all right, "The captain is here." All I have to do is go out and play the best big man who's ever been around. Not with two legs but one leg.
A. Dave Cowens   B. Walt Bellamy   C. Willis Reed
Answer: C. Reed, before Game 7 of the 1970 Finals against the Lakers.

1425. They say I changed what a center does. "He's so mobile and quick," they'd say. One writer said I had the feet of a dancer and the touch of a surgeon. That's nice, I'm glad I was able to win a title or two.
A. Dave Cowens   B. Hakeem Olajuwon   C. Moses Malone
Answer: B. Some say his "Dream Shake" was the most unguardable move by a center. He won consecutive titles with the Rockets in 1994 and 1995.

1426. Some people say the skyhook was the single most potent weapon in the history of the game. I could get into a rhythm with that shot. I don't know why more people didn't try that.
A. Kareem Abdul-Jabbar   B. Hakeem Olajuwon   C. Shaquille O'Neal
Answer: A. Abdul-Jabbar, who some people think is the greatest player ever, won three MVPs in his first six seasons and led the Bucks to a title in just three years, the fastest expansion team ever to win.

1427. They say "Nobody roots for Goliath." I would score 70 points or grab 40 rebounds. People just didn't see why I didn't win all the time. I did win one time in 1967, and then again in 1972. But I didn't always have the best players around me.
A. Nate Thurmond   B. Wilt Chamberlain   C. Walt Bellamy
Answer: B. Chamberlain explaining that no matter what he accomplished in the way of individual exploits, people would still attack him.

1428. I didn't notice some of the accomplishments. But I see I led the league in assists per game five seasons. The last guy to do that was Jason Kidd and before that John Stockton, who did it nine times.

A. Chris Paul   B. Russell Westbrook   C. Steve Nash   D. Rajon Rondo

Answer: C. All five times Nash led the league were after 30 years old. He was picked for the 75th Anniversary Team. The free throw percentage was over 90 percent, and the field goals were at 49 percent.

1429. I averaged a triple-double one season in my younger days. The title came in later years.

A. Jerry West   B. Russell Westbrook   C. Oscar Robertson

Answer: C. He also led the league in assists seven times. In 1971 he teamed with Kareem Abdul-Jabbar to win his only title.

1430. So I'm first in points, I have more than 10,000 assists, and more than 10,000 rebounds. I don't know about this GOAT title that people talk about all the time, but those are some fine numbers.

A. LeBron James   B. Michael Jordan   C. Wilt Chamberlain
D. Kareem Abdul-Jabbar

Answer: A. He is first in points with 38,652, and second among active players in assists with 10,420 and in rebounds with 10,667. He has carried the Cavaliers, Heat, and Lakers to NBA titles.

1431. We lost Baylor to retirement after nine games in the 1971–72 season. So I teamed with West and he scored 25.8 points and I got him by a 10th of a point with 25.9. Look at all those assists he got, like 9.7 to lead the league. Didn't Wilt win the Finals MVP?

A Happy Hairston   B. Gail Goodrich   C. Jim McMillian
D. Keith Erickson

Answer: B. The Lakers finished 69-13, won the division by 18 games over the Warriors, and then won 33 in a row from November to January. Wilt did win Finals MVP, averaging 19 points and 23 rebounds a game.

1432. I was elated to win that Finals MVP in 1974. It had been a while since we won a title. The Knicks, the Lakers, and Bucks were all winning. Jabbar hit that 15-foot baseline skyhook in the second overtime in Game 6.
A. Jo Jo White   B. Dave Cowens   C. John Havlicek   D. Don Nelson
Answer: C. "Hondo" posted 26.4 points, 7.7 rebounds, and 4.7 assists and the Celtics won in Milwaukee 102–87 to grab Game 7 and their first championship since Russell retired in 1969.

1433. I had spent seven years there, so I wanted to bring them a title. But when we fell behind three games to one it didn't look good. We were behind in Game 7 but we made the plays—a block, a last-second shot.
A. J. R. Smith   B. LeBron James   C. Kyrie Irving   D. Kevin Love
Answer: B. "King James" brought Cleveland its first title in 2016, wrapping it with a triple-double: 27 points, 11 rebounds, and 11 assists in a 93–89 win. The city had been without a title in baseball since 1948 and in football since 1964. It was the Cavs' 46th year and they had their first championship.

1434. I got 55 points in one game. We barely won. I had the green light, and the jump shots were there. I had 43 and 46 in two other games and we lost. I averaged 41 for the series but we lost in six to the 76ers and Chamberlain.
A. Hal Greer   B. Rick Barry   C. Nate Thurmond   D Jeff Mullins
Answer: B. Barry is the all-time ABA leader with 33 points per game in the playoffs and averaged 27 in the NBA.

1435. I had 27 at the half, which is what the Suns had, and we led 57–27 at the half of Game 7 of the 2022 Western Conference semis. We were down 2-0 but won the series with two blowouts in Games 6 and 7. It was different in the Western finals against the Warriors.
A. Jalen Brunson   B. Reggie Bullock   C. Luka Dončić
D. Spencer Dinwiddie
Answer: C. He is the active leader with 32 career points per game and second all-time behind Jordan.

1436. They're both Finals MVPs, so I don't know if one is better than the other. I'll take the first, since the Warriors had lost the title to LeBron and the Cavs. Then I helped to get it back. I don't think I ever shot the ball more consistently. It's not every day that you hit 55 percent of your shots and average 35 points, eight rebounds, and five assists. Then it was four straight the next year. So maybe those are the two highlights.

A. Klay Thompson   B. Stephen Curry   C. Kevin Durant
D. Draymond Green

Answer: C. At 35, he shows few signs of decline as he heads toward 30,000 points and maintains a high shooting percentage.

1437. You know that night when Wilt scored 100? I was the leading scorer for the other team.

A. Dave Budd   B. Willie Naulls   C. Cleveland Buckner   D. Richie Guerin

Answer: Guerin tallied 39 points, eight rebounds, and six assists. The 76ers won 169–147 in Hershey, Pennsylvania, on March 2, 1962. The Iona College graduate was elected to the Hall of Fame in 2013.

1438. Can you imagine that there were three seconds left in the game and our team had only scored nine points in the fourth quarter? I had all nine, so you figured if we'd score any more points, I would get them, right?

A. Scottie Pippen   B. Michael Jordan   C. John Paxson
D. B. J. Armstrong

Answer: B. Wrong. Horace Grant threw it out to Paxson who hit the 3-pointer to give the Bulls a 99–98 win over the Suns and a third straight title. The Bulls scored just 12 in the quarter but won. Jordan averaged 41 points, eight rebounds, and six assists for the series.

WHO SAID IT?

1439. "Is he a great free throw shooter? Is he a great three-point shooter? Is he a great dribbler? So you're saying the GOAT, but he ain't even great in all those categories."
A. Ray Allen   B. Tim Duncan   C. Jalen Rose   D. Charles Barkley
Answer: A. Ray Allen on why LeBron James is not the greatest player of all time.

1440. "Man, I'm just gonna say this. Any media person that I see in person for the rest of my life who tries to tell me that LeBron James is as good as Michael Jordan, I'm just gonna slap the hell out of him right on the spot. Right on the same spot, no question asked, and I will take my chances with the judicial system."
A. Shaquille O'Neal   B. Charles Barkley   C. Jalen Rose
D. Scottie Pippen
Answer: B. Charles Barkley, Hall of Fame forward and commentator.

1441. "I never played with Wilt Chamberlain. I never played with Jerry West. To now say that one is greater than the other is a little unfair."
A. Scottie Pippen   B. Oscar Robertson   C. Kareem Abdul-Jabbar
D. Michael Jordan
Answer: D. Michael Jordan, talking to Marvin Shanken, publisher of *Cigar Aficionado*.

1442. "No, I made my money. I have my fans. People understand what I did. If they don't understand it, it's OK."

A. Oscar Robertson   B. Jerry West   C. Michael Jordan

D. Kareem Abdul-Jabbar

Answer: D. Abdul-Jabbar, being asked by radio host Dan Patrick "Do you care where you're ranked all-time?"

1443. "The greatest of all time is right here."

A. Jerry Lucas   B. Bill Russell   C. Clyde Drexler   D. Elgin Baylor

Answer: C. Clyde Drexler, being interviewed on TNT in Cleveland during the NBA 50th Anniversary Weekend and gesturing toward Wilt Chamberlain.

1444. "I wouldn't be on the podium if it wasn't for this guy. He gave me the vision man. You know, you want to be fast like Isiah, you wanna shoot like Bird, rebound like Barkley, pass like Magic, be dominant like Shaq, but man, I wanted to be like Mike. I remembered the first time I played against him. I walked out on the court and I looked at him and for the first time in my life a human being didn't look real to me. I don't know if you all watch the *Chappelle Show*, but he talked about a certain incident where somebody seen Rick James and I literally seen this aura. And it look like he was glowing. I'm like 'man that's Mike.' And I can't stop looking at him. I'm looking at his shoes and I'm like 'Man, he's got on the Jordans.'"

A. Steve Nash   B. Gary Payton   C. Allen Iverson   D. Byron Scott

Answer: C. Iverson at his Hall of Fame induction in 2016.

1445. "Someone asked me, 'What was the toughest arena to play in?' I said the Boston Garden. It was so tough to win there. You couldn't make a mistake with them. If you turned your head. Or you didn't rotate on defense, those guys made you pay. And it was him. He was a savant on the court, like two plays ahead on everything."

A. Joe Dumars   B. Isiah Thomas   C. Bill Laimbeer   D. John Salley

Answer: A. Dumars recalling the difficulty of getting past the Celtics and playing against Larry Bird.

1446. "When we won our first championship, I told the team, 'We have to win four or five of these or we didn't do our job.' I always thought that we left them on the table. You hate to blame injuries but like in '87 there were so many guys hurt. I'm sure the Lakers had injuries too."
A. Larry Bird   B. Robert Parish   C. Dennis Johnson   D. Kevin McHale
Answer: A. Bird lamenting that the Celtics didn't win more than three titles.

1447. "Being long is an advantage on the court. So people admire people like Michael Jordan and LeBron who can overcome their relative lack of height and still get stuff done. That's spectacular and people are attracted to that type of athletic talent. But tall people dominate this game, still."
A. Jerry West   B. Tim Duncan   C. Isiah Thomas
D. Kareem Abdul-Jabbar
Answer: D. One of the tallest at 7'2", Abdul-Jabbar was responding to a question about how people are disappointed in the careers of some big people such as Wilt Chamberlain and Shaquille O'Neal.

1448. "If I was starting a franchise, I would choose Bill Russell. He played on 11 championship teams in 13 years."
A. Bob Cousy   B. Tommy Heinsohn   C. Bob Pettit   D. Elgin Baylor
Answer: D. Baylor, Hall of Fame forward for the Lakers, when asked by broadcaster Rick Eisen who was the best player he ever played against.

1449. "I think when you put the greatest of all time right at the top of the list, Michael Jordan combined some elements that I haven't seen in a basketball player. The totality of his game is enormous. People, because Michael had that swagger, he had killer look in his face—someone I greatly admire."
A. Jerry Lucas   B. Karl Malone   C. Jerry West   D. John Stockton
Answer: C. West, Hall of Fame guard for the Lakers, asked on the *Dan Patrick Show* if the greatest of all time was Jordan.

1450. "Who was that Alex Hannum coaching [when Wilt scored 100 points on March 2, 1962]? He told them every time down throw the ball to Wilt. I played with guys who needed to get the ball. If I got double-teamed, I gave it up. I tried to play a team game and people didn't resent the fact that coaches wanted me to shoot those high percentage shots, because when the defense sagged, I'd pass the ball and we got shots on the perimeter."
A. Shaquille O'Neal   B. Nate Thurmond   C. Kareem Abdul-Jabbar
Answer: C. Abdul-Jabbar explaining the way he saw the game as a team endeavor. Frank McGuire was coaching the Warriors in 1962, not Hannum.

1451. "They thought I was coming in to take over the team. I told them on the first day of training camp 'I'm here to help you.' I said to him on the first day, 'Where do you like the ball? Do you like it high, do you like it in the middle of your chest? 'He said, 'I like it high.' I said, 'That's where it will be every time.' I'm here to help you be more successful."
A. Magic Johnson   B. James Worthy   C. Norm Nixon
Answer: A. Johnson recalling his meeting with Kareem Abdul-Jabbar in 1979.

1452. "He was just getting started in Golden State. But we loved the Chief [Robert Parish]. He was a great player and a very determined person."
A. Bill Walton   B. Kevin McHale   C. Larry Bird   D. Chris Ford
Answer: A. Walton on teammate Robert Parish, who averaged double digits in points and rebounds for eight years as part of the greatest front line ever.

1453. "If Willis Reed was undersized, Cowens was *definitely* undersized. Yes, I don't think there was a night when Cowens didn't compete at 100 percent of his athletic talent. He always played to his potential. Any loose ball on the floor was his."
A. Red Holzman   B. Jack Ramsay   C. Hubie Brown
Answer: C. Brown, then assistant coach with the Bucks, on 6'8" Dave Cowens.

1454. "I was always a bully, until one day in fifth grade. I threw something at the chalkboard and this kid rats me out. Prior to that, my father said, 'If you get suspended again, I'm gonna kill you. I'm gonna beat you like you never been beat before because you're irresponsible.' So I know what I'm getting when I get home. But before I get home, I'm gonna whup your ass. So I'm beating this kid up, and he has an epileptic seizure. It's just me and the kid out there and now he's on the ground shaking and I think 'Uh, oh.' So then a guy comes and saves the kid. So I go home and my mother pulls me to the side and says, 'You're too big and too strong, you can't ever do that again.' That kind of stayed with me and I thought 'I don't want to do that no more.'"
A. Wilt Chamberlain   B. Shaquille O'Neal   C. Shawn Kemp
Answer: B. O'Neal explaining why he didn't bully other players.

1455. "If I said, 'Michael Jordan,' what would you say? I think unbelievable. One time I turned and he jumped and his knees almost hit me in the chin. That's when I realized this guy is pretty special. Of course, jumping ability. But cat quick. He closed out a passing lane as fast as anybody I had ever seen. Just a phenomenal player."
A. Robert Parish   B. Larry Bird   C. Isiah Thomas
Answer: B. Bird relaying to Magic Johnson his recollections of Michael Jordan.

1456. "I just tried to keep him away from the basket. He would position himself so magnificently for rebounds. Like Rodman and Barkley and all the great rebounders, he knew where the ball was going. And he would go get it and stick it back in."
A. Dave Cowens   B. Nate Thurmond   C. Bill Walton   D. Bob Lanier
Answer: C. Bill Walton on Moses Malone's irrepressible nature under the backboard.

1457. "If I had a vote, I would have selected Walt Frazier, maybe because I'm a big Walt Frazier fan. Four or five guys on our team deserved to win [the Finals MVP]."
A. Willis Reed   B. Earl Monroe   C. Dave DeBusschere
Answer: A. Willis Reed, at Mamma Leone's restaurant, accepting his second Finals MVP Award in 1973.

Walt Frazier

1458. "He set the table for everybody. He came in and showed it wasn't about just being big but about being skilled and being smart. It's not the biggest strongest guy who wins all the time. Shaq and Wilt (by 1996) have only two titles between them in 18 years of play. They're phenomenal players but look where the titles are—with Russell, Mikan, Jabbar. The titles are with Magic, Bird, Jordan, Hakeem, Isiah."
A. Bob Ryan   B. Bill Walton   C. Kareem Abdul-Jabbar   D. Hubie Brown
Answer: B. Bill Walton on 6'10" George Mikan, center for the five-time champion Minneapolis Lakers.

1459. "People like to mention things in threes—you know, Larry, Magic, and Michael."
A. Isiah Thomas   B. Charles Barkley   C. Kevin McHale
Answer: A. Isiah Thomas, noting Moses Malone's being mentioned in the hallowed company of the greatest centers.

1460. "He was the best I ever played. He set the standard. The opponent's entire game plan had to be what you were going to do with Jabbar."
A. Bill Walton   B. Moses Malone   C. Robert Parish   D. Bob Lanier
Answer: A. Bill Walton, center for the Trail Blazers, who swept the Lakers in the 1977 conference finals. Walton averaged 19 points and 15 rebounds for the series, while Abdul-Jabbar averaged 30 points and 15 rebounds. The story was written as if Abdul-Jabbar was outplayed.

1461. "I came to Milwaukee in 1973. Kareem was 26. He won another MVP (his third) that first season. Three MVPs at age 26. How many guys turned around a franchise like that?"
A. Larry Brown   B. Hubie Brown   C. Gene Shue   D. Billy Cunningham
Answer: B. Hubie Brown, assistant coach to Larry Costello for the Bucks. The Bucks were 27-55 in 1969. In Jabbar's first season they leapt to 56-26. The following season they won a title in just their third season in the league.

1462. "I was with Wilt as a rookie guard on that 76er title team in 1967, when he changed his style because of the types of players he was surrounded by. I think even though all those years Wilt seemed to get the better of Russell statistically—Wilt was a scorer and Russell was not and both were great rebounders, shot blockers, and defenders—Wilt publicly and through the media always took the hit because Russell's teams eventually won the championship."

A. Hal Greer   B. Matt Guokas   C. Wali Jones   D. Bob Weiss

Answer: B. Guokas, a teammate of Chamberlain's in 1967, when Wilt averaged 24 points, 24 rebounds, and eight assists per game and the 76ers won the title.

1463. "But we were playing for love of the game, something today's players don't know a lot about."

A. Jerry Lucas   B. Oscar Robertson   C. Wilt Chamberlain
D. Bill Russell

Answer: C. Wilt Chamberlain, recalling in his 1992 book *A View from Above* that players were making about $9,000 when he started.

1464. "This may sound corny, but I know this means a lot to Willis and us. We don't want to come in the back door."

A. Jerry West   B. Gail Goodrich   C. Wilt Chamberlain   D. Elgin Baylor

Answer: A. West, before Game 7 of the 1970 Finals, on the importance of playing the Knicks with Willis Reed in the lineup.

1465. "Michael is the greatest player ever. Michael's been injured one time. He never asked to sit out. He never asked me anything. He only asked for respect and money. If Michael played in this era, he would average 50."

A. Scottie Pippen   B. Dennis Rodman   C. Bill Wennington
D. Toni Kukoč

Answer: B. Rodman played with Jordan from 1995 through 1998.

1466. "Coach Wooden had a very famous saying. 'It's not how high you jump, it's where you are when you jump. It's not a game of size and strength; it's a game of skill, timing and position.' That fits George Mikan to a tee. People say he wouldn't be able to do it today, but he was about 6'10" and 250. I don't see why he wouldn't be a talented player. All the great players from the past would be great ones today. The reason they got to be great was how hard they worked, how smart they were, and their competitive greatness and that's something you can't measure."
A. Kareem Abdul-Jabbar   B. Gail Goodrich   C. Bill Walton
D. Lucius Allen
Answer: C. Bill Walton on George Mikan in his own time and in today's game.

1467. "He was probably the hardest teammate I've ever played with. But it was really productive because he was able to raise the level of our competitiveness and our confidence. Every practice was almost harder than the game because you had to deal with him. Michael was so dominant. Everyone felt more a sense of 'We're going to win because we have Michael.' We would scrimmage every day, and those scrimmages were battles."
A. Steve Kerr   B. Ron Harper   C. Toni Kukoč   D. Randy Brown
Answer: A. Steve Kerr recalling that the practices on the Bulls were tougher because you didn't "want to get on his bad side."

1468. "I went 51 straight games without missing a minute, then came out for three minutes. In one other game I came out for four minutes. Think Patrick Ewing or David Robinson could ever match that?"
A. Bill Russell   B. Moses Malone   C. Wilt Chamberlain
D. Kareem Abdul-Jabbar
Answer: C. Chamberlain, from his book *A View from Above*, recalling his 1962 season.

1469. "He played 82 games at 40 years old. The crazy part is he would never sit out a practice. [Coach] Doug Collins had to try and kick him off the floor. He wouldn't leave. Playing 82 games was a badge of honor. And this man is doing it at 40 years old. C'mon man. Talk about dedication to the game. It doesn't get any better than that."
A. Ty Lue   B. Christian Laettner   C. Charles Oakley   D. Bryon Russell
Answer: A. Lue was Jordan's teammate with the Wizards in 2002 and 2003.

1470. "For ten years, I had the opportunity to play with Willis Reed in the NBA. There is no player more deserving of the honor of being elected to the Basketball Hall of Fame than Mr. Reed. He was the captain and the leader of the New York Knicks during two championships in 1970 and 1973, in addition to being selected as the league's Most Valuable Player in 1970. His past exploits while injured are well known to the public, but they are merely a small indication of the tremendous 'heart' that he exhibited throughout his basketball career. I wholeheartedly endorse Willis Reed's nomination to the Basketball Hall of Fame."
A. Bill Bradley   B. Dave DeBusschere   C. Walt Frazier   D. Phil Jackson
Answer: A. Letter from Bill Bradley, senator and teammate of Willis Reed, to the Basketball Honors Committee in November 1980. Reed was inducted in 1982.

1471. "Michael said 'I'm gonna get you a ring.' I was one of the only guys in that building without one. John Paxson said 'I'm going to give you some advice. If he drives and he hits you with that pass, don't miss.'"
A. Bobby Hansen   B. Craig Hodges   C. Cliff Levingston   D. Stacey King
Answer: A. Hansen, playing in his ninth and last season in 1992, got his ring when the Bulls beat the Blazers in six. In the fourth quarter of Game 6, the Bulls outscored the Blazers 33–14 to win 97–93. Hansen took and made a 3-pointer.

1472. "Kareem dropped that shot in, right hand or left hand, whenever the game was on the line. In our half-court offense, we went into Kareem in the low post so often it was an act of arrogance. We didn't even try to disguise it. It was like saying, 'Here's what we're going to do. It's what we always do. We don't think you can stop it.'"
A. Magic Johnson   B. James Worthy   C. Pat Riley   D. Jamaal Wilkes
Answer: C. Pat Riley, coach of the Lakers, explaining the go-to scorer in his book *Show Time*.

1473. "Michael Jordan was a scorer, first, second, and third. He was a phenomenal finisher of the game. He stopped facilitating. He was the game's greatest finisher, because he had no weakness in his game."
A. B. J. Armstrong   B. Rex Chapman   C. Pete Myers   D. Stacey King
Answer: A. Armstrong, Jordan's teammate from 1990 through 1995.

1474. "At various points in my career I led the league in scoring, assists, and blocked shots. Show me one other player in the history of the game that did all that and maybe I'll admit that you found someone better than or as good as I was."

A. Bob Pettit   B. Kareem Abdul-Jabbar   C. Wilt Chamberlain
Answer: C. Chamberlain, in his book *A View from Above*. He left out rebounds, which he led the league in 11 times. He never led the league in assists, as Guy Rodgers led in assists in 1967, the year Wilt averaged 7.9 per game.

1475. "[To get free throws] you got to know how to use your body, draw the contact, get fouled."

A. Karl Malone   B. Dolph Schayes   C. Adrian Dantley   D. Moses Malone
Answer: D. Moses Malone on maneuvering in traffic. He made 9,018 free throws, second only to Karl Malone in NBA history.

1476. "People say 'He was a tyrant.' I never looked at it that way. He was a guy who was trying to motivate his teammates."

A. Jud Buechler   B. Will Perdue   C. Luc Longley   D. Craig Hodges
Answer: B. Perdue also caused a fistfight in practice with Jordan after Perdue set consecutive legal screens and Jordan bounced off and hit the floor.

1477. "Unseld was our inspirational leader. His outlet passing and rebounding—he was always dependable. He would go 40–46 minutes, setting picks and doing all the little things you need done. He was the established leader of that team. He reinforced that leadership with his style of play and mannerisms on the court, and by age too."

A. Bob Dandridge   B. Elvin Hayes   C. Greg Ballard   D. Phil Chenier
Answer: D. Phil Chenier, three-time All-Star guard for the Bullets and Unseld's teammate on the 1978 team that won the title.

1478. "Me and four guys from Petersburg High [in Virginia, Malone's hometown] could beat the Celtics."

A. Calvin Murphy   B. Robert Reid   C. Moses Malone
D. Rudy Tomjanovich
Answer: C. Moses Malone, crowing before the 1981 Finals. "I don't regret the statement," Moses later said. "We were just 40-42 that year and look what we did." The Celtics beat the Rockets four games to two.

1479. "Every training program now involves stretching. People used to look at me like I was a male dancer. They would say, 'What is that, ballet?' It certainly contributed to my playing 20 years. I could not have played as long without it. I didn't get the injuries people usually have as their years advance. Now everyone does it."

A. Hakeem Olajuwon   B. Robert Parish   C. Kareem Abdul-Jabbar

Answer: C. Kareem Abdul-Jabbar, explaining his training regimen.

1480. "Kareem was the ultimate team player. He was the pivotal force behind the defense of those great [Lakers] teams. Very few centers would leave their man to help on traps and double teams. He anchored those defenses and made them great teams."

A. Hubie Brown   B. Walt Frazier   C. Larry Brown   D. Pat Riley

Answer: A. Two-time Coach of the Year Hubie Brown was an assistant coach to Larry Costello with the Bucks when Abdul-Jabbar led the Bucks to a title in just their third year.

1481. "I saw the best defenders in the league just shredded. Shredded. This kid here was the greatest. I'm including Kareem in his heyday. Wilt. Can't you tell from these highlights? He was shredding people like it was nobody's business."

A. Will Perdue   B. Brad Sellers   C. Sam Vincent   D. Bill Cartwright

Answer: B. Center Brad Sellers, Jordan's teammate from 1987 through 1989.

1482. "Russell only had to play Wilt Chamberlain; I had to play the whole Celtics' team."

Answer: Wilt Chamberlain on the difference between his teams and Russell's Celtics.

1483. "Wilt got tricked. Most fans and writers emphasized points, so he went out and got points. Then they said rebounds, so he went out and got the most rebounds [55]. In his mind he had done everything required of a player, because he led in all the categories they had told him about. And he still could not win."

A. Tom Gola   B. Bill Russell   C. Bob Cousy   D. Jerry West

Answer: B. Rival Bill Russell explaining Chamberlain's unsolvable difficulties as a player.

1484. "Next to Bird, Barry is the greatest passing forward ever to play the game. His assist numbers are the same as John Havlicek's (4.9 per game). And he lifted that 1975 championship Golden State team on his back."
A. Mike Gminski   B. Hal Greer   C. Clifford Ray   D. Jamaal Wilkes
Answer: A. Forward Mike Gminski, recalling the Finals sweep of the Bullets when the Warriors won twice by one point and Barry averaged 29 points.

1485. "Once he crossed that line in practice, he was a maniac. We took him out. We physically beat the hell out of him. And he took it. The games for him were pretty much easier than practice was."
A. Dave Corzine   B. Orlando Woolridge   C. Gene Banks
D. Charles Oakley
Answer: C. Gene Banks, small forward on the Bulls in 1986 and 1987, recalling Michael Jordan's demeanor.

1486. "I think it's a travesty that the NBA can't just tell these guys to play basketball two days in a row. It's just a joke to me. We flew commercial, and we were able to play back-to-back."
A. Charles Barkley   B. Larry Bird   C. Magic Johnson   D. Julius Erving
Answer: A. Part of Barkley's charm is that he can ridicule other players and laugh at himself.

1487. "People will say 'He wasn't a nice guy. He may have been a tyrant.' But that's you, because you never won anything."
A. Bill Russell   B. Michael Jordan   C. LeBron James
D. Kareem Abdul-Jabbar
Answer: B. Michael Jordan, in the 2020 documentary *The Last Dance*, talking about the attitudes of his teammates and others.

1488. "I started [my career] with Dr. J and I ended with Michael. Oh yeah. Both of those brothers played so hard in practice and in the game. Oh yeah."
A. George Gervin   B. Roger Brown   C. Billy Paultz   D. Alvin Robertson
Answer: A. Gervin began his career in 1972, with the Virginia Squires of the ABA when Julius Erving reigned. He finished with the Bulls in 1986 when Jordan reigned.

1489. "Michael Jordan didn't beat Larry Bird. The highlight where he dropped 63 in the playoff game, they got swept."
A. Isiah Thomas   B. Bill Laimbeer   C. Robert Parish
Answer: A. Thomas reminding radio host Stephen A. Smith that the Celtics were better than the Bulls when Bird scored a playoff record 63 points in April 1986.

1490. "I think he is probably going big game hunting because he's coming out with a book. So he's going after Phil Jackson, Michael Jordan, me, you're just going big game hunting because you know it's gonna get some clicks and sell some books."
A. Charles Barkley   B. Isiah Thomas   C. Shaquille O'Neal
Answer: A. Barkley explaining why Scottie Pippen was promoting his new book by attacking prominent people in basketball.

1491. "Even myself, when people get talking about me, they get to talk about stupid things I did. Whatever happens, happens. You don't get to get mad about it. The stuff that Michael said in *The Last Dance* was true."
A. Shaquille O'Neal   B. Charles Barkley   C. Dennis Rodman
Answer: B. Barkley defending the documentary about Michael Jordan and the Chicago Bulls, despite its recalling some of the foolish things Scottie Pippen did in his career, such as sitting out a play in the playoffs against the Knicks when Phil Jackson called a last-second shot for Toni Kukoč, not Pippen.

1492. "As much as I love LeBron, he's amazing. Listen, Michael and Kobe will kill you. And it's just a mindset. Giannis is closer to Michael and Kobe, and Anthony Davis is closer to LeBron. LeBron is a great player and a nice guy. I don't think anybody ever said Michael and Kobe are nice guys, because they don't care about that. They are out there to kill you."
A. Charles Barkley   B. Shaquille O'Neal   C. Kevin McHale
Answer: A. Barkley answering an interviewer's question about Anthony Davis and whether he had a killer instinct to win.

1493. "When you talk about some of the greatest athletes to even play in the NBA, I think Dennis Rodman is in that category, you think about the stamina, the way he could run."
A. Michael Jordan   B. Scottie Pippen   C. Steve Kerr
D. Alonzo Mourning
Answer: C. Kerr talking about his teammate. Rodman was tireless; after games ended, Rodman would often be seen on the Stairmaster for an hour.

1494. In a 2019 anonymous poll in *The Athletic*, 117 players voted on who was the best player of all time. Rank the following players by how those picks went.
A. LeBron James   B. Michael Jordan   C. Kobe Bryant
D. Kareem Abdul-Jabbar   E. Magic Johnson   F. Allen Iverson
G. Kevin Durant
Answer: 1-B, 73 percent of the vote; 2-A, 11.9 percent; 3-C, 10.9 percent; 4-D, 1.9 percent; 5-E, F, G, 1 percent each.

1495. "It's a movie. It's a big movie. Being able to just sit back, eat your popcorn and watch."
A. Al Horford   B. Marcus Smart   C. Jaylen Brown   D. Robert Williams III
Answer: B. The Celtics guard, after Jayson Tatum connected for 51 points, a playoff record, to defeat the 76ers in Game 7 of the 2023 Eastern Conference semifinals.

1496. "Me and James can't win alone."
A. Joel Embiid   B. Tyrese Maxey   C. Tobias Harris   D. P. J. Tucker
Answer: Joel Embiid reflects on the 76ers' series loss to the Celtics in the 2023 Eastern Conference semifinals. The remarks were surprising, since Embiid hit a miserable 5 of 18 shots and James Harden connected on only 3 of his 11 in a humiliating 112–88 drubbing.

1497. "It's really freakin' hard to get to the Eastern Conference finals."
A. Jimmy Butler   B. Bam Adebayo   C. Eric Spoelstra   D. Kyle Lowry
Answer: C. Heat coach Spoelstra made the remark after a 96–92 win against the Knicks that gave the Heat a six-game victory and landed them in the conference finals against the Celtics in 2023.

1498. "You're not going to be great in every game. No one is."
A. Jalen Brunson   B. Quentin Grimes   C. Julius Randle
D. Tom Thibodeau
Answer: D. After the Knicks' six-game defeat in the 2023 Eastern Conference semifinals, coach Thibodeau replied to a reporter's remark that, besides Brunson, the Knicks' four starters hit just 5 of 32 three-point attempts in the elimination game.

1499. "I definitely think this team maxed out."
A. Steve Kerr   B. Stephen Curry   C. Draymond Green   D. Jordan Poole
Answer: C. In a postgame interview, Green said the Warriors didn't play like a championship team in their six-game defeat to the Lakers in the 2023 Western Conference semifinals.

1500. "It only feels that way because we get asked about it."
A. Draymond Green   B. Klay Thompson   C. Stephen Curry
D. Steve Kerr
Answer: C. Curry was responding to a reporter asking, "Does it feel like this is the last dance?"

1501. One more: "A challenging year to say the least, but at the end of the day, we kept powering through, our vibes stayed positive, once we righted the ship and switched out some pieces, we came together, and I'm just happy and thankful that I get to sit in this seat and enjoy the ride."
A. LeBron James   B. Darvin Ham   C. Anthony Davis   D. Austin Reaves
Answer: B. The Lakers coach was appraising the team's up-and-down 2022–23 season in which they were just the second number seven seed to reach the conference finals since seeding began in 1984, joining the 1987 Seattle SuperSonics.

ACKNOWLEDGMENTS

Many people have shared in my love of basketball, and I want to acknowledge them here. My involvement with basketball began, suddenly, with the ascendancy of the New York Knicks during the 1968–69 season, a year before their first championship. The New York Yankees were the other team I rooted for, but the excitement surrounding the Knicks was greater, as it seemed their winning a title was imminent. I listened to Marv Albert on the radio and used his inimitable broadcasts to keep score by recording the points, rebounds, and season averages of all 12 players.

My father, though a fervent fan of the Brooklyn Dodgers and later of the Mets, had no attachment to basketball until those Knicks teams seized the attention of New York. I recall watching games between the Knicks and Baltimore Bullets with him, appreciating the matchups at each position: Walt Frazier against Earl Monroe, Willis Reed battling Wes Unseld. Neither of us had ever seen anything like this. We watched the Knicks win two titles in 1970 and 1973. I then went to St. Bonaventure, a hotbed of basketball enthusiasm, where students and the entire town descended on the Riley Center in Olean, New York, to support our Division I team. But I always felt closer to the pro game during that time.

Later, I would get into basketball conversations with my brothers, sister, and nephews. I worked for Total Sports Publishing. I am grateful to publisher John Thorn, who trusted me with *Total Basketball: The Ultimate Basketball Encyclopedia*. When Sports Media Group (in Toronto) took over the publication of the book, we had produced the largest encyclopedia ever, a distinction it still holds.

After I wrote *Strong to the Hoop: 1,501 Basketball Trivia Questions, Quotes, and Factoids from Every Angle* for Lyons Press, I was fortunate to meet Ken Samelson, an ever cheerful, conscientious, and skilled editor. I also want to thank the professionalism of managing editor Janice Braunstein from Rowman & Littlefield Publishing Group, whose skills were invaluable in seeing this book through to its completion.

ABOUT THE AUTHOR

Kenneth A. Shouler is a full professor of philosophy at the County College of Morris in Randolph, New Jersey. He has published 12 books in five categories: sports, philosophy, religion, politics, and business. His basketball books include *The Experts Pick Basketball's Best 50 Players in the Last 50 Years*, which he self-published in 1996, on the 50th anniversary of the NBA, and was later picked up by Addax Press. That book led to his editing and writing *Total Basketball: The Ultimate Basketball Encyclopedia*, which at 1,475 pages is the most complete basketball volume ever published. He has also written on basketball for *ESPN*, *Hoop*, *Inside Sports*, *Sport*, *Cigar Aficionado*, and other periodicals.

Since 2007, he has been writing the *Baseball Trivia Calendar* for Workman Publishing, devising 312 questions per year.